WordPress® For Dummies

Cheat Sheet

Real Quick Tour of the Administration Panel

These brief descriptions of the main menu items on the WordPress Administration panel apply across all versions of WordPress. Each version of WordPress varies in the options available for your settings, however.

The WordPress Administration Panel Menu at a Glance

Menu Option	Description
Dashboard	Find basic information and statistics about your blog along with information from the WordPress Development Blog. You'll also find other posts and information from blogs run by those involved with WordPress development or resources.
Write	Write posts and categorize them by topic; upload images; create post excerpts; send trackbacks; manage custom fields; and create static pages for your blog.
Manage	Edit/delete posts and pages; view/edit/delete your uploads; manage your categories; view/edit files; import from another blogging platform; and export your blog data.
Comments	Manage comments here by viewing, editing, or deleting them; also manage your comment moderation queue and comment/trackback spam.
Blogroll	Manage your blogroll by editing, deleting, or categorizing your links. Add links, edit links, and import links here.
Presentation	Manage your WordPress themes by viewing them, activating them, and editing them in the Theme Editor. Use your Sidebar Widgets here, too, if you have them activated.
Plugins	View a listing of plugins installed in your WordPress blog. Activate, deactivate, and edit them here.
Users	Manage your users and subscribers and edit your own profile here.
Options	Set the general options for your blog in this section. You find settings for blog posts, RSS feed, discussion options, privacy, and permalinks here.

Finding WordPress Community Support

This book covers three versions of WordPress, and each version is represented by support forums run by volunteers from the WordPress community. In these forums, you can ask questions and get answers from seasoned users of the software.

Pick the Right WordPress Support Forum

If You Are . . .	This Is the Right Forum for You . . .
A user of the hosted solution provided by the fine folks at WordPress.com	http://forums.wordpress.com
Running the single-user version of WordPress on your own Web server (self-hosting)	http://wordpress.org/forums
Managing and maintaining a community of users on your domain using the WordPress MU software	http://mu.wordpress.org
Wanting to find a repository of information regarding the overall use of WordPress	http://codex.wordpress.org

For Dummies: Bestselling Book Series for Beginners

WordPress® For Dummies®

Cheat Sheet

Where to Find WordPress Plugins

Name	On the Web at...
WordPress.Org — Extend Plugins	http://wordpress.org/extend/plugins
WordPress Plugin Database	http://wp-plugins.net
WordPress Codex	http://codex.wordpress.org/plugins
WP Plugins	http://wpplugins.org
WordPress Plugin Repository	http://dev.wp-plugins.org
Blogging Pro	http://bloggingpro.com/archives/category/ wordpress-plugins
WordPress MU Plugins	http://wpmudev.org/plugins.php

Find Free Themes for Your WordPress Blog

Name	On the Web at...
WordPress Theme Viewer	http://themes.wordpress.net
WordPress Codex — Themes List	http://codex.wordpress.org/Using_Themes/Themes_List
Alex King's Themes Directory	http://alexking.org/projects/wordpress/themes

Find Skilled Designers Experienced with WordPress

Name	On the Web at...
E.Webscapes Design Studio	http://ewebscapes.com
Moxie Design Studios	http://moxiedesignstudios.com
The Blog Studio	http://theblogstudio.com
Cr8d Design	http://www.cre8d-design.com
Hop Studios	http://hopstudios.com

For Dummies: Bestselling Book Series for Beginners

WordPress®

FOR

DUMMIES®

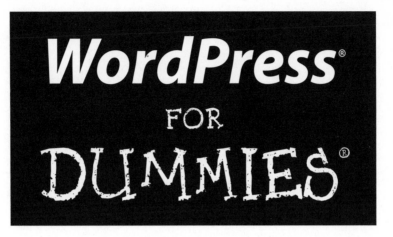

WordPress®
FOR
DUMMIES®

by Lisa Sabin-Wilson

Foreword by Matt Mullenweg
Co-Founder of WordPress

Wiley Publishing, Inc.

WordPress® For Dummies®

Published by
Wiley Publishing, Inc.
111 River Street
Hoboken, NJ 07030-5774
www.wiley.com

Copyright © 2008 by Wiley Publishing, Inc., Indianapolis, Indiana

Published by Wiley Publishing, Inc., Indianapolis, Indiana

Published simultaneously in Canada

For general information on our other products and services, please contact our Customer Care Department within the U.S. at 800-762-2974, outside the U.S. at 317-572-3993, or fax 317-572-4002.

For technical support, please visit www.wiley.com/techsupport.

Wiley also publishes its books in a variety of electronic formats. Some content that appears in print may not be available in electronic books.

Library of Congress Control Number: 2007936103

ISBN: 978-0-470-14946-1

Manufactured in the United States of America

10 9 8 7 6 5

WILEY

About the Author

Lisa Sabin-Wilson has worked with the WordPress software since its inception in 2003 and has built her business around providing technical support, hosting, and design solutions for bloggers who use WordPress. She reaches thousands of people worldwide with her WordPress services, skills, and knowledge regarding the product.

Lisa operates a few blogs online, all of which are powered by WordPress. Her personal blog (justagirlintheworld.com) has been online since February of 2002; her design business at E.Webscapes (ewebscapes.com) has been online since 1999. She also provides a successful Web hosting service, Blogs About Hosting (blogsabout.com), which caters to blogs and bloggers on a global scale.

When she can be persuaded away from her computer, where she is usually hard at work providing design solutions for her WordPress clients, she sometimes emerges for public speaking appearances on the topics of design, blogging, and WordPress. She has appeared at conferences such as the annual South By Southwest Interactive Conference.

Lisa consults with bloggers both large and small. Bloggers come in thousands of different flavors, from business to personal, from creative to technical, and all points in between. Lisa is connected to thousands of them worldwide and appreciates the opportunity to share her knowledge through *WordPress For Dummies.* She hopes you find great value in it, as well!

When she's not designing or consulting with her clients, you can usually find her either at her favorite coffee shop sipping espresso, on a mountaintop somewhere hitting the slopes with her family, or 100 feet beneath the ocean waters, scuba diving with her husband and swimming with the fishes.

Dedication

For the amazing man who is my husband, whose patience, encouragement, and unwavering belief in my abilities never end. For every line you read, for each and every concept we discussed, and for every deadline I obsessed over (while you did the dishes and laundry), you had my back every step of the way. I love you.

Author's Acknowledgments

Many, many thanks and kudos to Matt Mullenweg, the core development team from Automattic, and every single person involved in making WordPress the best blogging platform available on the Internet today. To the volunteers and testers who destroy all those pesky prerelease bugs for every new version release, the WordPress community thanks you! And to each and every WordPress plugin developer and theme designer who donates his or her time, skills, and knowledge to provide the entire WordPress community of users with invaluable tools that help us create dynamic blogs, thank you a thousand times! Every person mentioned here is an invaluable asset to the overall WordPress experience; I wish I could name you all, individually, except that there are literally thousands of you out there!

A few individuals who are not directly connected to this book but whose contributions, by way of providing interviews, input, and encouragement I would like to acknowledge are Susie Gardner, Aaron Brazell, Mark Jaquith, Chris Pearson, Ben Eastaugh, Scott Wallick, Ghyslain Armand, Rebecca Wei, Alex King, Leanne Wildermuth, Lindsey Hardegree, Chelle Killilea, Andrew Billits, Dave Powers, Peter Flaschner, Joelle Reeder, and Kathy Scoleri. If any of you want to know what I'm thanking you for, drop me a line! Special thanks to Tom Naughton for those much-needed sanity breaks.

Huge thanks to Melody Layne, Steve Hayes, Susan Christophersen, and Heidi Unger from Wiley Publishing for their support, assistance, and guidance during the course of this project. Just the mere fact that Susan and Heidi had to read every page of this book means that they deserve the Medal of Honor! Also, many thanks to technical editor Paul Chaney and other editors of the project who also worked hard to make sure that I look somewhat literate here.

To any family members and friends whom I have neglected during the process of writing this book, thank you for not abandoning me!

Finally, I thank my family — my husband, Chris; my children, Ben and Melissa; and my parents, Donald and Penny Sabin — for their unending support through this project.

Publisher's Acknowledgments

We're proud of this book; please send us your comments through our online registration form located at www.dummies.com/register/.

Some of the people who helped bring this book to market include the following:

Acquisitions, Editorial, and Media Development

Project Editor: Susan Christophersen

Executive Editor: Steve Hayes

Sr. Acquisitions Editor: Melody Layne

Copy Editors: Heidi Unger, Virginia Sanders

Technical Editor: Paul Chaney

Editorial Manager: Jodi Jensen

Editorial Assistant: Amanda Foxworth

Sr. Editorial Assistant: Cherie Case

Cartoons: Rich Tennant
(www.the5thwave.com)

Composition Services

Project Coordinator: Erin Smith

Layout and Graphics: Claudia Bell, Stacie Brooks, Carl Byers, Stephanie D. Jumper, Barbara Moore, Laura Pence, Melanee Prendergast

Proofreaders: Todd Lothery, Toni Settle

Indexer: Potomac Indexing, LLC

Anniversary Logo Design: Richard Pacifico

Publishing and Editorial for Technology Dummies

    Richard Swadley, Vice President and Executive Group Publisher

    Andy Cummings, Vice President and Publisher

    Mary Bednarek, Executive Acquisitions Director

    Mary C. Corder, Editorial Director

Publishing for Consumer Dummies

    Diane Graves Steele, Vice President and Publisher

    Joyce Pepple, Acquisitions Director

Composition Services

    Gerry Fahey, Vice President of Production Services

    Debbie Stailey, Director of Composition Services

Contents at a Glance

Table of Contents

Foreword

There used to be a program from Microsoft called FrontPage that was the first visual interface for creating Web sites that I saw. It worked like Word or Publisher, so with very little knowledge, I was able to hack together the world's worst Web site in just a few hours without worrying about what was going on under the hood.

Years later when I look back at that Web site, I cringe, but at the time it was incredibly empowering. The software, though crude, helped me publish something anybody in the entire world could see. It opened up a world I had never imagined before.

Now, using software like WordPress, you can have a blog or Web site light-years beyond my first one in both functionality and aesthetics. However, just as my first Web experience whetted my appetite for more, I hope that your experience entices you to explore the thousands of free plugins, themes, and customizations possible with WordPress, many of which are explained in this book.

WordPress is more than just software; it is a community, a rapidly evolving ecosystem, and a set of philosophies and opinions about how to create the best Web experience. When you embrace it, you'll be in good company. WordPress users include old media organizations such as CNN, *The New York Times*, and *The Wall Street Journal*, along with millions of personal bloggers like myself for whom a WordPress blog is a means of expression.

Matt Mullenweg
Co-founder of WordPress

Introduction

* *

*L*et's see . . . it was 2003 when I first discovered the wonders of WordPress. Way back then (and in Internet years, that's actually a lot of time), I was using Movable Type as my blogging platform. My friend Chelle introduced me to the WordPress software. "Try it," she said. "You'll really like it," she insisted.

Being somewhat of a creature of habit, I felt reluctant to make the change. However, a growing buzz around the WordPress software made me curious. Shortly thereafter, Six Apart, the makers of Movable Type, made a drastic change in the licensing requirements. All of a sudden, software that used to be free cost money. As soon as Six Apart made that move, a mass exodus from Movable Type to WordPress seemed to occur. All the cool kids were doing it, so I decided to give it a shot.

I have not looked back since. I've been with WordPress since then.

2004 was the year blogging was recognized and touted in the media as the latest Internet trend. Mainstream media looked on — open-mouthed — as bloggers attained press credentials to major events; bloggers got book deals and press attention; bloggers earned five-figure monthly incomes from in-blog advertising; blogs were recognized and read by the general public; and blogs became an accessory as ubiquitous for the young as the latest cell phone. In 2005, businesses caught on to the phenomenon and began to embrace it. Major PR companies launched campaigns that included, or were entirely focused on, blogs; CEOs and Fortune 500 companies joined the fray.

2006 was the year that blogs went from trend to mainstay. No longer a novelty, blogs are now a natural extension of daily communication, frequently replacing the e-mail newsletter. Blogs are here to stay. Today's authors, students, new parents, business owners, academics, hobbyists — you name it — are using blogs as a matter of course.

The number of new blogs has doubled six times every five-and-a-half months for the past three years, putting the number of U.S. blogs at around 102.9 million in the latter half of 2007. Studies show that more than 175,000 new blogs are started daily.

To a brand-new user, some aspects of WordPress can seem a little bit intimidating. However, after you take a look under the hood, you begin to realize how intuitive, friendly, and extensible the software is. This book presents an in-depth look at all three flavors of WordPress:

> ✔ The hosted version available at WordPress.com
>
> ✔ The self-hosted version available at WordPress.org
>
> ✔ The multiuser version of WordPress MU for multiuser blogging communities

If you're interested in taking a detailed look at the blogging and Web site services provided by WordPress, you happen to have just the right book in your hands.

About This Book

This book covers all the important aspects of WordPress that new users need to know to begin using the software for their own blog (or blogs). I cover the three free versions that WordPress makes available and highlight all the important parts, such as:

> ✔ Setting up and using a hosted blog at WordPress.com
>
> ✔ Locating good hosting services for those who wish to use the self-hosted version available at WordPress.org, as well as the multiuser version of WordPress MU
>
> ✔ Installing and setting up the WordPress.org software
>
> ✔ Installing and setting up the WordPress MU software
>
> ✔ Touring the Administration panels, settings, and options for all three versions of WordPress
>
> ✔ Introducing you to templates and tags needed to work with themes and templates for WordPress
>
> ✔ Installing, activating, and managing WordPress plugins
>
> ✔ Finding great themes, plugins, and consultants that can help you create _just_ the blog you want
>
> ✔ Discovering the potential pitfalls associated with each version
>
> ✔ Understanding the challenges you'll face when running a WordPress-powered site, such as dodging comment and trackback spam and developing a regular blogging routine
>
> ✔ Exploring RSS feed syndication
>
> ✔ Trying out special blog technologies such as podcasting, videoblogging, and photoblogging
>
> ✔ Migrating your existing blog to WordPress (if you are using a different blogging platform such as Blogspot, Movable Type, or Typepad)

✔ Discovering the power of WordPress as a content management system (CMS) to create a full Web site, not just a blog

✔ Finding out how and where to obtain ongoing support, tips, and resources for using the WordPress software

With WordPress, you can truly tailor a blog to your own tastes and needs. All the tools are out there. Some of them come already packaged within the WordPress software; others come in the form of third-party plugins and add-ons created by members of the WordPress user community. It takes a little research, knowledge, and time on your part to put together the blog you want that is unique to your needs and provides your readers with an exciting visitor experience that keeps them coming back for more.

Conventions Used in This Book

Throughout the book, I apply the following typography conventions to help guide you through some of the information I present:

✔ When I ask you to type something on your computer, you'll see the text that you're supposed to type in **bold**.

✔ When I suggest a keyword that you might want to plug in to a search engine, that term appears in *italics.*

✔ Text that appears in this `special font` is certain to be a URL (Web address), e-mail address, filename, folder name, or code.

✔ When I use a term that I think you might not be familiar with, I apply *italics* to that term to let you know that I go on to define it next.

✔ In some instances, I give you a basic idea of what a Web address or block of code looks like. For situations in which the text that you see might be different, depending on your settings and preferences, I apply *italics* to that text.

What You Are Not to Read

Don't read supermarket tabloids. They're certain to rot your brain.

As I explain previously, this book covers the details of how to set up, use, and maintain the software for the three free versions of WordPress. I don't intend for you to read this book from cover to cover. (Unless you're my mother — then I won't forgive you if you don't.) Rather, hit the Table of Contents and the index of this book to find the sections that contain the information you need.

If you never intend to run a multiuser WordPress MU community, you can completely skip Chapters 12, 13, and 14.

If you have no interest in setting up a hosted blog at WordPress.com, skip Chapters 3, 4, and 5.

Long story short: Take what you need and leave the rest.

Foolish Assumptions

I'll never know what assumptions you've made about me, at this point. However, I can tell you a few things that I've already assumed about you:

✔ You know what a computer is. You can turn it on and you understand that if you spill coffee on your keyboard, you'll have to run out and get a replacement.

✔ You understand how to hook yourself into the Internet and know the basics of using a Web browser to surf Web sites and blogs.

✔ You have a basic understanding of what blogs are and you're interested in using WordPress to start your own blog. Or you already have a blog and are using WordPress and want to better understand the program so that you can do more cool stuff and stop bugging your geeky best friend whenever you have a question about something. Or even better, you already have a blog on another blogging platform and want to move your blog to WordPress.

✔ You know what e-mail is. You know what an e-mail address is. You actually have an e-mail address and send and receive e-mail on a semi-regular basis.

If, when you approach your computer, you break out into a cold sweat and look similar to a deer caught in headlights and say to yourself "Here goes nothing!" before you even sit down in front of your monitor, you might want to brush up on your basic computer skills before you begin this book.

How This Book Is Organized

This book is made up of six parts that introduce you to WordPress and cover each of the fascinating and free versions available today:

✔ **Part I: Introducing WordPress** gives you an overview of WordPress and the advantages of making it your blogging platform. You might think of WordPress as coming in three "flavors": vanilla (WordPress.com hosted solution), chocolate (WordPress.org self-hosted solution), and Neapolitan (WordPress MU, the multiuser solution). In this part, you also discover some of the fun and aspects of blogging, such as RSS feed syndication and reader interaction through the use of comments.

✔ **Part II: Using the WordPress Hosted Service** takes you through signing up for a blog with the hosted service. In this part, you take a tour of the Administration panel, explore writing and managing your blog, find out how to change to the various themes available in this version, and discover how to enhance your blog with widgets.

✔ **Part III: Self-Hosting with WordPress.org** explores the single-user version of the WordPress software available at WordPress.org. This is software that you install on your own hosted Web server, so I give you valuable information about domain registration, Web hosting providers, and a few of the basic tools, such as FTP, that you need to install and set up a WordPress blog. I also familiarize you with the WordPress Administration panel, where you personalize your settings and explore many of the menu options and settings that you need to manage and maintain your WordPress-powered blog.

After you get everything set the way you like it, you can continue with the rest of the part, where I tell you how you can organize and archive your posts, add links to other sites, edit your blog URLs in a way that suits your needs, create your own blog designs, extend your blog's functionality with plugins, and hire a professional for advanced blogging services.

Many established WordPress users may find this part of the book especially helpful and enlightening. Representing my years of providing technical support, design solutions, and consulting services to my clients, the information contained in this chapter answers about 90 percent of the questions and queries my clients have about WordPress.

✔ **Part IV: Going Multi-User with WordPress MU** is for those of you who want to create and build a multi-user blogging community that is housed within one domain. This part covers the unique hosting and server setup needs for this software, as well as how to install the software on your Web server. Also, I give you lots of instructions for performing the administrative tasks that your community members will expect you to do and tell you how to get the latest updates on the software so that you can properly maintain your community.

✔ **Part V: Flexing and Extending WordPress** tells you how to move a blog that you might have in another blogging platform — such as Blogspot or Moveable Type — to WordPress. The second chapter in this part tells you how you can use WordPress as a full-blown content management system (CMS). WordPress isn't just for blogs anymore.

✔ **Part VI: The Part of Tens** is in every For Dummies book that you will ever pick up. This part introduces you to ten popular, free WordPress themes that you can use to create a nice, clean look for your blog. In this part, you also discover ten great WordPress plugins that you can use to provide your visitors (and yourself) with some great functionalities.

Icons Used in This Book

Icons are those little pictures in the margins of the book that emphasize a point to remember, a warning to be aware of, or a tip that I think you might find helpful. Those points are illustrated as such:

These are little bits of information that you may find particularly useful, but aren't necessarily obvious for the casual user or beginner.

This is kind of like when your mother warned you, "Don't touch that pan, it's hot!" but you touched it anyway. That is how you learned the meaning of "ouch!" Yeah, that is when I use this warning icon. I fully expect that, out of curiosity, you may very well touch the hot pan, but you can't say that I didn't warn you!

All geeky stuff goes here. Even though there is an aura of geek surrounding the use of the WordPress software, I surprised myself by not using this icon very much in this book. But I do use it in certain places, and when I do, it probably has to do with technical mumbo jumbo that would make your eyes glaze over if I had elaborated. Luckily for you, these little icon bits are short and sweet, but I don't promise that they won't bore you to death. Good thing I use them sparingly, hey?

When you see this icon, read the text next to it two or three times to brand it into your brain so that you remember whatever it was that I thought, at the time, you need to remember.

Where to Go from Here

As I mention in the "What You Are Not to Read" section of this chapter, take what you need and leave the rest. This book is a veritable smorgasbord of WordPress information, ideas, concepts, tools, resources, and instruction. Some of it will directly apply to what you want to do with your WordPress blog. Some of it may be something you're only mildly curious about, and you might skim through those pages.

Part I

Introducing WordPress

The 5th Wave   By Rich Tennant

"Hi all. Turns out that the rash I posted about last night _is_ contagious..."

In this part . . .

Ready to get started? I know I am! This part of the book provides a brief introduction to WordPress and blogging. WordPress is unique in offering three versions of its software, and I tell you about each version so that you can choose the one that's right for you.

Chapter 1

What WordPress Can Do for You

*I*f you believe that your ideas are important enough to publish on the World Wide Web for the entire world to see, then you, my friendly reader, are the perfect blogger, and WordPress is your perfect tool! How else can you get your message out with the potential of reaching a vast audience of millions worldwide for the cost of exactly nothing? There might be no free lunch in this world, but you can bet your bottom dollar that there are free blogs to be had. And WordPress serves it all up in one nifty package.

The software's ease of use and the speed at which you can get your blog up and running on the Internet are the best reasons to use WordPress to power your personal or business blog. In this chapter, I introduce you to the WordPress software so that you can begin to discover how effective it is as a tool for creating your blog or Web site.

Discovering the Benefits of WordPress

I work with first-time bloggers all the time, folks who are new to the idea of publishing on the Internet. One of the most frequently asked questions I get is, "How can I run a blog? I don't even know how to code or create Web sites."

Enter WordPress. You no longer need to worry about knowing the code, because the WordPress blogging software does the code part for you. When you log in to your blog, you have only these simple things to do in order to publish your thoughts and ideas:

1. Write your article.

2. Click a button to publish your article.

And that's it!

WordPress, which is open source blogging software, is uniquely positioned to be the blogging tool of choice for many new bloggers — as well as for those who already have blogs, because migrating to a new blogging tool is a common occurrence. *Open source* means that the code used to power the software is completely open for public consumption. So you, or I, or the lady who serves your kid lunch in the school cafeteria can take the WordPress code and play with it, change it, adapt it, repackage it, and redistribute it if we have the technical ability and means to do so.

Open source also means that the use of the software, in all of its forms, is free. Anyone can use WordPress. It doesn't matter whether you're using it to start a blog about how a really good cup of espresso can make you weak in the knees, or to build a Web site for a Fortune 500 company. And whether you decide to use the hosted version of WordPress at WordPress.com, install the WordPress software on your own hosted account, or use WordPress MU (MU stands for Multi-User) to run a network of blogs, the cost of WordPress itself is absolutely nothing.

At times, there can be some costs associated with running a WordPress blog. For instance, if you choose to host your own blog on your own domain, you have the costs associated with Web hosting and domain registration (see Part III for more about hosting your own domain). And, of course, if you hire a designer to create a custom template for your blog, you need to pay that person as well. (See Chapter 11 for information about hiring a design professional for your WordPress blog.)

In addition to being open source, WordPress brings the following competitive advantages with it as the most popular blogging tool on the market:

- **Diversity:** Three versions of WordPress are available to suit nearly every type of blogger: a hosted turnkey solution; a version to install on the Web server of your choice; and a multi-user version that allows you to offer blogs across a group or organization.

- **Ease of use:** WordPress setup is quick and the software is easy to use.

- **Extensibility:** WordPress is extremely extensible, meaning that you can easily obtain plugins and tools that let you customize it to suit your purposes.

- **Community of users:** WordPress has a large and loyal members-helping-members community through public support forums, mailing lists, and interactive blogs geared toward the use of WordPress.

The following sections fill in a few of the details about these aspects and point you to where in the book you can find out more about them.

A little something for everyone

One of the most satisfying benefits of choosing WordPress as your blogging platform is the fact that WordPress supplies you with three different flavors of blogging software (well, four flavors when you count the Enterprise version, which isn't free). The developers of WordPress are forward thinkers and provide something for everyone. Find out which variety is likely to fully meet your blogging needs:

- ✔ **WordPress.com (see Part II):** This version is a hosted, turnkey solution for WordPress bloggers. You can go to `http://wordpress.com`, sign up for a blog hosted by WordPress, and be up and running with several key WordPress features within a matter of minutes. You can choose your own username to individualize your new blog. For example, if you want the username *souptonuts*, your WordPress.com blog is assigned the following domain: `http://souptonuts.wordpress.com`. That is, of course, if someone hasn't already beaten you to the punch in nabbing the souptonuts username. If someone has, you need to choose one that is available in the WordPress.com system.

- ✔ **Self-installed WordPress (see Part III):** Available at `http://WordPress.org`, this version is software that you download from the WordPress Web site and install on your own Web server to run on your own domain. It requires you to get into the inner workings a bit, but it also offers much more flexibility than the hosted version. The nice thing about this version is that just about anyone can use it, from novices to experts. You can get as involved with the code as you want — or avoid the code altogether and still run a fully functional blog on your own domain.

- ✔ **WordPress MU (see Part IV):** Found at `http://mu.wordpress.org` and pronounced *em-you,* where MU stands for Multi-User. With this version of WordPress, you can perform one installation of WordPress MU and run several hundred to thousands of blogs on one domain. WordPress MU isn't meant for the individual blogger, but it's perfect for corporations, groups, and organizations to maintain a network of blogs on one server and one domain. There is an enterprise version of WordPress MU, known as the "KnowNow WordPress Enterprise Edition" (KWEE). This version of WordPress MU caters to the corporate world and Fortune 500 companies, is not free, and comes with consulting fees and services to help you manage and maintain your WordPress MU environment.

Easy to set up and use

WordPress is one of the only blog platforms that can brag about a five-minute installation — and stand behind it! Choosing to sign up for the hosted version of WordPress yields approximately the same amount of time during the signup process. WordPress MU takes a bit longer to install and get it up and running. I recently installed it in approximately 20 minutes from start to finish.

Mind you, those are *approximate* installation times, which don't include the time it takes to set up the different options and settings within the Administration panel.

After you complete the installation, the world of WordPress awaits you. The design of the Administration panel is intuitive, well organized, and easy on the eyes. Everything is clear and logical — easy for even a first-time user to see where to go to manage settings and options.

The WordPress software surely has enough meat to it to keep the most experienced developer busy and happy. However, at the same time, it's intuitive and friendly enough to make a novice user giddy at how easy it is to get started. Each time you use WordPress, you can find out something exciting and new.

Flex and extend WordPress capabilities

I've found that the most exciting and fun part about running a WordPress blog is the flexibility of the software, with hundreds of plugins available to create a blog that functions the way *you* need it to.

If you think of your blog as a vacuum cleaner, plugins are the attachments. The attachments don't function alone. However, when you add the attachments to your vacuum cleaner, you add to the functionality of your vacuum, possibly improving the performance of your vacuum. By and large, plugins are available at no charge to you. You can find more about WordPress plugins and where to get them in Chapter 10. Also, in Chapter 18, you'll find a listing of my choice of the ten popular WordPress plugins available for download.

For the most part, every WordPress blog is the same at its core. By using WordPress plugins, you can truly individualize your blog, making it stand out by providing additional features and tools to benefit you and your readers. When you come upon a WordPress blog on the Internet and see some really different and cool functions on it, 98 percent of the time you can include that function on your blog using a WordPress plugin. If you don't know what plugin that blog is using, feel free to drop the blog owner an e-mail or leave a comment. WordPress blog owners are usually eager to share the cool tools they discover.

You can also embellish your WordPress blog with templates and themes. WordPress comes prepackaged with two default themes to get you started. Shown in Figure 1-1 is the famous Kubrick theme, created by Michael Heilemann from `http://binarybonsai.com`, which is the default theme that is displayed after you've installed and set up your blog.

Its default form is blue and white, but the theme creator gives you a handy application built right into the theme preferences so that you can change the color of the top header.

This default theme includes all the basic elements that you need when starting a new WordPress blog. You can extend your WordPress blog in a hundred different ways with the use of plugins and themes that have been released by members of the WordPress community, but the Kubrick theme is a nice place to start.

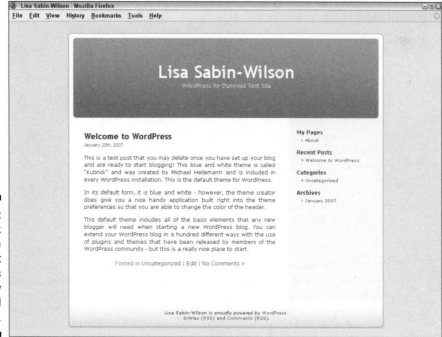

Figure 1-1:
Kubrick theme, the default WordPress theme by Michael Heilemann.

Taking part in the community

Allow me to introduce you to the fiercely loyal folks who make up the user base, better known as the vast WordPress community. This band of merry ladies and gentlemen comes from all around the globe, from California to Cairo, Florida to Florence, and all points in between and beyond.

By March 2005, Matt Mullenweg of WordPress proudly proclaimed that the number of WordPress downloads had reached 50,000. This was an exciting landmark in the history of the WordPress blogging software. By August 2006, the real excitement occurred when WordPress logged 1 million downloads.

Don't let the sheer volume of users fool you. The WordPress community has the bragging rights to the most helpful blogging community on the Web today. You can find users helping other users in the WordPress support forums at `http://wordpress.org/support`. You can also find WordPress users contributing to the very helpful WordPress Codex (a collection of How To documents) at `http://codex.wordpress.org`. In the blogosphere, you can find multiple blogs written on the topic of WordPress — users sharing their experience and WordPress war stories, published in the hopes of helping the next user who comes along.

You can subscribe to various mailing lists, too. They offer WordPress users the opportunity to become involved in various aspects of the WordPress community, as well as the future development of WordPress software.

Don't worry if you're not yet a member of the WordPress community. It's easy to join by simply starting your own WordPress blog using one of the three software options WordPress has available. If you're already blogging on a different blogging platform, such as Blogspot or Movable Type, WordPress makes it simple for you to migrate your current data from that platform into a new WordPress setup. (See Chapter 15 for information about moving your existing blog into WordPress.)

Your publishing history

WordPress lets you sort and organize everything you publish in an order that you, and your readers, can access by date and category. This archiving process occurs automatically with every post you publish to your blog.

You can create as many categories as you want for filing your blog posts away by topic. However, you don't have to use the Category feature if you'd rather not.

Engaging in blog talk

Want to engage in a lively conversation with your readers? For many bloggers, that's what blogging is all about. With WordPress you can get instant feedback from your readers the moment you make a post to your blog. People can leave a note for you that gets published to your site, and you can respond and engage your readers in conversation about the topic at hand. Having this function included on your blog creates the opportunity for others to expand on the thoughts and ideas that you presented in your blog post.

You have full administrative control over who can and can't leave comments. In addition, you can edit the comment or delete it altogether. You're also free to choose not to allow any comments on your blog.

Many blog users will say that a blog without comments is not a blog at all. This is a commonly held belief among those in the blogging community because experiencing visitor feedback through the use of comments is part of what has made blogging so popular today.

Feeding your readers

An *RSS feed* is a basic standard that readers of blogs have come to expect from blogs on the Internet today.

RSS stands for Really Simple Syndication. An *RSS feed* is a basic standard that blog readers have come to expect. The resource site WebReference.com (www.webreference.com/authoring/languages/xml/rss/intro/) defines RSS as "a lightweight XML format designed for sharing headlines and other Web content. Think of it as a distributable 'What's New' for your site."

WordPress has built-in RSS feeds in several different formats. Because it's built in to the software platform, you don't need to actually do anything in order to provide your readers with an RSS feed of your content. Check out Chapter 8 to find out more about using RSS feeds within the WordPress program.

Chapter 2

Blogging Basics

Among the realities of running a blog today is the veritable feast of possibilities from which to choose the right software platform that will perform the way you need it to. You want to be sure that the platform you choose has all the options you're looking for. WordPress is unique in that it offers three different versions of its software. Each version is designed to meet the various needs of bloggers. The three different versions of WordPress are the following:

✔ The hosted version at WordPress.com. (Part II of this book focuses on this version.)

✔ The self-installed and self-hosted version available at WordPress.org. (Part III focuses on this version.)

✔ The multi-user version, WordPress MU, available at `http://mu.word press.org`. (Part IV focuses on this version.)

In this chapter, I discuss the advantages and disadvantages of each WordPress version in relation to the others to help you discover which is right for you. This chapter also covers some of the various blogging technologies that will help you on your way to running a successful blog, such as the use of comments and RSS feed technology, as well as information about combating spam.

Choosing the Hosted Version from WordPress.com

WordPress.com is a free service. If downloading, installing, and using software on a Web server sounds Greek to you — and something you'd rather avoid — the WordPress folks provide a solution for you at WordPress.com.

WordPress.com is a *hosted solution,* which means that there is no software requirement. No downloads. No installation or server configurations. It's all done for you on the back end, behind the scenes. You don't even have to worry about how it happens. It happens quickly, and before you know it, you're making your first blog post using a WordPress.com blog solution.

WordPress.com has some limitations, however. You can't install plugins or custom themes, and you can't customize the base code files (the PHP files that power the foundation of the blog). However, even with its limitations, WordPress.com is an excellent starting point for a brand-new blogger who might be a little intimidated by the software and configuration requirements of the self-installed WordPress.org software.

The good news is this: If you find you outgrow your WordPress.com hosted blog in the future and want to take a swing at the self-hosted WordPress.org software, you can. You can even take all the content from your WordPress.com hosted blog with you and easily import it into your new setup with the WordPress.org software.

So in the grand scheme of things, you're really not that limited.

Self-Hosting with WordPress.org

The self-installed version from WordPress.org (covered in Part III) requires you to download the software from the WordPress Web site and install it on a Web server. Unless you own your own Web server, you need to lease one — or lease space on one.

Using a Web server is typically referred to as *Web hosting,* and unless you know someone who knows someone, it's generally not free. That being said, Web hosting doesn't cost a whole lot, either. You can usually obtain good Web hosting services for anywhere from $5–$10 per month. (Chapter 6 gives you the important details you need to know about obtaining a Web host.) You do, however, need to make sure that any Web host you choose to work with has the required software installed on the Web server. Currently, the minimum software requirements for WordPress include:

  ✔ PHP version 4.2 or greater
  ✔ MySQL version 4.0 or greater

After you have WordPress installed on your Web server (see the installation instructions in Chapter 6), you can start using it to blog to your heart's content. With the WordPress software, you can install several different plugins that can extend the functionality of the blogging system, as I describe in Chapter 10. You also have full control over the core files and code that WordPress is built on. So if you have a knack for PHP and knowledge of MySQL, you can work within the code to make changes that you think would be good for you and your blog.

You don't need design ability to make your blog look great. Members of the WordPress community have created more than 1,600 WordPress themes (designs), and you can download them for free and install them on your WordPress blog (see Chapter 9). Additionally, if you're creatively inclined, like to create designs on your own, and have knowledge of CSS, you have full access to the template system within WordPress and can create your own custom themes (see Chapter 9).

Running a Network of Blogs with WordPress MU

Although the WordPress.com hosted service runs on the WordPress MU software and the end-user configuration settings are very similar, setting up, administering, and managing this version of WordPress differ a great deal from the WordPress.com or WordPress.org versions.

WordPress MU allows you to run thousands of blogs on one installation of its software platform, on one domain. Its biggest claim to fame, of course, is the hosted version of WordPress.com, which uses the MU platform to run more than one million blogs and climbing.

When you install and use WordPress MU, you become administrator of a network of blogs. The administration interface for WordPress MU differs from WordPress.com or the software from WordPress.org in that you're configuring options and settings for your blog as well as multiple blogs across your network.

WordPress MU does everything the original software from WordPress.org does, so you can provide bloggers with all of the functionality that WordPress users have come to expect and enjoy.

WordPress MU isn't meant for the casual user or beginner. It's also not meant for bloggers who want to run 5–10 of their own blogs on one domain. Who is it meant for, then?

✔ Blog networks (such as edublogs.org) that currently have more than 150 blogs.

✔ Newspapers and magazines such as *The New York Times,* and universities such as Harvard Law School that currently use WordPress MU to manage the blog sections of their Web sites.

✔ Niche-specific blog networks, such as Edublogs.org, that use WordPress MU to manage their full networks of free blogs for teachers, educators, lecturers, librarians, and other education professionals.

In addition, in 2006, Automattic, Inc. (the folks behind the WordPress machine), started offering enterprise-level support to companies that need assistance with using the WordPress software. Automattic partnered with KnowNow to form the KnowNow WordPress Enterprise Edition (KWEE), a special version of WordPress MU for business and corporate setups.

In Part IV of this book, I introduce you to the basics of the setup, installation, and management of a WordPress multi-user community network of blogs.

Understanding the Differences in WordPress Versions

Certain features are available to you in every WordPress blog setup, whether you're using the software from WordPress.org, the hosted version at Word Press.com, or the multi-user version of WordPress MU (see Table 2-1 for a comparison of the three WordPress versions). These features include but aren't limited to the following:

✔ Quick-and-easy installation and setup

✔ Full-featured blogging capability, allowing you to publish content to the Web through an easy-to-use Web-based interface

✔ Topical archiving of your posts, using categories

✔ Monthly listings archiving feature

✔ Comment and trackback tools

✔ Automatic spam protection through the use of Akismet

✔ Great community support

✔ Unlimited amount of static pages, allowing you to step out of the blog box and into the sphere of running a fully functional Web site

✔ RSS capability with RSS 2.0, RSS 1.0, and Atom support

✔ Tools for importing content from different blogging systems (such as Blogger, Movable Type, and LiveJournal)

Table 2-1	Exploring the Differences among the Three Versions of WordPress		
Feature	*WordPress.org*	*WordPress.com*	*WordPress MU*
Cost	Free	Free	Free
Software download	Yes	No	Yes
Software installation	Yes	No	Yes
Requires Web hosting	Yes	No	Yes
Custom CSS control	Yes	$15/year	Yes — for the MU administrator, not for the end user
Template access	Yes	No	Yes — for the MU administrator, not for the end user
Sidebar widgets	Yes	Yes	Yes
RSS syndication	Yes	Yes	Yes
Access to core code	Yes	No	Yes — for the MU administrator, not for the end user
Ability to install plugins	Yes	No	Yes
WP themes installation	Yes	No	Yes
Multi-author support	Yes	Yes	Yes
Unlimited number of blog setups with one account	No	Yes	Yes
Community-based support forums	Yes	Yes	Yes

This Crazy Little Thing Called Blog

The practice of blogging is an evolutionary process, and it's my strong feeling that blogs have evolved beyond personal journals to become tools for real journalism, business, and authorship.

A blog is a fabulous tool to use to publish your personal diary of thoughts and ideas; however, blogs also serve as excellent tools for business, editorial journalism, news, and entertainment. Here are some ways that people use blogs:

- ✔ **Personal:** This type of blogger creates a blog as a personal journal or diary. You're considered a personal blogger if you use your blog mainly to discuss topics that are personal to you or your life — for example, your family, your cats, your children, or other topics of great interest to you, such as technology, politics, sports, art, or photography.

- ✔ **Business:** This type of blogger uses the power of blogs to promote her company's business services and/or products on the Internet. Blogs are very effective tools for promotion and marketing, and these blogs usually offer helpful information to readers and consumers, such as ad tips and product reviews. Blogs also allow readers to provide feedback and ideas, which can help a company improve services. Search engines (such as Google, Yahoo!, and MSN) really like Web sites that are updated on a regular basis, and using a blog for your business allows you to regularly update your Web site with content and information that your readers and consumers might find helpful. At the same time, you can increase your company's exposure in the search engines by giving the search engines a lot of content to sift through and include in the search results.

- ✔ **Media/journalism:** More and more, popular news outlets such as Fox News, MSNBC, and CNN are adding blogs to their Web sites to provide information on current events, politics, and news on a regional, national, and international level. These news organizations often have editorial bloggers, as well. For instance, editorial cartoonist David Cagel maintains a blog at MSNBC at `http://cagle.msnbc.com/news/blog`, where he blogs about his cartoons and feedback he receives from readers.

- ✔ **Citizen journalism:** There was a time when I might have put these bloggers in the Personal Blogger category; however, blogs have really opened up the possibility of average citizens having a great effect on the analysis and dissemination of news and information on a national and international level. The emergence of citizen journalism saw the swing from old media to new media. In old media, the journalists and news organizations were the ones to direct the conversation about news topics.

  With the popularity of blogs and the millions of bloggers who exploded onto the Internet, old media felt a change in the wind. Average citizens, using the power of their voices on blogs, changed the direction of the conversation, with many of these bloggers fact-checking news stories and exposing inconsistencies with the intention of keeping the media or local politicians in check. Many of these bloggers are interviewed on major cable news stations as the mainstream media recognizes the importance of the emergence of the citizen voice through blogging.

✔ **Professional:** These bloggers are a rare breed, but they're out there. This category of blogger is growing every day. This blogger is hired and then paid to blog for an individual company or Web site. There are blog networks, such as WeblogsInc.com, that hire bloggers to write a blog on a certain topic of interest. Recently, I've noticed a few new services on the Internet, such as ReviewMe.com, that put advertisers together with bloggers, whereby the advertisers hire bloggers to make blog posts about their products. The blogger then gets paid for this. Is it possible to make money as a blogger? Yes, and it's becoming more and more common these days.

Dipping In to Blog Technologies

The WordPress software is a personal publishing system that uses a PHP and MySQL platform, which provides you with everything you need for creating your own blog to publish your own content, dynamically, without having to know how to program those pages yourself. In short, all of your content is stored in a MySQL database on your hosting account.

PHP stands for PHP Hypertext Preprocessor, and it's a server-side scripting language for creating dynamic Web pages. When a visitor opens a page built in PHP, the server processes the PHP commands and then sends the results to the visitor's browser. MySQL is an open source, relational, database management system (RDBMS) that uses Structured Query Language (SQL), the most popular language for adding, accessing, and processing data in a database.

Every time a visitor goes to your blog to read your content, he makes a request that's sent to your server. The PHP programming language receives that request, obtains the requested information from the MySQL database, and then presents the requested information to your visitor through his Web browser.

In using the term *content* as it applies to the data that's stored in the MySQL database, I'm referring to your blog posts, comments, and options that you set up in the WordPress Administration panel. The theme (design) you chose to use for your blog, whether it's the default theme, one you create for yourself, or one that you have custom designed for you, isn't part of the content in this case. Those files are a part of the file system and aren't stored in the database. So it's always a good idea to create and keep a backup of any theme files that you're currently using. Refer to Chapter 9 for further information on WordPress theme management.

TIP

When you look for a hosting service, you should keep an eye out for the hosts who provide you with daily backups of your site, just in case something does happen and your content/data is lost. Web hosting providers who offer daily backups as part of their service can save the day by restoring your site to its original form.

Archiving your content

Packaged within the blogging software is the capability to maintain chronological and categorized archives of your publishing history, automatically. WordPress uses PHP and MySQL technology to sort and organize everything you publish in an order that you, and your readers, can access by date and category. This archiving process is done automatically with every post you publish to your blog.

When you create a post on your WordPress blog, you can file that post under a category that you specify. This feature makes for a very nifty archiving system in which you and your readers can find articles/posts that you've placed within a specific category. For example, my personal blog at `http://justagirlintheworld.com` contains a section called Categories, and there you find a list of categories I've created for my blog posts. Clicking the Photography link under my Categories heading takes you to a listing of posts that I wrote on that topic (see Figures 2-1 and 2-2).

Categories
where i put stuff

- Blog Design
- Blogging
- Blogs About Hosting
- Color
- Cooking
- CSS
- Current Events
- Design
- E.Webscapes
- Family/Friends
- Fun N' Frolic
- Geeky Things
- General
- Goals
- Green Thumb
- Him n' Her
- Holidays/Travel
- Movies/TV
- Music/Books
- Nursing
- Paid Reviews
- Photography

Figure 2-1:
A list of categories in a WordPress blog site.

Figure 2-2:
A page
with a list of
posts made
in my Photo-
graphy
category.

WordPress lets you create as many categories as you want for filing your blog posts away by topic. I've seen blogs that have just one category and blogs that have up to 1,800 categories — it's all about personal preference and how you wish to organize your content. On the other hand, using WordPress categories is your choice. You don't have to use the category feature if you'd rather not.

Interacting with your readers through comments

One of the more exciting and fun features of blogging with WordPress is getting instant feedback from your readers the moment you make a post to your blog. Referred to as *blog comments,* this feedback is akin to having a guest book on your blog. People can leave notes for you that are published to your site, and you can respond and engage your readers in conversation about the topic at hand. (See Figures 2-3 and 2-4.) Having this function included on your blog creates the opportunity to expand the thoughts and ideas that you presented in your blog post by allowing your readers the opportunity to add their two cents.

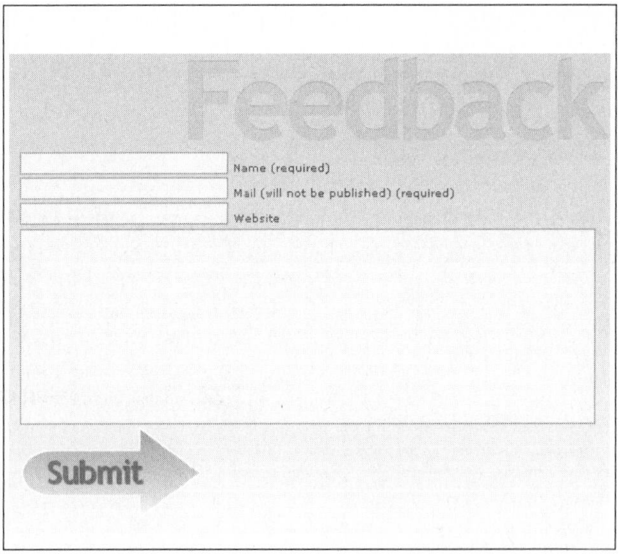

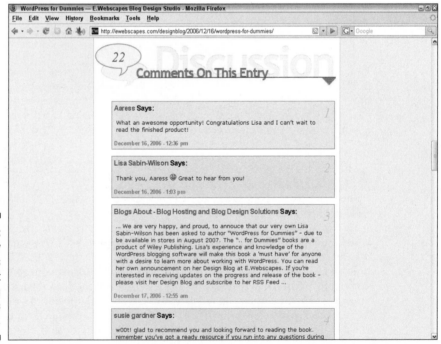

Figure 2-3:
Readers use
the form to
leave their
comments.

Figure 2-4:
My
blog fans
comment
on my blog
about this
book.

In the WordPress Administration panel, you have full administrative control over who can and can't leave comments. In addition, if someone leaves a comment with questionable content, you can edit the comment or delete it altogether. You're also free to make the choice not to allow any comments on your blog.

Many blog users say that a blog without comments isn't a blog at all. This is a commonly held belief among those in the blogging community because experiencing visitor feedback through the use of comments is part of what has made blogging so popular. It's a personal choice. Publishing a blog without comments allows your readers to passively partake in your published words. Allowing comments on your blog invites your audience to actively involve themselves in your blog by creating a discussion and dialogue about your content. By and large, readers find this to be a more satisfying experience when they visit blogs, making them part of the discussion.

Tracking back

The best way to define trackbacks is to think of them as comments, except for one thing: *Trackbacks* are comments that are left on your blog by other blogs, not by actual people. Sounds perfectly reasonable, doesn't it?

Actually, it does.

It happens when you make a post on your blog, and within that post, you provide a link to a post made by another blogger, on a different blog. When you publish that post, your blog sends a sort of electronic memo (a *network ping)* to the blog you've linked to. That blog receives the memo and posts an acknowledgement of receipt in a comment to the post that you linked to.

That memo is sent via a method called a *network ping* (a tool used to test, or verify, whether a link is reachable across the Internet) from your site to the site you link to. This works as long as both blogs support trackback protocol. WordPress does. Almost all of the major blogging platforms do, except Blogspot. Blogspot users need to sign up and use a third-party program called HaloScan in order to have trackback functionality on their blogs.

Sending a trackback to a blog is a nice way of telling the blogger that you like the information she presented in her blog post. Every blogger out there appreciates the receipt of trackbacks to their posts from other bloggers.

Dealing with comment and trackback spam

Ugh. The absolute *bane* of every blogger's existence — comment and trackback spam. When blogs became the "It" thing to do on the Internet, spammers saw an opportunity beyond spamming via e-mail. If you've ever received spam in your e-mail, the concept is similar and just as frustrating.

Before blogs came onto the scene, you could often see spammers filling up Internet guest books with their links — but not leaving any relevant comments. The reason for this is simple: Web sites can receive a higher ranking in the major search engines if they have multiple links coming into their site from other sites on the Internet. Enter blog software with the comment and trackback technologies — and this was prime breeding ground for millions of spammers to live.

Because comments and trackbacks are published to your site publicly — and usually with a link to the commenter's Web site — spammers started to take advantage of getting their Web site links posted on millions of blogs throughout the Internet by creating programs that automatically seek out Web sites with commenting systems in place and then hammering the comment system with tons of comments that contain links back to their site.

No blogger likes spam. As a matter of fact, blogging systems such as WordPress have spent untold hours all in the name of stopping these spammers in their tracks. And, for the most part, they've been successful. Every once in a while, however, spammers sneak through. Many of them are offensive. All of them are frustrating because they don't contribute to the ongoing conversations that occur on blogs.

As you read about the different versions of software available from WordPress, I tell you how to combat comment and trackback spam. However, all WordPress systems have one very major, very excellent thing in common. It's called Akismet, and it kills spam dead. Chapter 10 tells you more about Akismet, which is brought to you by Automattic, the makers of WordPress.com.

Distributing new content to readers with RSS feeds

RSS stands for Really Simple Syndication. An *RSS feed* is a standard feature that blog readers have come to expect. So, what is it, really?

The resource site WebReference.com (`www.webreference.com/authoring/languages/xml/rss/intro/`) defines RSS as "a lightweight XML format designed for sharing headlines and other Web content. Think of it as a distributable 'What's New' for your site."

Readers can use tools called *feed readers* to download your feed — that's to say that their feed readers are set up to automatically discover new content (such as posts and comments) from your blog and download that content for their consumption. Of the many feed readers on the market today, Table 2-2 lists some of the more popular ones.

Table 2-2	Popular RSS Feed Readers	
Reader	*Source*	*Description*
Bloglines	`http://blog lines.com`	A free online service for searching, subscribing to, and sharing RSS feeds. There is no software to download or install, as it's all Web based. You do need to sign up for an account with Bloglines in order to use this service.
Google Reader	`http://google. com/reader`	A free online service provided by Internet search giant, Google. With Google Reader, you can keep up with your favorite blogs and Web sites that have syndicated (RSS) content. There is no software to download or install in order to use this service. This service does require you to sign up for an account with Google.
FeedDemon	`http://feed demon.com`	This service does require a software download that you install on your computer. It isn't a free service — at the time of this writing, you can download a free trial. When that trial is over, it does carry a fee of $29.95.
FeedLounge	`http://feed lounge.com`	This Web-based service allows you to subscribe to your favorite blogs or Web sites and carries the cost of $5 per month.

In order for your blog readers to stay updated with the latest and greatest content you post to your site, they need to subscribe to your RSS feed. Most blogging platforms allow the RSS feeds to be *autodiscovered* by the various feed readers — meaning, the reader needs only to enter your site's URL, and the program will automatically find your RSS feed.

 Most browser systems today will alert visitors to the RSS feed on your site by displaying the universally recognized orange RSS feed icon, shown here in the margin.

Moving On to the Business of Blogging

Making the choice as to which variety of WordPress is best for you requires you to take a long look at your big plans for your Web site. A word of advice: Organize your plan of attack before you start. Have a good idea about what type of information you want to publish, how you'd like that information to be presented and organized, and what type of services and interaction you want to provide to your audience.

It doesn't matter if you're planning to start a personal blog with a diary of your daily life or a business blog that provides useful information to readers interested in your area of expertise. All potential bloggers have ideas of what type of information they want to present, and you wouldn't be considering starting a new blog if you didn't want to share that information (no matter what it is) with the rest of the world via the Internet. So having a plan of attack is helpful when starting out.

Say this out loud: "What am I going to blog about?" Go ahead, say it. Do you have an answer? Maybe you do, maybe not — either way, it's all right. There's no clear set of ground rules you must follow. Having an idea of what you're planning to write about in your blog makes planning your attack a little easier. Will you write about your personal life? Maybe you're planning to share only some of your photography, with very little commentary to go along with it. Are you a business owner planning to blog about your services and current news within your industry?

Having an idea of what your subject matter will be helps you determine how you want to deliver that information. For instance, my design blog is where I write about Web design projects, client case studies, and news related to design and blogging. You won't find pictures of my cats there, but you will find those pictures on my personal blog. I keep the two separate much in the same way that most of us like to keep a distinct line of separation between our personal and professional lives, no matter what industry we work in.

With your topic in mind, ask yourself these questions:

- ✔ How often will I update my blog with new posts? Daily? Weekly?
- ✔ Do I want to encourage discussion by allowing my readers to comment on my blog posts?
- ✔ Do I want to make every post available for public display? Am I okay with my boss or my family finding and reading my blog posts?
- ✔ How will I categorize my posts?
- ✔ Do I want the full content of my posts, or just a partial excerpt, published in my RSS feed?
- ✔ Do I want my blog posts to be easily found by search engines?

With your topic and plan of delivery in mind, you can move forward and adjust your blog settings to work with your plan.

Part II

Using the WordPress Hosted Service

The 5th Wave   By Rich Tennant

"He saw your laptop and wants to know if he can post a new blog."

In this part . . .

*I*f installing software on a Web server and hosting your own blog sound like things you'd like to avoid, WordPress.com may be your answer. In this section, you find out how to get — and use — a free hosted blog from WordPress.com.

Chapter 3

Getting Started with WordPress.com

In This Chapter

▶ Signing up for a blog

▶ Familiarizing yourself with the Administration panel

▶ Reviewing important settings

*I*f installing software on a Web server sounds like something you'd rather avoid at all costs, WordPress.com has an alternative for you.

Part I of this book gives you a glimpse into the three different software versions in the WordPress family, along with an overview of blogging with Word-Press. This part takes a complete look at the hosted service offered at WordPress.com, and in this chapter, you discover how to obtain a free blog using this service. You also find out how to get your hosted blog up and running.

Don't confuse this part with the blogging software available for download at WordPress.org! The two were created and developed by the same folks, and they do share the same name; however, they are each a different variety of WordPress. (See Part III for information on installing and using the self-hosted version of WordPress.org.)

Creating a WordPress.com Account

To create your WordPress.com user account, follow these steps:

1. **In your browser, enter the URL** `http://wordpress.com`.

2. **On the page that appears, click the big Sign Up Now! button (shown in Figure 3-1).**

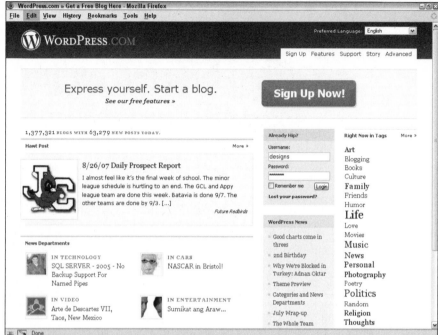

Figure 3-1:
On the
WordPress.
com main
page, click
the Start
Your
WordPress
Blog link.

This takes you to the WordPress.com signup page at `http://word press.com/signup`.

3. **In the Username text box, enter the name you will use to log in to your blog from now until forever.**

   This username cannot be changed for the blog you are creating right now. You can, in the future, sign up for a new account with WordPress.com with a new username; this will also mean that you'll be starting over with a new blog.

4. **Enter a password of your choice in the Password box.**

   This is the password you'll use to log in to your new WordPress.com account. Choose, and then type, a password that you will remember, but not one that would be easy for any outside users to guess. Type it once more in the Confirm box.

5. **Enter your e-mail address in the Email Address box.**

   This address is not made public on your blog; rather, it's used for communication between you and WordPress.com. You can change this address later, under the Options tab in your WordPress.com Administration panel.

6. **Select the check box in the Legal Flotsam section.**

   Selecting the Legal Flotsam box lets the WordPress.com folks know that you've read their Terms of Service.

7. **Select either Gimme a Blog! or Just a Username, Please.**

   The Gimme a Blog! option signs you up with a WordPress.com account and sets you up with a new WordPress.com blog. The Just a Username, Please option just signs you up with a new WordPress.com account, without the blog setup part. You may want only to reserve a username in WordPress.com for now, which is why you might choose the second option.

8. **Click the Next button.**

9. **Enter what you choose as your blog domain name in the Blog Domain text box.**

   Whatever you enter here will be the URL address of your blog. It must be at least four characters (letters and numbers only), and you can't change it later, so choose carefully! (The domain name of your blog does not have to be the same as your username, although WordPress.com already fills in this text box for you, with your username. You can actually choose any domain name that you want here — WordPress.com will let you know whether that domain name is available within its network.)

10. **In the Blog Title text box, enter the name you've chosen for your blog.**

    Your blog title doesn't have to be the same as your username, and you can change it later in the Options section of your Administration panel.

11. **Select your language preference in the Language drop-down menu.**

    This is the language that you will be primarily blogging in.

12. **Select the Privacy check box if you want your blog to be public. Deselect this box if you want your blog to be private — that is, not show up on search engines.**

    Some bloggers actually do not want their blog to be indexed by search engines, amazingly enough. For instance, you may want to run a private blog for which you decide who can, and cannot, view the contents of your blog.

13. **Click the Sign-Up button and you're done!**

    Clicking this button loads a new page, which displays a confirmation message that your WordPress.com account is now active. An e-mail is also sent to you that contain your username, password, and some important links (for instance, links to where you go to write new posts to your blog, a link to your Administration panel, and other information).

Your new blog is yours to use for the life of your blogging career at WordPress.com. You can log in to your blog any time by going to http://wordpress.com and filling in the Already Hip? box (shown in Figure 3-2) on the main page with your WordPress.com username and password.

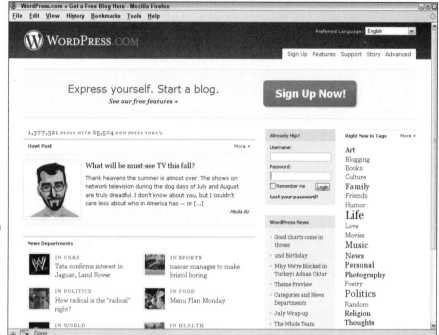

Figure 3-2:
Already hip?
Go ahead
and log
in to your
new blog.

Have you ever signed up for services on the Web, only to later forget your username and/or password for that service mere weeks after the fact? Yep, me, too. It is a *very* good idea to file that e-mail from WordPress.com in a safe place for future reference. Just make sure that you remember where you put it. Or you can tell WordPress.com to remember you each time you enter the site. To do so, select the Remember Me check box, and WordPress.com places a cookie in your browser files that tells it to remember your login credentials the next time you visit the site (you need to have cookies enabled in your browser configurations in order for this to work).

Logging In to WordPress.com

When you've successfully logged in to your new account, WordPress returns you to the main WordPress.com Web site — only this time, you see something slightly different at the top. The page now displays the WordPress.com menu bar, as shown in Figure 3-3. The WordPress.com menu bar contains some short-cut links to some important areas of your Administration panel.

Figure 3-3:
The
WordPress.
com menu
bar.

The WordPress.com menu bar also appears at the top of any WordPress.com blog you surf to, as long as you are logged in to your WordPress.com account. This menu bar provides you with fast access to your own WordPress.com Administration panel and account.

The WordPress.com menu bar consists of several helpful quick links for you to access your account, your Administration panel, and various options. From left to right, these quick links include:

✓ **My Account:** Hover your mouse pointer over this link in the menu bar and you see a drop-down menu that consists of the following:

- *Global Dashboard:* Takes you to the Dashboard panel.

- *Tag Surfer:* Takes you to the Tag Surfer, where you can find out what people are talking about based on keywords.

- *My Comments:* Takes you to the My Comments section of the WordPress Administration panel, where you can view all comments you've left anywhere within the WordPress.com network of blogs.

- *Edit Profile:* Takes you to the Your Profile section of your Administration panel, where you can edit your own user profile.

- *Contact Support:* Click this if you need assistance from the folks who run WordPress.com.

- *WordPress.com:* Takes you to the main WordPress.com Web site.

- *Logout:* Click this to logout.

✔ **My Dashboard:** Click this tab to go into your WordPress.Com Administration panel, to the Dashboard page.

✔ **New Post:** Click this tab to go into your WordPress.com Administration panel, to the Write Post page, where you can write and publish a new post to your blog.

✔ **Press This:** This is a nifty feature in WordPress.com. When you are surfing other users' blogs on WordPress.com, you can click the Press This link in the menu bar and in the same window, the Write Post page loads with the title of the page you were on automatically inserted in the title field, with a link to the page you were on embedded into the Post text box.

✔ **Blog Info:** Hover your mouse over this tab to see a drop-down a menu with the following elements:

- *Random Post:* Loads a random post from the blog you are visiting in the same window.

- *Subscribe to Blog:* Loads the Blog Surfer page within your Administration panel, allowing you to subscribe to the blog you're visiting.

- *Add to Blogroll:* Automatically adds the blog you are visiting to your blogroll.

- *Report as Spam:* Reports the blog to the WordPress.com administration as a spam blog.

- *Report as Mature:* Reports the blog to the WordPress.com Administration as a blog containing mature content.

If you delete your cookies in your browser and then visit WordPress.com again, you won't see the WordPress.com menu bar and will have to log in again. Likewise, after deleting the cookies in your browser, when you visit your new blog, it will appear to you as if you are a visitor (that is, you'll see no menu bar with quick links to log in to your Administration panel). In this case, you have to revisit the WordPress.com main site to log in again.

The WordPress.com Dashboard

When you click the My Dashboard link in the WordPress.com menu bar (covered in the previous section), you go directly into your new WordPress.com Administration panel, starting at the Dashboard tab. (See Figure 3-4.)

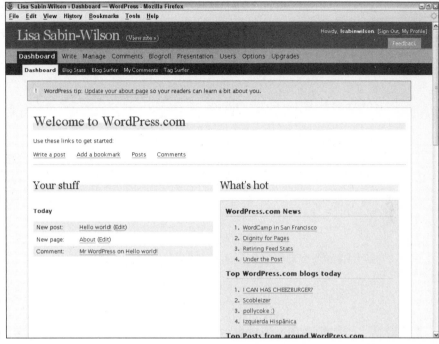

Figure 3-4:
The
Dashboard
page
serves as
the control
center for
your blog.

The upper-left part of the page contains the following areas:

- ✔ **Write a Post:** Click this link to go to the Write Post section, where you can write and publish new posts to your blog.

- ✔ **Add A Bookmark:** Click this link to go to the Add Link page, where you can add a link to your blogroll. A *bookmark* is a link to another blog or site that you favor and would like to share, publicly, on your blog.

- ✔ **Posts:** Click this link and you find a list of the posts you've made, with options to allow you to manage them.

- ✔ **Comments:** Click this link and the Comments opens with a list of all the comments that visitors have made on your blog. The page also includes options to allow you to manage the comments.

In the Your Stuff area of the page, you see the following sections:

- ✔ **Today:** Click the links here to go to a page with options that allow you to manage today's posts. Contains new or updated posts you've made on your blog on the current day.

- ✔ **A While Ago:** Click the links here to go to a page with options that allow you to manage posts and updates you've made on past days.

And finally, the What's Hot section provides you with information about the happenings in and around WordPress.com, including WordPress news, top blogs, and so on. It also tells you how much spam WordPress.com has prevented from showing up on your blog.

Important Options to Set before You Blog

The options in this section help you get started and well on your way to managing your own WordPress.com blog. In this section, you discover the steps to take to set the primary options that personalize your blog, including creating your user profile, setting the date and timestamp for your blog (based on your own time zone settings), and uploading a picture of yourself.

Setting your General options

To begin personalizing some of the settings and options for your Word Press.com blog, follow these steps:

1. **Click the My Dashboard tab on the menu bar of the WordPress.com main page.**

   This takes you into your WordPress.com Administration panel, starting in the Dashboard panel.

2. **Click the Options tab on the Administration panel.**

   The Options page, shown in Figure 3-5, appears.

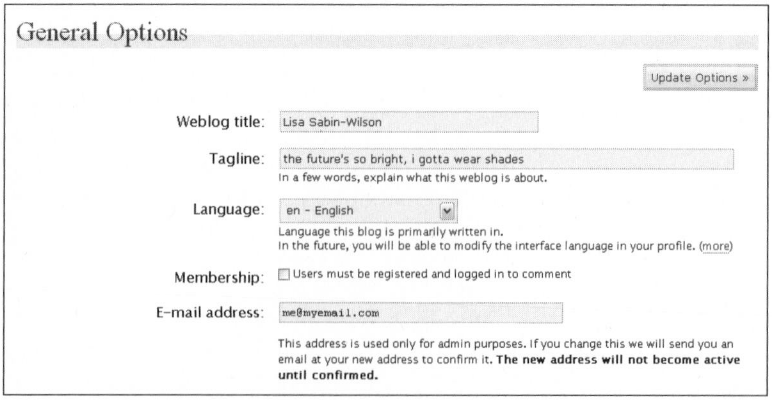

Figure 3-5:
Setting the
General
options for
your blog.

General Options

Update Options »

Weblog title: Lisa Sabin-Wilson

Tagline: the future's so bright, i gotta wear shades
In a few words, explain what this weblog is about.

Language: en - English
Language this blog is primarily written in.
In the future, you will be able to modify the interface language in your profile. (more)

Membership: ☐ Users must be registered and logged in to comment

E-mail address: me@myemail.com

This address is used only for admin purposes. If you change this we will send you an email at your new address to confirm it. **The new address will not become active until confirmed.**

3. **Enter the name of your blog in the Weblog Title text box.**

   This is the name of your blog. You can revisit this page again at anytime in the future and change this as often as you'd like.

4. **In the Tagline text box, enter a slogan or a motto that describes you or your blog.**

   The tagline should be a short, one-liner that sums up the tone and premise of your blog. As you can see in Figure 3-5, I used a quote from a song by a group called Timbuk 3: "The future's so bright, I gotta wear shades." Although my tagline doesn't really give you a description of what my blog is about, it does give you an idea about the optimistic nature of the blog's author.

5. **Click the drop-down menu next to Language to choose the language in which you want to publish your blog.**

6. **Select the check box next to Membership if you want to allow comments on your blog only from users who have registered and logged in as members of your blog.**

   If you would like to open your blog to comments from anyone who surfs in, don't select this option. (You can find more information about managing members and users in Chapter 4.)

7. **Type your e-mail address in the E-mail address box.**

   The e-mail address that you signed up with appears here. You can change this e-mail address, but be warned: If you change the e-mail address here, it won't become active until you confirm that you are, in fact, the owner of said e-mail address. This is accomplished through a simple process whereby WordPress.com sends an e-mail to that address and gives you a link to click and confirm that you are the owner. This e-mail address is used for administrative purposes only, which consists mainly of communication between you and WordPress.com.

Adjusting your Date and Time settings

After you set up the General options that I discuss in the preceding section, you can use the last part on this page to set your local time so that your blog posts are published with a time stamp in your own time zone, no matter where in the world you currently live. Use the following options to establish your settings in this area, as shown in Figure 3-6.

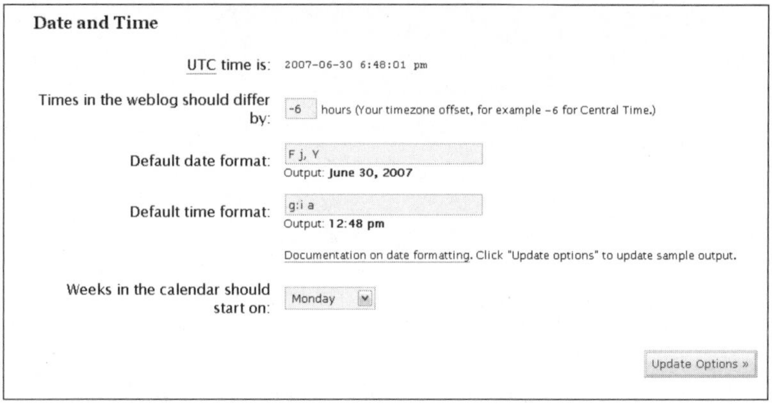

Date and Time

UTC time is: 2007-06-30 6:48:01 pm

Times in the weblog should differ by: `-6` hours (Your timezone offset, for example −6 for Central Time.)

Default date format: `F j, Y`
Output: June 30, 2007

Default time format: `g:i a`
Output: 12:48 pm

Documentation on date formatting. Click "Update options" to update sample output.

Weeks in the calendar should start on: `Monday ⌄`

Update Options »

Figure 3-6:
Date
and Time
settings
for your
WordPress.
com blog.

✔ **Times in the Weblog Should Differ By:** With this option, you can choose the number of hours that your local time differs from the Coordinated Universal Time (UTC) displayed directly above this option. This ensures that all your blog posts and comments left on your blog are time stamped with the correct time output. For example, if you are lucky enough to live, as I do, in the frozen tundra of Wisconsin, which is in the Central Time Zone (CST), you enter **−6** in this text box. If you're unsure what your time zone offset is, you can look it up on the Greenwich Mean Time Web site (`http://wwp.greenwichmeantime.com`).

✔ **Default Date Format:** Choose this option to have your date appear using the default format "F d, Y," where F is the full textual representation of the month, (as in January), d is the two-digit representation of the day (01), and Y is the four-digit representation of the year (2007), making the date appear in this format: January 01, 2007.

✔ **Default Time Format:** Set the way you want the time to appear in "g:i a" format, where g is the 12-hour format for the hour, i is the two-digit representation of the minutes, and a is the lowercase ante meridiem (am or pm), giving you a time output of, for example, 12:00 pm.

✔ **Weeks in the Calendar Should Start On:** Choose the day of the week you want your calendar to start on here. If you plan to display the WordPress calendar on your blog, you can set it to start on any day of the week.

You can format the time and date any of several different ways. Go to `http://us3.php.net/date` to find the format potentials at the PHP Web site.

After you're done with setting up your general options and the date/time format, click the Update Options button at the bottom of this page. Performing this last step saves the options you just selected.

Setting your profile: Tell us a little about yourself

The next set of options you need to update is your profile. This area lets you configure your personal settings in order to individualize your WordPress.com blog and tell the world a little more about yourself. This blog is, after all, all about you, and this is your opportunity to brag and promote!

Make sure that you've clicked the My Dashboard tab to get into the Administration panel. There, click the Users tab and then click the Your Profile subtab to see the Your Profile and Personal Options page. Here, you can adjust all sorts of personal settings that will allow your visitors to get to know you better. You can be as liberal with the information you want to share, or as stingy as you want. It's *your* blog, after all.

If you don't want people to know your real name, use a nickname here. If you don't want to share a picture of yourself in fear of shattering computer monitors worldwide, you can choose not to upload any picture at all or upload a picture of something that reflects the essence of you. (For example, post a picture of a book if you're an avid reader, a picture of a camera if you're a photographer, and so on.) The options here are endless, and there are no real rules that apply to what type or how much personal information you should, or should not, share with the rest of the Internet world.

Make it your own. Stake your claim and mark your territory in this section! Figures 3-7 through 3-9 show the areas of the Your Profile and Personal Options page, where you can provide this personal information.

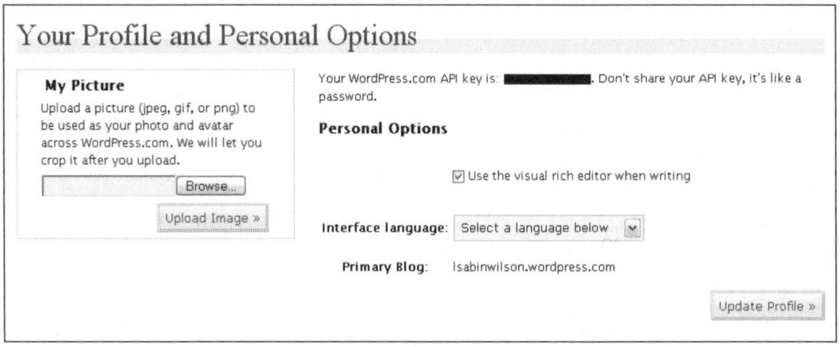

Figure 3-7: Upload a picture and set personal options.

Your Profile and Personal Options

My Picture
Upload a picture (jpeg, gif, or png) to be used as your photo and avatar across WordPress.com. We will let you crop it after you upload.

[Browse...]
[Upload Image »]

Your WordPress.com API key is: ▓▓▓▓▓▓▓. Don't share your API key, it's like a password.

Personal Options

☑ Use the visual rich editor when writing

Interface language: [Select a language below ▾]

Primary Blog: lsabinwilson.wordpress.com

[Update Profile »]

Choosing a language to administrate with

In Figure 3-7, the Interface Language option refers to the language that you want to set for the Administration panel only. Don't confuse this with the Language option (shown previously in Figure 3-5). That option is the language you want to publish your blog in. If you want to view the settings in your WordPress Administration panel in Italian but want your published, public blog in English, you set the Interface Language option (shown in Figure 3-7) to Italian and the Language option (shown in Figure 3-5) to English. *Capiche?*

My Picture

In the My Picture section of the Your Personal Profile and Personal Options page, you can upload a picture (also called an avatar, which is a graphical image of you) of yourself or an image that represents you.

The picture/avatar that you insert into your WordPress.com is used in a number of different ways:

✔ The WordPress.com Blog of The Day page at `http://botd.word press.com/top-posts`, which lists the Top Posts from the Top Blogs of the Day. If your blog is included in these lists, a smaller version of the picture you've uploaded to your profile appears next to the listing.

✔ WordPress.com also lists a Hawt Post (or "Hot" post) on its main page at `http://wordpress.com`. If the WordPress spotlight shines in your direction, your picture will be displayed here for your own 15 minutes of WordPress.com fame.

✔ WordPress.com also keeps a directory (by topic) of its community blogs. This directory is called the Tags page (`http://wordpress.com/tags`). Bloggers on WordPress.com can tag their posts with keywords that help define the topic of their post, and WordPress.com collects all those tagged posts and sorts them by name on the Tags page.

For example, on the Tag: Blogging page at `http://wordpress.com/tags/blogging`, you find the most recent posts that WordPress.com bloggers have made on the topic of blogging. If your blog appears in this directory, so does a thumbnail of your picture.

Follow these steps to insert a picture or avatar into your profile:

1. **Choose the image you want to attach to your profile and save it to your computer.**

   To be safe in your image selection, be sure to upload an image that is at least 128 pixels in width and 128 pixels in height: 128 x 128. Later in these steps, you see how you can crop a larger image down to the perfect size.

2. **In the My Picture section of the Your Profile and Personal Options page, click the Browse button.**

This opens the Choose File dialog box from your own computer, where you can choose the image file from the files stored on your computer.

3. **Double-click the file.**

The name of the image you chose appears in the text box to the left of the Browse button.

4. **Click the Upload Image button.**

No matter what size image you have used, WordPress.com crops the image for you to the correct size, and lets you decide which part of your image will be used for your picture display. When you click the Upload Image button, the Crop Uploaded Image page appears, and you can crop (cut) your chosen picture to the right size to be used as an avatar or icon.

5. **Use the Crop Tool to highlight the area of the picture that you'd like to remain after cropping.**

In Figure 3-8, you see the box with a dotted line (the Crop Tool) on my mug shot. This dotted outline indicates the size the picture will be when you're done cropping it. You can move that dotted box around to choose the area of the image you want to use as your avatar.

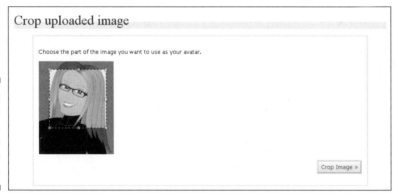

Figure 3-8: Using the WordPress. com Image Crop interface.

6. **When you have chosen the area, click the Crop Image button.**

You receive a message from WordPress.com that states: "Your avatar image has been uploaded and you should start seeing it appear around WordPress.com soon!"

Name, rank, and serial number, please!

Figure 3-9 shows the next section in the Your Profile and Personal Options section. Here, you can provide your name, e-mail address, and other contact information to tell your visitors who you are and where they may contact you.

Fill in the boxes with the information requested. Note that E-mail is the only required field here. This is the e-mail address that WordPress uses to notify you when you have new comments or new user registrations to your blog. Make sure you use a real e-mail address so that you get these notifications.

The Nickname field is for the name that appears publicly on your blog. You may wish to use your real name or develop a nickname (or pseudonym).

Figure 3-9:
Give up your name and contact information.

Name		Contact Info	
Username: (no editing)		E-mail: (required)	
lsabinwilson		lisa@justagirlintheworld.com	
First name:		Website:	
Lisa			
Last name:		AIM:	
Sabin-Wilson			
Nickname:		Yahoo IM:	
lsabinwilson			
Display name publicly as:		Jabber / Google Talk:	
lsabinwilson			

Share and protect

Figure 3-10 reveals the last section of the Your Options and Personal Profile section. Fill in the About Yourself text box with a short snippet that describes you.

The next section is the Update Your Password section. You can change your password here by typing the new password in the New Password text box and typing it again in the Type It One More Time text box.

Make it a regular practice to change your password frequently . I can't recommend this strongly enough. There are people on the Internet who make it their business to attempt to hijack blogs for their own malicious purposes. If you change your password monthly , you lower your risk by keeping them guessing.

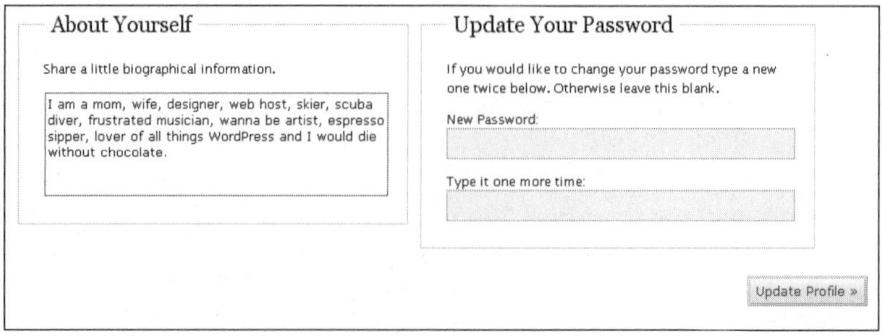

Figure 3-10:
Tell the world about yourself and update your password.

About Yourself	Update Your Password
Share a little biographical information.	If you would like to change your password type a new one twice below. Otherwise leave this blank.
I am a mom, wife, designer, web host, skier, scuba diver, frustrated musician, wanna be artist, espresso sipper, lover of all things WordPress and I would die without chocolate.	New Password:
	Type it one more time:
	Update Profile »

Chapter 4

Writing and Managing Your Blog

· ·

In This Chapter

▶ Writing your first post and making it look nice

▶ Uploading images and videos to a post

▶ Creating and categorizing your blogroll

▶ Inviting friends and establishing their permissions

▶ Moderating a discussion — even when you aren't logged in

▶ Combating comment spam on your blog

▶ Expressing your preference on what shows up on your front page

▶ Displaying your posts in RSS feeds

▶ Protecting your blog's privacy and initiating trusting relationships with OpenID

· ·

*T*he first chapter in this part covers the signup process and a few important settings and options that you configure when you first log in to your new WordPress.com blog. Now it's time to make a blogger out of you. In this chapter, I show you the tools you need to write your first post. After you understand that process, the blogging world is right at your fingertips.

This chapter also shows you the basics of categorizing your posts and links, uploading images to your blog posts, setting discussion and reading options for your blog, using static pages, and managing your users and authors. I don't have the space in this chapter to cover every option available, but I hit the high points of what you need to know.

Ready? Set! BLOG!

In the Administration panel, click the Write tab to display the page where you write, organize, and publish your first post. Start by thinking up a name for your post and entering it in the Title text box, shown in Figure 4-1. You can make the name snappy and fun if you want, but don't be cryptic. Use titles that give your readers a basic idea of what they're about to read in the posts.

Of course, no set of hard-and-fast rules exists when it comes to creating titles for your blog posts; these are just my recommendations. Have fun with your title and allow it to reflect your personality and style of writing.

Figure 4-1:
The area in which you write your post.

By default, the area in which you write your post is in the Visual Editing mode, as indicated by the Visual tab that appears above the text. The Visual Editing mode is how WordPress provides WYSIWYG (what you see is what you get) options for formatting. Rather than have to embed HTML code within your post, you can simply type your post, highlight the text you'd like to format, and click the buttons, shown in Figure 4-1, that appear above the box in which you type your post.

If you've ever used a word processing program, such as Microsoft Word, you'll recognize many of these buttons. They are as follows:

- ✔ **Bold:** This embeds the `<strong> </strong>` HTML tag to emphasize the text in bold. Example: **Bold Text.**

- ✔ **Italics:** This embeds the `<em> </em>` HTML tag to emphasize the text in italics. Example: *Italics Text.*

- ✔ **Strikethrough:** This embeds the `<strike> </strike>` HTML tag that puts a line through your text. Example: `Strikethrough Text.`

- ✔ **Unordered List:** This embeds the `<ul><li> </li></ul>` HTML tags that create an unordered, or bulleted, list.

- ✔ **Ordered List:** This embeds the `<ol><li> </li></ul>` HTML tags that create an ordered, or numbered, list.

- ✔ **Outdent:** This moves the paragraph or section of text you've selected to the left.

- ✔ **Indent:** This inserts the `<blockquote> </blockquote>` HTML tag that moves the paragraph or section of text you've selected to the right.

- ✔ **Align Left:** This inserts the `<p align="left"> </p>` HTML tag that lines the paragraph or section of text you've selected up against the left margin.

- ✔ **Align Center:** This inserts the `<p align="center"> </p>` HTML tag that positions the paragraph or section of text you've selected to the center of the page.

- ✔ **Align Right:** This inserts the `<p align="right"> </p>` HTML tag that positions the paragraph or section of text you've selected up against the right margin.

- ✔ **Insert/Edit Link:** This inserts the `<a href=" "> </a>` HTML tag around the text you've selected to create a hyperlink to a URL.

- ✔ **Unlink:** This removes the URL (hyperlink) from the selected text, if it has been previously linked.

- ✔ **Insert/Edit Image:** This allows you to insert an image in your post by using the image URL. You can set options for this image by setting the alignment, dimensions, borders, and spacing around the image here.

- ✔ **Split Post with More Tag:** This inserts the `<!--more-->` tag that allows you to split the display on your blog page. It publishes the text written above this tag with a Read More link, which takes the user to a page with the full post. This is good for really long posts.

- ✔ **Toggle Spellchecker:** Perfect for the typo enthusiasts! Checking your spelling before you post is always a good idea.

- ✔ **Help:** This opens a new browser window where you see the Rich Editing Basics page that contains helpful information on Rich Editing.

At this point, you can skip to the "Publishing your post" section of this chapter for information on publishing your post to your blog, or continue with the following sections to discover how to include images in your blog post and refine the options for your post.

WordPress.com has a nifty, built-in autosave feature that saves your work while you're typing and editing a new post. If your browser crashes or you accidentally close your browser window before you've saved your post, it will be there for you when you get back. Those WordPress.com folks are so thoughtful!

Uploading and using images in your post

Pictures and images can greatly enhance the content of a post by adding a visual effect to the words that you've written. You can transfer images to WordPress.com from your computer by using the image upload feature. To upload an image, follow these steps:

1. **On your WordPress Administration panel, click the Write tab.**

   The Write Post page appears; this is the page on which you write your blog post.

2. **Scroll down to the Upload section.**

   This area is directly beneath the Save and Continue Editing, Save, and Publish buttons. The file types that WordPress lets you upload are listed to the right of the Browse button, as shown in Figure 4-2.

3. **Click the Browse button to open a window from your own computer that shows a list of files for you to select. Double-click the file you want to upload.**

   If you find a picture on a Web site or in your e-mail that you want to upload to your site, save it to your hard drive first. After you double-click the file you want, the window closes and you return to the page you were on, the Write Post page.

4. **Fill in the Title and Description text boxes.**

   The title and description are automatically inserted into the image code within your post. Use whatever you want for these boxes; these fields are very helpful from an SEO standpoint on your blog. You can read more about these and other SEO techniques in Chapter 16.

5. **Click the Upload button.**

   WordPress selects the Browse tab and shows your image, its filename, and options pertaining to how you'd like to display and link to the image.

6. **In the Show area (shown in Figure 4-3), click one of the three radio buttons to choose how you'd like to display the image in your blog post, as follows:**

   • *Thumbnail:* Display a smaller-sized version of the original.

   • *Full Size:* Display the full-sized image.

   • *Title:* Display the image's title, hyperlinked to the image on another page.

7. **In the Link To area (also shown in Figure 4-3), click one of the three radio buttons to choose how you want to link the image.**

   • *File:* Links the image to the original file location on your server. After it's published, when a visitor clicks the image, the file opens in its own browser window.

   • *Page:* Links the image to a formatted page within your blog — with a unique permalink (URL).

- *None:* Does exactly what you'd expect. Nothing. The image isn't linked at all.

8. Click the Send to Editor button.

This embeds the necessary HTML code to make sure that the image appears in your post when you publish it to your blog.

Figure 4-2:
WordPress.
com image
uploader.

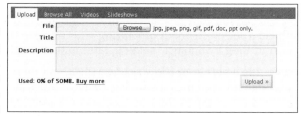

Figure 4-3:
Setting
parameters
for the
image after
you've
uploaded it.

WordPress.com gives you 3 gigabytes of disk space with your free blog, and while it would take a lot of files to use up that amount of space, if you upload large images, it could go faster than you think. Keep the actual file size of the images you upload in mind when using this feature; you can eat that disk space up before you know it.

There are three other tabs in the image upload section:

- ✔ **Browse All:** Displays all the images you've ever uploaded to your WordPress.com blog, allowing you to reinsert them later if you want.

- ✔ **Videos:** Gives you instructions (and the correct code) for inserting a video from YouTube or Google Video into your blog post.

- ✔ **Slideshows:** Gives you instructions (and the correct code) for inserting slideshows from these services: RockYou, SlideShare, Splide, and SplashCast.

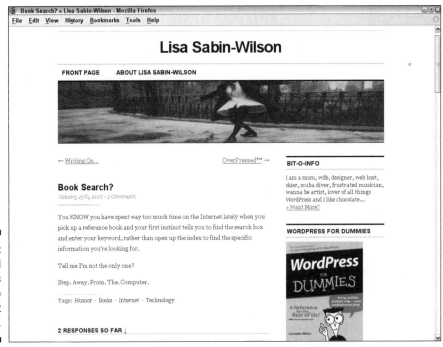

Figure 4-4:
Successful
blog posts
make it to
your front
page.

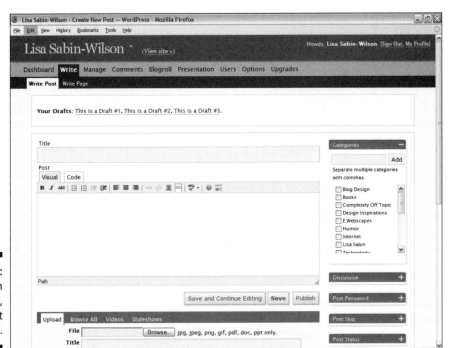

Figure 4-5:
Posts with
draft status,
not yet
published.

Organizing Your Blog by Subject

Categorizing your posts in WordPress provides an organizational structure for your blog. Each blog post that is assigned to a category is grouped with other posts in the same category. When your blog is a few months old, this structure creates a nice, topical directory of posts for you and your readers.

Category lists generally appear in two places on your blog, allowing your readers to find all of your posts by subject very easily. First, almost all WordPress themes list categories within the blog post itself. Most themes also provide a list of your categories in the sidebar of your blog so that your readers can click a topic of interest.

Each category that exists within a WordPress.com blog has its own RSS feed, making it easy for your readers to subscribe to a feed and keep updated on what you have to say about a certain topic on your blog.

Creating categories and subcategories

A brand-new WordPress.com blog has only two categories to begin with: Blogroll and Uncategorized, as shown in Figure 4-6. You can create new categories (and categories within those categories) by following these steps:

Figure 4-6:
The Categories manager in the Administration panel.

1. **On the Administration panel, click the Manage tab and then click the Categories subtab.**

   The Categories page appears.

2. Click the Add New link at the top of the page.

WordPress scrolls down to the Add Category section of the Categories page, shown in Figure 4-7.

3. In the Category Name text box, enter the category you want to create.

4. Leave the default option (None) in the Category Parent field.

The Category Parent drop-down menu lets you create subcategories. For instance, if you have a main category called Books, you'll see it in the Category Parent drop-down menu. To create a subcategory of the Books category, follow Steps 1–3 and then select Books from the Category Parent drop-down menu.

5. (Optional) Enter a description of the category in the Description text box.

Do this so that later on, you know what you were thinking of when you first created this category. A short summary will do. (Also, some Word-Press themes are coded to display the category description in the sidebar of your blog).

6. Click the Add Category button.

Add Category

Category name:	
Category parent:	None ▼
Description: (optional)	
	Add Category »

Figure 4-7:
Add a new category to your blog.

WordPress.com also calls these categories *tags* because your posts get tagged with topical keywords (based on your category name) and your posts show up in the WordPress Tag Surfer. Visitors to the Tag Surfer can easily find your posts that pertain to the topic they're interested in. You can find the Tag Surfer on the front page of the WordPress.com main site by clicking the More button on the top right, next to Right Now in Tags.

Categories you create now aren't set in stone. You can edit or delete them in the future just by revisiting this page and clicking the Edit link in the Action column to the right of each category.

Filing posts in categories and subcategories

The previous section tells you how to create categories and subcategories. To place your post in a category you've created, follow these steps:

1. **Click the Manage tab on the Administration panel.**

   The Posts page appears, and you see a table showing the Post ID, title, category, and author of each post on your blog.

2. **To the right of the post information, click the Edit link for the post you'd like to categorize.**

   A page appears with all the same options you had when you originally wrote the post.

3. **In the Categories section on the right side of the page, click the plus (+) sign to view the entire section, if it isn't already open.**

4. **Select the check box next to the category or subcategory (you can select more than one category and/or subcategory) that you'd like to assign to the post.**

   You can also use the Categories section before you publish a new post to assign it to the categories you'd like.

5. **Click the Save button.**

   You return to the Manage Posts table, which now reflects your changes.

Categorizing links in your blogroll

This section shows you how to add and manage the links in your blogroll. A *blogroll* is a list of links displayed on your blog — typically, links that you find interesting.

On the WordPress Administration panel, click the Blogroll tab to display the Blogroll Management page, as shown in Figure 4-8.

By default, you'll see the links for WordPress.com and WordPress.org in there.

If you want to remove a link from your blogroll, click the Delete link to the right.

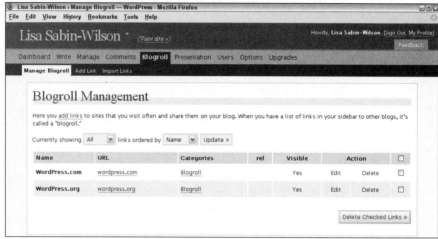

To add a new link to your blogroll, click the Blogroll tab and then the Add Link subtab in the Administration panel, which takes you to the Add Link page shown in Figure 4-9.

Figure 4-9:
Add a link to
your blogroll
using this
tool from
WordPress.
com.

Follow these steps to add your new link:

1. **In the Name text box, type the name of the Web site you're adding.**

2. **In the Address text box, type the URL (Internet address), making sure to include the `http://` part of the URL.**

3. **(Optional) Type a short description of the Web site in the Description text box.**

   For the Categories box on the right (not shown in Figure 4-9), leave the Blogroll category selected.

4. **Click the Add Link button.**

5. **Click the Blogroll subtab on the Administration subpanel.**

   The link you just added is now included as part of your blogroll. If you're using the Links widget to display your blogroll, you now see the link you just added under the Blogroll heading on your live blog.

You can create multiple categories for your links in the WordPress.com Administration panel if you want to have more than one link list. For example, sometimes having a large list of links under the Blogroll heading Blogroll is just too generic, and you may want to separate your list of links under different headings that will further define the links you've added to your blog. You can do this by creating subcategories under the Blogroll category in the Administration panel and then assigning links to the appropriate categories as you add them. You can create Blogroll categories by following these steps:

1. **On the Administration panel, click the Manage tab.**

2. **Click the Categories subtab.**

   The Categories page appears.

3. **Click the Add New link that appears next to the Categories heading.**

4. **Follow the steps given previously in this chapter for adding new categories.**

   To add a new Blogroll category, be sure to select Blogroll in the Category Parent drop-down menu. This tells WordPress.com that this is a Blogroll category, not a post category, and it will appear in the category option box on the Add Link page. (But it won't appear in the category option box on the Write Post page.)

Managing and Inviting Users

What's a blog without blog users? Of course, there is always at least one user for every WordPress.com blog — you. To see your list of users, click the Users tab in the Administration panel. On the Administration subpanel, notice the Authors & Users, Your Profile, and Invites subtabs two of which are described in the following sections. (See Chapter 3 for information on the Your Profile subtab.)

Managing authors and users

The Authors & Users page includes the User List by Role section, where you can manage current users and authors by setting their user roles and viewing (and editing, if necessary) their profiles. Also in the User List by Role section, you can look at a table that includes each user's ID, username, and e-mail address, which helps you manage your user accounts. This page also has the

Add User from Community section, where you can add a new user to your blog. (By *user,* WordPress means simply a person who is a member of your blog, either as a contributor, author, editor, or administrator.)

To manage user accounts, you need to understand the differences in the user roles. See the list that follows for an explanation of the type of access each role provides:

- **Contributor:** Can upload files and write/edit/manage her own posts. However, when a Contributor writes a post, that post is saved as a draft to await administrator approval; Contributors can't publish their posts. This is a nice way to moderate content written by new authors.

- **Author:** In addition to having the same access and permissions as a Contributor, an Author can publish her own posts without administrator approval. Authors can also delete their own posts.

- **Editor:** In addition to having the same access and permissions as an Author, an Editor can moderate comments, manage categories, manage links, edit pages, and edit other Author's posts. Editors can also read and edit private posts.

- **Administrator:** Has the authority to change any of the Administration options and settings within the WordPress blog.

WordPress.com lets you have multiple users and authors on one blog, which is a nice feature if running a multi-author blog is something you'd like to do.

To manage a user's account, find that person's username in the User List by Role section of the Authors & Users page and click the Edit link to the far right. You're taken to the Edit User page, where you find that you can edit the profile details for a user, including her e-mail address and password.

To view all the posts made by an author, click the corresponding View Posts link on the Authors & Users page.

At the bottom of this page, in the Add User From Community section, you can add new users to your blog. Enter the person's e-mail address, assign a user role, and click the Add User button. The user you add must be a registered user within the WordPress.com system. However, if you enter someone who isn't already registered, WordPress.com notices that and gives you the option to send that person an invitation to become a member. They've just thought of everything, haven't they?

Inviting friends to WordPress.com

Now that you've experienced the fun, ease, and excitement of having your very own WordPress.com blog, why not tell your friends, so they can tell their friends, and their friends can tell their friends, and so on?

Click the Invites subtab and you can do just that. Figure 4-10 shows the form that allows you to invite people you know to sign up for WordPress.com accounts. You can also tell WordPress to add a user to your blogroll after he joins. Additionally, you can tell WordPress to add the new member to your own blog as a Contributor, if you'd like. (This is especially helpful if you're setting up new users or authors for your own WordPress.com blog.)

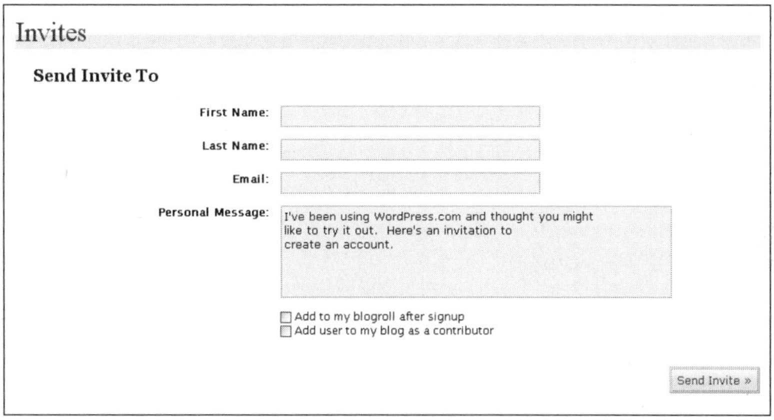

Figure 4-10:
WordPress.
com Invites
page.

> Invites
>
> **Send Invite To**
>
> First Name:
> Last Name:
> Email:
> Personal Message: I've been using WordPress.com and thought you might like to try it out. Here's an invitation to create an account.
>
> ☐ Add to my blogroll after signup
> ☐ Add user to my blog as a contributor
>
> Send Invite »

Follow these instructions to invite as many people as you want to join WordPress.com:

1. **On the Administration panel, click the Users tab and then click the Invites subtab.**

2. **In the appropriate text boxes, type the user's first name, last name, and e-mail address.**

3. **Type a personal message to the prospective member, or use the default message WordPress.com provides, in the Personal Message text box.**

4. **(Optional) Select the Add to My Blogroll after Signup check box if you also want to add this person to your own WordPress.com blogroll.**

5. **(Optional) Select the Add User to My Blog as a Contributor check box if you want to add this user as a Contributor on your blog after he signs up.**

6. **Click the Send Invite button to send the invitation to the prospective member via e-mail.**

When you complete these steps, WordPress sends you confirmation that the invitation was sent.

Managing Comments and Comment Spam

As I describe in Chapter 2, comments provide a great way for readers to interact with the site owner, and vice versa. Readers of your blog can post comments by using the comment form that appears on the same page as each of the published blog posts on your blog. You need to be able to exercise control over the comments that appear on your blog, however.

Viewing comments

You open the Comments page by clicking the Comments tab on the Administration panel. The Comments page shows all the comments to your blog, from the very first day you started. Here, you can view the comments, edit them, mark them as spam, or just flat-out delete them.

If you've set your Comments options so that comments aren't published on your blog until you approve them, you can approve comments in this section, as well. Of course, you have to have comments on your blog in order to accomplish this, and if your blog is brand new, you may not have any yet. Check out Figure 4-11 to see what a comment looks like in this area.

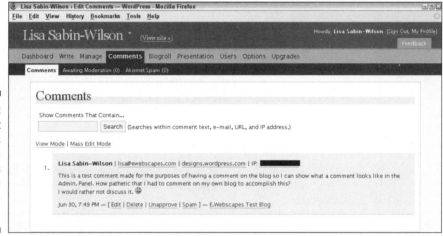

Figure 4-11: Looking at comments on the Comments page in the Administration panel.

To manage a comment in this area, find the comment you'd like to edit, delete, unapprove (or remove it from your blog page), or mark as spam. If you need to, you can find a specific comment by using the search feature. Just type a keyword into the Show Comments That Contain text box and click the Search button.

When you've found the comment you'd like to manage, click the link for the action you want to take and respond to any dialog box or new page that WordPress might show you next.

Setting discussion options for your blog

On the Discussion Options page, you can set the options, such as notification settings, for your posts and how comments and comment spam are handled on your WordPress.com blog. There are five sections on the Discussion Options page with settings for you to configure for your blog:

- ✔ **Usual Settings for an Article:** This is where you tell WordPress.com how you want post notifications to be handled on your blog. Three options are available to you here:

  - *Attempt to Notify any Weblogs Linked to from the Article (Slows down Posting.)* Enabled by default, this option makes your blog send a notification, via a ping, to any site you've linked to in your blog post. This is very similar to a trackback (which I discuss in Chapter 2). This can slow down the process of posting just a bit because of the time it takes for your blog to talk to another blog to let it know that you're talking about it.

  - *Allow Link Notifications from other Weblogs (Pingbacks and Track-backs.)* Enabled by default, this option tells WordPress that you want your blog to be notified — via pings and trackbacks — that other people have linked to you. WordPress lists any ping and trackback notifications on your site as comments in the Comments section. If you deselect this option, your ears may tingle, but you won't know when other people are talking about, or linking to, you on other blogs.

  - *Allow people to post comments on the article.* Enabled by default, this option lets people leave comments on your blog.

- ✔ **E-mail Me Whenever:** The two boxes here, Anyone Posts a Comment and A Comment Is Held for Moderation, are selected by default. This feature tells WordPress that you want to receive an e-mail anytime anyone leaves a comment on your blog and/or anytime a comment is awaiting your approval in the moderation queue. This feature can be very helpful, particularly if you don't visit your blog daily. Everyone likes to get comments on his blog posts — and it's good to be notified when it happens so that you can revisit that post, respond to your readers, and keep the conversation active. You can disable this feature, however, by deselecting the boxes here.

- ✔ **Before a Comment Appears:** The three options in this section tell WordPress how you want WordPress to handle comments before they appear on your blog.

- *An Administrator Must Always Approve the Comment.* Selecting this option holds every new comment on your blog in the moderation queue until you log in and approve it. This feature is particularly helpful if you want to review the content of comments before they're published to your blog.

- *Comment Author Must Fill Out Name and E-Mail.* This option is selected by default. Having this enabled creates a bit more work for comment spammers when they attempt to spam your blog with useless comments. WordPress doesn't verify that the name and e-mail address are valid ones, so this option doesn't serve as a hard-core comment spam protection measure — but it does make those Internet nuisances work a little harder.

- *Comment Author Must Have Previously Approved Comment.* With this box selected, the only comments that are approved and published on your blog are those that have been left by commenters who have already been approved by you previously. Their e-mail addresses are stored in the database, and WordPress runs a check on their e-mail. If the e-mail address matches a previously approved comment, the new comment is automatically published. If no match occurs, WordPress places the comment in the moderation queue, awaiting your approval. This is yet another measure to help prevent comment spam.

✔ **Comment Moderation:** In this section, you can set options to specify what type of comments are held in the moderation queue to await your approval. Frequently, comment spammers try to spam your blog with just a *ton* of links in hopes of promoting their own sites using your comment form. You can set the number of links that are allowed in a comment before it is tossed into the moderation queue to await approval. The default is 2. Give that a try, and if you find that you're getting lots of spam comments with multiple links, you may want to revisit this page and increase that number.

The text box underneath the link setting is where you can set keywords, URLS, e-mail addresses, or IP addresses to be flagged for moderation. For example, one of the popular topics that comment spammers like to spam with is Viagra. Basically, they fill their comments with links to sites where you can purchase Viagra. Really, if you wanted to know, wouldn't you seek it out? Well, that's beside the point. If you're getting a lot of Viagra spam, you can enter **Viagra** in the Comment Moderation list in this box rather than the Comment Blacklist below because you might actually receive a legitimate comment with the word *Viagra* in it that you would like to approve. A visitor to my blog left a comment that said, "Espresso is Viagra for my brain!" on a post I made about my love for espresso. That is a legitimate comment but probably got thrown into my moderation queue because I have that term in my Comment Moderation list.

✔ **Comment Blacklist:** In contrast to the Comment Moderation list above, the Comment Blacklist is a list of words, URLs, e-mail addresses, and IP addresses that you want to flat-out ban from ever making it to your blog. Items placed here don't even make it into your comment moderation queue — they're filtered as spam by the system and completely disregarded. The words I have placed in my Blacklist are not family friendly and have no place in a nice book like this.

Are you getting the feeling that comment spam is a real issue for bloggers? It's huge — probably bigger than you imagine it to be. Much of the comment spam prevention is done behind the scenes, so you don't even see half of what's going on. All the options on the Discussion Options page are geared toward decreasing or completely eliminating comment or trackback spam from your blog. If, during the course of your blogging experience on Word Press.com, you find that you're having an issue with spam, you may want to revisit these options and make adjustments.

When you're done setting up your options here, be sure to click the Update Options button to make the changes take effect. You can revisit this page as often as you need to in order to keep your settings current and to your liking.

Awaiting moderation

If you have the option set to approve any comments that come through to your blog, you can approve or disapprove of comments on the Awaiting Moderation page. If you have comments awaiting moderation, just log in to your Word Press.com account, click the My Dashboards tab in the menu bar to enter your WordPress.com Administration panel, click the Comments tab on the Administration panel, click the Awaiting Moderation subtab, and manage those comments.

A comment awaiting moderation won't show up on your blog until you approve it.

Managing comment spam with Akismet

Comment spam, as I discuss in Chapter 2, is a sneaky method that spammers are fond of using to post links to their sites on yours. Akismet is the answer to combating comment and trackback spam — it kills spam dead. Created by the Automattic team, headed by Matt Mullenweg, Akismet is a "collaborative effort to make comment and trackback spam a non-issue and restore innocence to blogging, so you never have to worry about spam again," according to Akismet.com.

Click the Akismet Spam subtab to view the Caught Spam page, where you'll see the comments and trackbacks that were caught by Akismet's spam filters, if any. Akismet does keep the last two weeks of comments and trackbacks that were stopped by their filters because the rare legitimate comment can get caught up in the spam filters. If that happens, you can visit this section and de-spam the comment by clicking the Not Spam button.

I usually don't have to visit the Akismet Spam page. My readers are usually pretty quick to let me know if they've left a comment that didn't get published. In such a case, I check the Akismet Spam page to see whether it was caught in the spam filters. Then I de-spam it and move on.

Creating a Static Page

You can create pages on your blog that are treated differently than posts. Called a *static page,* this appears as a separate page on your blog rather than a post on your blog. You use nearly the same process of writing it as you do to write a post. You can easily create an unlimited number of static pages, and these can serve as a nice complement to your overall site content. You can create these pages by logging into your WordPress.com Administration panel and following these steps:

1. **Click the Write tab in the top menu and then click the Write Page subtab.**

   The Write Page page appears, where you can compose your static page.

2. **Type the title of your page in the Page Title text box.**

3. **Type the body of your page in the Page Content text box.**

4. **Set the options for your page using the various boxes that appear to the right of the Page Content text box.**

   To display these boxes, click the plus sign that appears in the top-right corner of each box. The following options appear:

   • *Discussion:* By default, the Allow Comments and Allow Pings boxes are selected. Deselect them if you don't want to allow comments or pings on this page.

   • *Page Status:* By default, the Draft status is selected. You can select Published, Draft, or Private here.

   • *Page Password:* If you selected Private in the Page Status area, enter the password of your choice in the Page Password box.

   • *Page Parent:* Select the page parent from the drop-down menu if you'd like to make this a subpage of another page you've created.

   • *Page Slug:* By default, WordPress.com creates a Post Slug from your page title. If you want a Page Slug that is different from your title, enter it here.

- *Page Template:* If the WordPress.com theme you are currently using has page templates available, select the template you wish to use for this page in the drop-down menu.

- *Page Author:* Select the author of this blog from the drop-down menu. This step isn't necessary if you're the only author on this blog; however, if you have multiple authors, you may find this helpful.

- *Page Order:* Enter a number in the text box that reflects the order in which you'd like this page to display in the listing of pages on your site. For example, if you want this page to be the third page listed, enter **3**.

5. **Click the Publish button under the Post Content text box to publish this page to your site, or click the Save and Continue Editing button or the Save button to save it as a draft.**

Your static pages aren't included in your Recent Posts list or in the category or monthly archive. You can use this feature to write a page called About Me, for example, on which you give all of the wild and wooly details about yourself. (See Figure 4-12 for an example of an About page.) If you use the Page Sidebar widget, the pages you create are listed in your sidebar. (See Chapter 5 for more about widgets.)

Figure 4-12: The author's About page.

Setting Up Your Front Page

On the Reading Options page (click the Options tab and then the Reading subtab), you can set how many blog posts show up on the front page of your blog and/or change your front page to a static page rather than the page with the list of your recent posts. (See the "Creating a Static Page" section, earlier in this chapter, for more information on creating pages.) You can also determine how many blog posts your readers can see in your RSS feed. Figure 4-13 shows the different options that are available here.

The Reading Options page gives you control of the settings that allow you to make these decisions for your blog:

✔ **Front Page:** Determines what appears on the front page of your site.

- *Your Latest Posts:* Select this option if you want your blog posts to display on the front page of your blog.

- *A Static Page:* Select this option if you want a static page to display on the front page of your blog.

- *Front Page:* If you choose to display a static page, select which page you'd like to display from this drop-down menu.

- *Posts Page:* If you choose to display a static page, use this drop-down menu to tell WordPress which page to display your posts on.

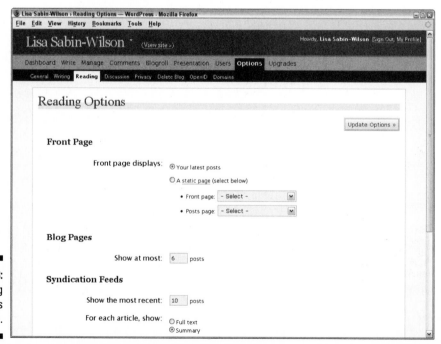

Figure 4-13:
The Reading
Options
page.

✔ **Blog Pages:** If you choose to display your blog posts on your front page, this is the step where you set the number of blog posts you'd like displayed per page. In Figure 4-13, you can see that I've decided to display only two posts to my front page. (My posts tend to be a little long, so I'd like to keep my front page posts to just two, allowing my readers to dig in to my archives, using the links in my sidebar, to read further into my blog, if they wish.)

✔ **Syndication Feeds:** Determines how your RSS feeds are displayed. Continue with the next section for details.

When you change any settings on the Reading Options page, make sure you click the Update Options button in the lower-right corner to save your preferences.

Setting Up Your RSS Feed

The next section on the Reading Options page (again, to get there, click the Options tab and then the Reading subtab in the Administration panel) allows you to set display options for your RSS feed. (I discuss RSS feeds in Chapter 2, if you'd like to visit that chapter to find out more.) On the Reading Options page, follow these steps to set the number of posts that visitors see in your RSS feed:

1. **On the Reading Options page, scroll down to the Syndication Feeds section.**

2. **Type the number of posts you'd like displayed in your RSS feed.**

   By default, the number is set to 10, but you can set that number to however many you wish.

3. **Indicate what portion of each post you'd like displayed in your RSS feed.**

   • *Full Text:* Select this option if you'd like the entire text of each post displayed in your RSS feed.

   • *Summary:* Select this option if you'd like only excerpts of your posts displayed in your RSS feed.

4. **Click the Update Options button to save your selections.**

There is no real rule as to whether you publish the full text or just a partial summary in your RSS feed. Everyone's mileage on this one varies. Some bloggers like the idea of publishing only a summary of the text because it requires the reader to click the title to actually visit your site in order to read the rest of the post. Other bloggers don't mind publishing the full text in their RSS feed. It's all a matter of personal preference.

The last option in the Syndication Feeds area of the Reading Options page asks for the character encoding you'd like to set for your blog and your RSS feed. *Character encoding* is basically code that facilitates the storage and transmission of text through telecommunication lines, such as those that carry you through the Internet via your Internet connection. This is real geek stuff if you start digging in to different character encoding options. For the purpose of getting started, your safest bet is to leave the default setting (UTF-8) in place, as it's the most commonly accepted character encoding and supports a wide range of languages.

Publishing a Public or Private Blog

This section contains one very simple option for you to set, and it allows you to determine how you want to deal with publicity on your blog. Figure 4-14 shows your choices. To access the privacy options for your blog, click the Options tab and then the Privacy subtab in your WordPress Administration panel. You can choose one of these three options:

Figure 4-14:
Blog
Visibility
options on
the Privacy
Options
page.

- ✔ **I Would Like My Blog to Appear in Search Engines Like Google and Sphere, and in Public Listings around WordPress.com.** Select this if you want to freely allow search engines to visit your blog and include its content in their search directories.

- ✔ **I Would Like to Block Search Engines, but Allow Normal Visitors.** Select this option if you don't want search engines to visit and include your site in their directories. This option is helpful if you want normal (read: human) visitors but don't want the publicity that search engines provide.

✔ **I Would Like My Blog to Be Visible Only to Users I Choose.** Select this option if you want to make your blog available only to the people you choose. This option keeps your blog completely private and away from prying eyes — except for those users you allow.

When you select and save this option, WordPress.com provides you with a form where you can enter the WordPress.com usernames for people you'd like to invite to view your private blog. (WordPress.com allows you to add up to 35 users. You can pay an annual fee to add more.)

When you have completed your decision, be sure to click the Update Options button to make the changes take effect.

Establishing Trust Relationships with OpenID

OpenID is a third-party, Internet community identification system that allows an Internet user to create an online identity that he can use anywhere on the Web where OpenID is supported. With WordPress.com, you already have an OpenID identity.

In the WordPress Administration panel, you click the Options tab and the OpenID subtab to see the Manage Your OpenID page, which tells you what your OpenID is. (It's usually your main WordPress.com domain: `http://username.wordpress.com`.) On this page, you can also add Web site URLs that you consider to be trusted sites. After you enter the URL of the trusted site and click the Add to List button, you aren't asked if you trust the site when you attempt to log in to it. In a nutshell, this means that you can use your WordPress.com OpenID to log in to any site on the Web that supports OpenID.

Chapter 5

Enhancing Your Blog with Themes, Widgets, and Upgrades

In This Chapter

▶ Giving your blog a new look

▶ Adding widgets to your sidebar

▶ Enhancing your free WordPress.com blog

▶ Finding the help you need

You don't want your blog to look identical to everyone else's, do you? Although WordPress.com doesn't give you the vast array of design options that you have by hosting your own blog, you do have some flexibility. In this chapter, you discover the WordPress.com themes that are available for you to choose a design and format for your blog. You also explore the fun of using Sidebar widgets to rearrange how your blogroll, category archive list, monthly archive lists, and page lists are displayed.

This chapter also discusses enhancing your blog with custom CSS, using a domain name of your choice, and increasing the amount of hard drive space on your WordPress.com account through its upgrade feature (which charges a fee). I also include some valuable resources that provide assistance with your WordPress.com account.

Understanding Your WordPress.com Design Options

When it comes to your blog design, the great thing about the WordPress hosted service is how easily you can change your theme to one of the alternative designs available. What's not so hot is that you can't create your own custom theme. As noted later in this chapter, you can pay a fee to customize the Cascading Style Sheet (CSS) of the template you've chosen to use, but you need to be familiar with CSS to use this upgrade. And there again, you're limited to the templates WordPress provides.

In the meantime, you have some fabulous themes to choose from, all created by WordPress users. At the time of this writing, 53 themes are available to choose from. Considering that WordPress.com has more than 600,000 users, that's a lot of blogs looking a lot like each other. However, if you find a favorite theme, you can submit a theme request to the fine folks at WordPress.com in the Ideas Forum at `http://forums.wordpress.com/forum.php?id=1&page`. Be sure to provide the URL for the theme you'd like to see included in the WordPress.com available themes, and offer some good reasons for the theme to be added.

Changing Your Blog's Look

It's time to move on to choosing the theme for your WordPress.com blog. It's worth noting that, in this case, the word *theme* is synonymous with the words *design* and *template*. All three words describe the very same things: the visual layout and appearance of your blog.

On your Administration panel, click the Presentation tab and then click the Themes subtab. What you see is a page full of themes (as shown in Figure 5-1), along with a small screenshot, or picture, of the theme so that you can get a basic idea of what it looks like.

Figure 5-1:
Choose
a look for
your blog.

When you find a theme you like, click its name. The end.

No really, it's just that easy. There's no more to it than that. If you get tired of that theme, go back to the Presentations tab and click a different theme name, and you're done. Each time you return to the Presentation Themes page, you see a screenshot in the Current Theme section that tells you which theme is currently active on your site.

If you want to take a sneak peek at what your WordPress.com will look like with one of the available themes — before you commit to activating the theme on your site — click the small screenshot, or the preview link, and WordPress.com pops up your blog with the new theme in a little preview window. From there, you can activate the theme on your blog by clicking the Activate This Theme link in the top-right corner of the window. If you don't want to activate the theme, click the X in the top-left corner to close the window.

Widget Wonder: Adding Handy Tools to Your Sidebar

WordPress widgets are wonderful! Say *that* ten times fast, why don't you? Widgets are so wonderful because they allow you to very easily arrange the display of content in your blog sidebar, such as your blogroll(s), recent posts, and monthly and category archive listings. With widgets, you can accomplish this arranging without needing to know a single bit of code or HTML.

Selecting and activating widgets

Click the Presentation tab on your Administration panel, and click the Widgets subtab on the Administration subpanel. The Sidebar Arrangement page loads and displays the following message, as shown in Figure 5-2: `Your theme will display its usual sidebar when this box is empty. Dragging widgets into this box will replace the usual sidebar with your customized sidebar.` This feature is a big draw for WordPress.com users because it lets you control what features you use and where you place them — all without having to know a lick of code.

By "usual sidebar," WordPress means the default. Every theme is slightly different on the layout of the default sidebar. Usually, the WordPress.com sidebar, without the use of widgets, contains a default display of the following items: a search box, a list of recent posts made to your blog, and your blogroll(s). When you start using widgets, you can add extra items to the sidebar display of your blog, such as monthly and category archive listings, and photos from your Flickr (`http://flickr.com`) account, if you have one. You can also rearrange the order in which these items are displayed.

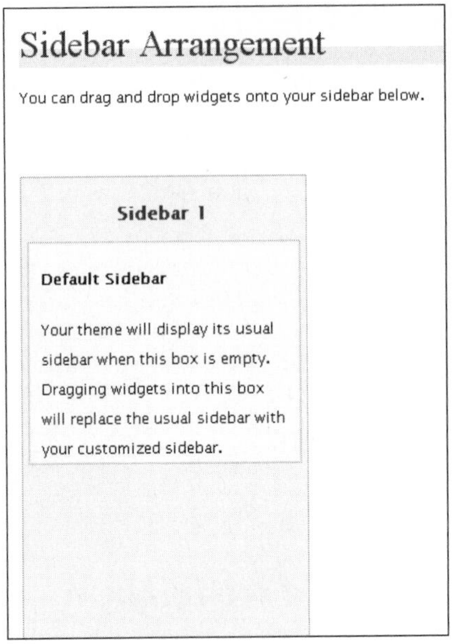

Sidebar Arrangement

You can drag and drop widgets onto your sidebar below.

Sidebar 1

Default Sidebar

Your theme will display its usual
sidebar when this box is empty.
Dragging widgets into this box
will replace the usual sidebar with
your customized sidebar.

Figure 5-2:
Sidebar
Arrange-
ment page.

Scroll down the Sidebar Arrangement page a bit to see the Available Widgets section, which contains a box representing each widget, as shown in Figure 5-3.

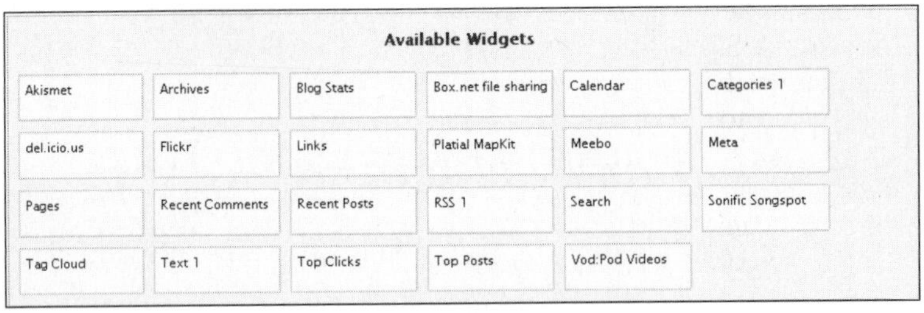

Available Widgets

Akismet	Archives	Blog Stats	Box.net file sharing	Calendar	Categories 1
del.icio.us	Flickr	Links	Platial MapKit	Meebo	Meta
Pages	Recent Comments	Recent Posts	RSS 1	Search	Sonific Songspot
Tag Cloud	Text 1	Top Clicks	Top Posts	Vod:Pod Videos	

Figure 5-3:
WordPress
widgets in
waiting.

Here is where widget magic happens. Click any one of those boxes and then drag it into the Sidebar box. See what happens? The widget settles into its new location, and the Default Sidebar box disappears. (Moving content in this way is called *drag-and-drop functionality.*) In Figure 5-4, you see the widgets I chose to drag and drop into my sidebar. They will appear on my blog in the same order that you see them here.

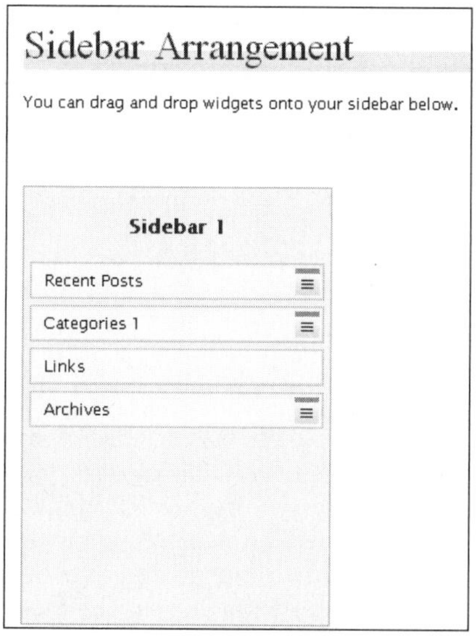

Sidebar Arrangement

You can drag and drop widgets onto your sidebar below.

Sidebar 1

Recent Posts

Categories 1

Links

Archives

Figure 5-4:
Selecting
the widgets
I want to
use.

When you have all the widgets you want to use in place, click the Save Changes button to the right. WordPress.com reloads the Sidebar Arrangement page with a confirmation message at the top that says `Options Saved View Site` (with the words "View Site" linked to your main blog page). Click the View Site link and you'll see that the sidebar display on your blog exactly matches the content (and order of the content) you've arranged in the sidebar on the Sidebar Arrangement page in the Widgets panel. How cool is that? You can go back to the Sidebar Arrangement page and rearrange the items, as well as add and remove items, to your heart's content.

Bloggers using the self-installed WordPress.org software also can take advantage of this widget wonderland — see Chapter 10 if you're considering switching to that version of the software.

Customizing widget options

In this section, I tell you how to work with some of the popular widgets — the staple widgets, if you will — and how to set their options.

First, the top four widgets that you see on almost every WordPress.com blog are the following:

- ✔ **Archives:** Contains hyperlinks to your post archives, by month, from the most recent month to the last.

- ✔ **Categories:** Displays the categories you set up in your blog, in alphabetical order, hyperlinked to the posts in those categories.

- ✔ **Recent Posts:** Displays the titles of the most recent posts you've made to your blog, hyperlinked to the posts.

- ✔ **Links:** Displays the links you've set up in your blogroll.

There are several other widgets you can use; however, those widgets can change pretty quickly because some of them rely on third-party services such as Flickr and Box.net. These third-party services and their associated WordPress widgets may not exist six months from now. Feel free to play around by dropping these widgets in your sidebar to discover what they do. If you have questions about a particular widget, visit the WordPress.com Support Forum (http://forums.wordpress.com) to post a question or search the forum for information about the widget.

You can adjust various settings for almost all the widgets. For example, when you're using the Recent Posts widget, you can control how many recent post titles are shown in your sidebar. To customize a widget, follow these steps:

1. **On your WordPress Administration panel, click the Presentation tab.**

2. **Click the Widgets subtab.**

   You see the Sidebar Arrangement page, with your active widgets in the Sidebar 1 box. Notice the icon with horizontal lines to the right of each widget name (if applicable), as shown in Figure 5-5. This is the Configure icon.

3. **Click the Configure icon for the widget you'd like to customize.**

   The Configure window opens, allowing you to set the widget options.

   For example, if you click the Configure icon for the Recent Posts widget, the Configure window for that widget, also shown in Figure 5-5, gives you the option to type a title in the Title box. This title is the heading that you want to appear on your blog, above the list of recent posts. You can also indicate how many recent posts you want the widget to link to from your sidebar; to do so, enter the number in the Use the Number of Posts to Show text box. (The maximum number you can enter is 15.)

4. **Click X in the top-right corner to close the Configure window.**

5. **When you've finished configuring your widgets, click the Save Changes button to the far right. Then visit your blog again to see the changes that have taken place with all of your widget play.**

The Sidebar Arrangement page reloads with a `Sidebar updated` confirmation message at the top of the page and a `View Site` link. Click that link to visit your site and see your changes.

At the very bottom of the Sidebar Arrangement page in the Widget panel are three drop-down menus that allow you to create even more widgets to play with, and you can create several of each widget, depending on your particular sidebar needs for your blog. Although I'm not even sure why the first type exists, I describe it, along with the other drop-down menus, as follows:

- **Categories Widgets:** At the time of this writing, there is no conceivable reason to have more than one Category widget on your blog. Because a Category widget already exists in the Available Widgets section, I don't know why WordPress.com gives you the ability to have up to nine Category widgets that all do the same thing: display a list of your category archives. (Check out this entry in the WordPress.com forums for more information on this confusing item: `http://en.forums.wordpress.com/topic.php?id=12848`.)

- **Text Widgets:** Allows you to insert your own text in the Widget Configuration so that you can display some of your own custom items in your sidebar display. Choose the number of text widgets you want to use (you can have up to nine) from the drop-down menu and then click the Save button. This reloads the Sidebar Arrangement page and displays additional text widgets in the Available Widgets section.

- **RSS Feed Widgets:** Allows you to display post links from other sites via RSS feed. (The RSS widget configuration options allow you to insert the RSS feed URL and title of the site you'd like to include.) Select the number of RSS widgets you want to use (you can have up to nine) from the drop-down menu and then click the Save button. This reloads the Sidebar Arrangement page and displays additional RSS widgets in the Available Widgets section.

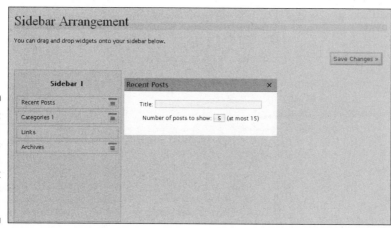

Figure 5-5:
Configuring the options for the Recent Posts widget.

Upgrading Your Hosted Service (For a Fee)

Although WordPress.com is a free service, it offers enhancements — for a fee. WordPress.com calls these items *upgrades,* and you can purchase credits for them at the cost of $1 (USD) per credit. (The prices I give here are current as of this book's printing, but they are, of course, subject to change.)

The following is a list of the current upgrades you can purchase to enhance your WordPress.com account; the prices listed here reflect the annual cost:

- ✔ **Custom CSS:** This upgrade allows you to customize the Cascading Style Sheets (CSS) for the theme you're currently using on the WordPress.com system. Recommended for users who understand the use of CSS, this upgrade currently costs 15 credits ($15 USD).

- ✔ **Unlimited Private Users:** With a free account, you're limited to 35 private users — if you choose to publish your WordPress.com blog as a private blog — giving access to only those users you authorize. This upgrade removes that limit, allowing you to have unlimited private users on your blog (provided that those users are already WordPress.com account holders). The cost is 30 credits ($30 USD).

- ✔ **Additional Space:** With the free WordPress.com blog, you have 3GB of hard drive space for use on your upload directory. The various space upgrades add more, letting you upload more files (images, videos, audio files, and so on). Currently, you can add 5GB for 20 credits ($20 USD), 15GB for 50 credits ($50 USD), or 25GB for 90 credits ($90 USD).

Naming Your Domain

The current URL for your WordPress.com blog is `http://username.word press.com`, with *username* being your username. My username is *designs* — therefore my WordPress.com domain is `http://designs.wordpress.com`.

WordPress.com enables you to use your own domain name for your Word Press.com blog. You can find more information about domain registration in Chapter 6; however, before you proceed further in this section, be aware that using the Domains feature in WordPress.com isn't free. At the time of this writing, it costs 10 credits per year to use this feature with WordPress.com (credits currently cost $1 each).

You can register your own domain using one of a variety of domain registration services, such as GoDaddy.com. For example, I could choose to register a domain called LisaSabin-Wilson.com. After doing so, I would go to my WordPress.com Administration panel, click the Upgrades tab and then the Domains subtab, and enter that domain name in the box provided there. I would then follow the prompts that WordPress.com gives to fully set up my own domain name.

When you've correctly configured your domain name, your old WordPress.com URL will redirect to your new domain name. In my example, my WordPress.com blog at `http://designs.wordpress.com` would redirect to `http://lisasabin-wilson.com`.

At the time of this publication, you don't pay WordPress.com for the Domain upgrade until after the domain is working correctly on your WordPress.com account.

Getting Help

I would be remiss if I didn't mention some of the places on the Internet you can visit to find more information on using WordPress.com — beginning with the super bunch of users within the WordPress.com community. See Table 5-1.

Table 5-1	WordPress.com Resources Online	
Resource	*Description*	*Location*
WordPress.com Forums	These forums, provided to the community by WordPress.com, are populated with users helping users. WordPress.com developers and staff members also sometimes provide help through these forums.	`http://wordpress.com/forums`

(continued)

Table 5-1 *(continued)*

Resource	Description	Location
WordPress Codex	This comprehensive online document repository covers everything WordPress — not just WordPress.com. You have to search and dig a little to find what you need, but you can find some valuable nuggets of information provided here, especially for new users.	`http://codex.wordpress.org/First_Steps_With_WordPress`
Need Help?	This little box of helpful links and information guides you to the forums, helpful documentation, the FAQ, and the page where you can send feedback to the WordPress.com team.	Appears at the bottom of every page in your WordPress.com Administration panel.

Part III

Self-Hosting with WordPress.org

The 5th Wave   By Rich Tennant

"He should be all right now. I made him spend two and a half hours reading prisoner blogs on the state penitentiary Web site."

In this part . . .

In this part, you really dig into the guts of WordPress.org. I tell you how to get your own domain name and Web host, take you through the features of the Administration panel that you'll want to know about when getting started, and tell you how to use plugins and themes to enhance your blog.

Chapter 6

Setting Up Blogging Base Camp

*B*efore you can start blogging with WordPress.org, you have to set up your base camp. Doing so involves more than simply downloading and installing the WordPress software. You need to establish your *domain* (your blog address) and your *Web hosting service* (the place that houses your blog). Although you initially download your WordPress software onto your hard drive, your Web host is where you install it.

Obtaining a Web server and installing software on it are much more involved projects than simply obtaining an account with the hosted version of WordPress that's available at WordPress.com (covered in Part II). There are many factors to consider with this undertaking, as well as a learning curve to expect because setting up your blog through a hosting service involves using some technologies that you might not, at first, feel comfortable with. This chapter takes you through the basics of those technologies, and by the last page of this chapter, you'll have WordPress successfully installed on a Web server with your own domain name.

Establishing Your Domain

You've read all the hype. You've heard all the rumors. You've seen the flashy blogs on the Web powered by WordPress. But where do you start?

The first steps toward installing and setting up a WordPress blog are to make a decision and then purchase the registration of a domain name. A *domain name* is the *unique* Web address that you type into a Web browser address bar in order to visit a Web site. Some examples of domain names are WordPress.org and Google.com.

Domain names: Do you own or rent?

In reality, when you "buy" a domain name, you don't really own it. Rather, you're purchasing the right to use that domain name for the period of time specified in your order. You can register a domain name for one year or up to 10 years. Be aware, however, that when your registration period ends and you don't renew that domain name, you lose it — and most often you'll lose it right away to someone who preys on abandoned or expired domain names. Some people keep a close watch on expiring domain names, and as soon as the buying window opens, they snap the names up and start using them for their own Web sites, in hopes of taking full advantage of the popularity that the previous owners worked so hard to attain for those domains.

I emphasize the word *unique* here because no two domain names can be the same. If someone else has registered the domain name you want, you can't have it. With that in mind, it can sometimes take a bit of time to find a domain that isn't already in use and is available for you to use. Of course, there are alternatives. You could contact the owner of the domain name you want and find out whether it's for sale and how much the owner will sell it for. However, chances are, with this approach you'll pay *way* more for the domain name than if you choose a domain name that's available for purchase through a domain registrar.

Registering a domain name

You register a domain name through a *domain registrar.* Domain registrars are certified and approved by the Internet Corporation for Assigned Names and Numbers (ICANN). Although hundreds of domain registrars exist today, the ones in the following list are popular because of their longevity in the industry, competitive pricing, and the variety of services they offer in addition to domain name registration (such as Web hosting and Web site traffic builders):

- ✔ **GoDaddy:** http://GoDaddy.com
- ✔ **Register.com:** http://register.com
- ✔ **Network Solutions:** http://networksolutions.com
- ✔ **NamesDirect:** http://namesdirect.com

Understanding domain name extensions

When registering a domain name, be aware of the *extension* that you want. The `.com`, `.net`, `.org`, `.info`, or `.biz` extension that you see tagged on the end of any domain name is the *top-level domain extension*. When you register your domain name, you're asked to make a choice about what extension you want for your domain. As long as it's available, that is.

A word to the wise here: Just because you have registered your domain as a `.com` doesn't mean that someone else doesn't, or can't, own the very same domain name with a `.net`. So, for example, if you register MyDogHasFleas.com and it becomes a hugely popular site among readers with dogs that have fleas, someone else can come along and register MyDogHasFleas.net and run a similar site to yours in hopes of riding the coattails of your Web site's popularity and readership.

You can register your domain name with all available extensions if you want to avoid this problem. For example, my business Web site has the domain name of EWebscapes.com. However, I also own EWebscapes.net, EWebscapes.biz, and EWebscapes.info.

Considering the cost of a domain name

Registering a domain costs you anywhere from $3 to $30 per year, depending on what service you use for a registrar and what options (such as privacy options and search engine submission services) you apply to your domain name during the registration process.

Keep in mind that when you pay the domain registration fee today, you will need to pay another registration fee when the renewal date comes up again in a year, or two, or five — however many years you chose to register your domain name for. (See the "Domain names: Do you own or rent?" sidebar.) Most registrars give you the option of signing up for a service called Auto Renew. This service automatically renews your domain name and bills the charges to the credit card you have set on that account. The registrar sends you a reminder, a few months in advance, telling you it's time to renew. If you do not have Auto Renew set up, you need to log in to your registrar account before it expires and manually renew your domain name.

Registering your domain name

No matter where you choose to register your domain name, here are the steps you can take to accomplish it:

1. **Decide on a domain name.**

   Doing a little planning and forethought here is necessary. Many people think of their domain name as their *brand* — a way of identifying their Web site or blog. Think of potential names for your site, and then you can proceed with your plan.

2. **Verify the domain name's availability.**

   From your Internet browser, enter the URL of the domain registrar of your choice. Look for the section on its Web site that will allow you to enter the domain name (typically, this is a short text field) you chose to see whether it's available. If it isn't available as a .com, try .net or .info.

3. **Purchase the domain name.**

   Follow the domain registrar's steps to purchase the name using your credit card. After you've completed the checkout process, you'll receive an e-mail confirming your purchase, so be sure to use a valid e-mail address during the registration process.

The next step is to obtain a hosting account, which I cover in the next section.

Some of the domain registrars out there do have hosting services that you can sign up for, but you don't have to use their hosting services. Often, you can find hosting services for a lower cost than most domain registrars offer. It just takes a little research.

Finding a Home for Your Blog

When you have your domain registered, you need to find a place for it to live. This is called *Web hosting,* and it's the second piece of the puzzle that you need to complete before you begin working with WordPress.

A *Web host* is a business, group, or individual that provides Web server space and bandwidth for file transfer to Web site owners who don't have it. Usually, Web hosting services charge a monthly or annual fee — unless you're fortunate enough to know someone who's willing to give you server space and bandwidth for free. The cost varies from host to host, but you can obtain quality Web hosting services for the price of $3 to $10 per month, to start.

Web hosts consider WordPress a *third-party application.* What this means for you is that the host typically won't provide you with technical support on the use of WordPress (or any other software application) because it isn't included as part of your hosting package. Although most Web hosts attempt to assist you with the use of the software, ultimately the responsibility for running it on your server account is all yours. This is one of the bigger reasons that some folks opt to run a WordPress-powered blog on the hosted version at Word Press.com. If you've chosen to go the self-hosted route with the WordPress.org software, you can find help and support on the use of WordPress in the WordPress support forums located at `http://wordpress.org/support/`.

Hosting services generally provide (at least) these services with your account:

- ✓ Hard drive space
- ✓ Bandwidth (transfer)
- ✓ Domain e-mail with Web mail access
- ✓ File Transfer Protocol (FTP) access
- ✓ Comprehensive Web site statistics
- ✓ MySQL database(s)
- ✓ PHP

Because you intend to run WordPress on your Web server, you need to look for a host that provides the minimum requirements needed to run the software on your hosting account, which are

- ✓ PHP version 4.2 (or greater)
- ✓ MySQL version 4.0 (or greater)

When considering a Web host, be sure that it has the minimum requirements needed to run the WordPress software on its machine. The easiest way to do that is to check the FAQ (Frequently Asked Questions) on the host's Web site, if it has one. If not, find the contact information for the hosting company and fire off an e-mail requesting information on exactly what it supports. Any Web host worth dealing with will answer your e-mail within a reasonable amount of time.

Getting help with hosting WordPress

The popularity of WordPress has given birth to services on the Web that put an emphasis on the use of the software. These services include WordPress designers, WordPress consultants, and, yes, Web hosts that specialize in using WordPress.

Many of these hosts offer a full array of WordPress features, such as an automatic WordPress installation included with your account, a library of WordPress themes, and a staff of support technicians who're very experienced in using WordPress.

Here is a list of some of those providers:

- ✔ **Blogs About Hosting:** `http://blogs-about.com`
- ✔ **Laughing Squid:** `http://laughingsquid.net`
- ✔ **AN Hosting:** `http://anhosting.com`
- ✔ **DreamHost:** `http://dreamhost.com`

A word about Web hosts and domain registration: A few Web hosting providers out there offer free domain name registration when you sign up for their hosting services. Research this topic and dig through those hosting providers' terms of service because that free domain name sometimes comes with a few conditions.

Many of my clients have gone this route only to find out a few months later — when they're unhappy with the unreliable hosting services and would like to change to another host — that the Web hosting provider has full control over the domain name and they aren't allowed to move that domain off their servers, either for a set period of time (usually a year or two), or for infinity. I feel it's always best to have the control in *your* hands, not someone else's, so I recommend registering your domain name yourself, with an independent domain registrar such as GoDaddy, and pay the few bucks it takes to make sure that you're the one in control of it.

Dealing with disk space and bandwidth

Web hosting services provide two very important things with your account:

- ✔ Disk space
- ✔ Bandwidth transfer

Think of your Web host as a garage that you pay to park your car in. The garage gives you the place to store your car (disk space). It even gives you the driveway so that you, and others, can get to and from your car (bandwidth). It won't, however, fix your rockin' stereo system (WordPress, or any other third-party software applications) that you've installed — unless you're willing to pay a few extra bucks for that service.

Managing disk space

Disk space is nothing more complicated than the hard drive on your own computer. Each hard drive has the capacity, or space, for a certain amount of files. An 80GB (gigabyte) hard drive can hold 80GB of data, no more. Your hosting account provides you with a limited amount of disk space, and the same concept applies. If your Web host provides you with 10GB of disk space, that's the limit on the file size that you're allowed to have. If you want more disk space, you need to upgrade your space limitations. Most Web hosts have a mechanism in place for you to upgrade your space limitations.

Time for a public service announcement: A good Web host has a system in place that sends you a warning (via e-mail) when you reach at least 80 percent of your total disk space capacity. This helps you manage the space on your hosting account. With this warning, you can plan on either doing some account maintenance of your own and clearing out some unnecessary files that might be taking up space or plan on getting in contact with your Web host to upgrade your account.

Choosing the size of your bandwidth pipe

Bandwidth refers to the amount of data that is carried from point A to point B within a specific period of time (usually only a second, or two). I live out in the country — pretty much the middle of nowhere. The water that comes to my house is provided by our private well that lies buried in our backyard somewhere. Between my house and the well are pipes that bring the water to my house. The pipes allow the free flow of water to our home so that everyone can enjoy their long, hot showers while I labor over dishes and laundry, all at the same time. Lucky me!

The very same concept applies to the bandwidth available with your hosting account. Every Web hosting provider offers a variety of bandwidth limits on the accounts it offers. When I want to view your Web site in my browser window, the bandwidth is essentially the pipe that allows your data to flow from your "well" to my computer and appear on my monitor. The bandwidth limit is kind of like the pipe connected to my well — it can hold only a certain amount of water before it reaches maximum capacity and won't bring the water from the well any longer. Your bandwidth pipe size is determined by how much bandwidth your Web host allows for your account — the larger the number, the bigger the pipe. For example, a 50MB bandwidth limit makes for a smaller pipe than does a 100MB limit.

Web hosts are pretty generous with the amount of bandwidth they provide in their packages. As is disk space, bandwidth is measured in gigabytes (GB). Bandwidth provision of 10–50GB is generally a respectable amount to run a Web site with a blog.

Web sites that run large files, such as video, audio, or photo files (check out Chapter 10 for information on podcasts, vblogs, and photoblogs) generally would benefit from a higher disk space than a site that doesn't involve large files. Keep this in mind when you're signing up for your hosting account. Planning ahead now will save you a few headaches down the road.

When you have successfully purchased your domain name and are all set with your new hosting account, it's finally time to get down to the business of installing WordPress on your hosting account. There is, however, one more piece of knowledge you need to have in order to make this happen. That piece of knowledge is called File Transfer Protocol (FTP), and it's how you transfer files from Point A to Point B.

File Transfer from Point A to Point B

This section introduces you to the basic elements of File Transfer Protocol (FTP). The ability to use FTP with your hosting account is a given on almost every Web host on the market today. *FTP* is the method you use to move files from one place to another — for example, from your computer to your Web hosting account. That method is referred to as *uploading*.

Using FTP to transfer files requires an FTP program, called an *FTP client*. There are many programs available for download; the following are some of the good, and free, ones:

- ✔ **WS_FTP:** www.ipswitch.com/_download/wsftphome.asp
- ✔ **SmartFTP:** www.smartftp.com/download
- ✔ **FileZilla:** http://sourceforge.net/projects/filezilla
- ✔ **FTP Explorer:** www.ftpx.com

Earlier in this chapter, you find out how to obtain a Web hosting account. Your Web host gave you a username and password for your account, including an FTP IP address. (Usually, the FTP address is the same as your domain name, but check with your Web host, as each might vary.) It is this information — the username, password, and FTP IP address — that you insert into the FTP program to connect it to your hosting account.

In Figure 6-1, you see my FTP client (FileZilla) connected to my hosting account. The directory on the left is the listing of files on my computer; the directory on the right shows the listing of files on my hosting account.

FTP clients, such as FileZilla, make it easy to transfer files from your computer to your hosting account by using a drag-and-drop method. You simply click the file on your computer that you want to transfer, drag it over to the side that lists the directory on your hosting account, and drop it. Depending on the FTP client you've chosen to work with, you can refer to its user manuals or support documentation for detailed information on how to use the program.

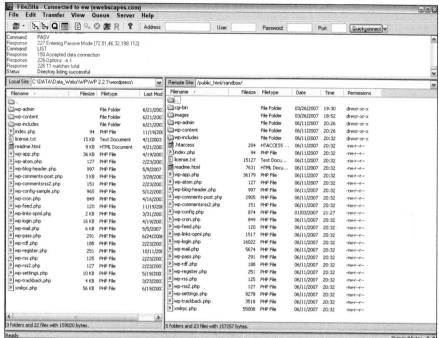

Figure 6-1:
FileZilla is a
popular FTP
client that
makes file
transfers
easy.

It's time to stop and do a quick checkpoint before moving on to the process of installing WordPress on your hosting account. At this point, you should have

✔ Purchased the domain name registration for your account.

✔ Signed up for and obtained a hosting service on a Web server for your blog.

✔ Established your hosting account username, password, and FTP address.

✔ Acquired an FTP client to transfer files to your hosting account.

If you've missed any of the items listed, you can go back to the beginning of this chapter to reread the portions you need.

In the next section, I'm diving directly into the installation procedure for WordPress.

Installing WordPress

Here's the portion of the book where the rubber meets the road — that is, you're putting WordPress's Famous Five-Minute Installation to the test. Set your watch and see if you can meet that five-minute mark.

By this point, you should have everything you need to perform the installation of WordPress on your hosting account. The first part of this section covers the steps you need to take to manually install WordPress on your Web server.

Some Web hosts now offer a "One-Click Installation" process for WordPress. If this is the case for you, you can simply follow the instructions provided by your Web host. The instructions that follow are for those of you doing a manual install of WordPress on your Web server.

Without further ado, go get the WordPress software here: `http://word press.org/download`.

WordPress gives you two compression formats for the software: zip and tar.gz. I recommend getting the zip file, as it's the most common format for compressed files.

Download the WordPress software to your computer and decompress (or unpack, or unzip) it to a folder on your computer's hard drive. These are the first steps in the installation process for WordPress. However, having the program on your own computer isn't enough. You need to *upload* (transfer) it to your Web server account (the one you signed up for and obtained in the first section of this chapter). Before installing WordPress on your Web server, you need to make sure that you have a MySQL database all set up and ready to accept the WordPress installation. The next section tells you what you need to know about MySQL.

Setting up the MySQL database

The WordPress software is a personal publishing system that uses a PHP and MySQL platform, which provide you with everything you need for creating your own blog and publishing your own content, dynamically, without having to know how to program those pages yourself. In short, all of your content (options, posts, comments, and other pertinent data) is stored in a MySQL database on your hosting account.

Every time visitors go to your blog to read your content, they make a request that's sent to your server. The PHP programming language receives that request, obtains the requested information from the MySQL database, and then presents the requested information to your visitors through their Web browsers.

Every Web host is different in how it gives you access to set up and manage your MySQL database(s) for your account. A popular account administration interface in use today is called cPanel (shown in Figure 6-2), and in this section, I use cPanel as the example. If your host provides a different interface, the same basic steps apply — just the setup in the interface that your Web host provides might be different.

To set up the MySQL database for your WordPress blog using cPanel, follow these steps:

1. **Log in to the administration interface with the username and password assigned to you by your Web host.**

   I'm using the cPanel administration interface, but your host might provide NetAdmin or Plesk, for example.

2. **Locate the MySQL Database Administration section.**

   In cPanel, click the MySQL Databases icon.

3. **Choose a name for your database and enter it in the Name text box. Be sure to make note of the database name because you will need it during the installation of WordPress later.**

Figure 6-2: cPanel is a Web hosting account manager provided by several Web hosting companies.

It doesn't really matter here what you choose for the database name, username, or password. However, for security reasons, make sure your password isn't something that sneaky hackers can easily guess. Usually, I give my database a name that I will easily recognize later. This is especially helpful if you're running more than one MySQL database on your account. If I name this database something like *WordPress* or *wpblog*, I can be reasonably certain — a year from now when I want to access my database to make some configuration changes — that I know exactly which one I need to deal with.

4. **Click the Create Database button.**

   You get a message confirming that the database has been created.

5. **Click the Go Back link or click the Back button on your browser toolbar.**

6. **Choose a username and password for your database and enter them in the Current Users text boxes; then click the Create User button.**

   You get a confirmation message that the username was created with the password you specified.

Make absolutely sure that you've made note of the database name, username, and password that you set up during this process. You *will* need them in the next section before officially installing WordPress on your Web server. Jot them down on a piece of paper, or copy and paste them into a text editor window — either way, just make sure you have them immediately handy.

7. **Click the Go Back link or click the Back button on your browser toolbar.**

8. **Under Add Users to Your Database heading, choose the user you just set up in the User drop-down menu. Then choose the new database from the Database drop-down menu.**

9. **Assign user privileges by selecting the All check box.**

   Under the drop-down menus is an area for you to assign privileges to the user. Because you're the administrator (owner) of this database, you need to make sure you assign all privileges to the new user you just created.

10. **Click the Add User to Database button.**

    You will receive a confirmation message that the user has been added to the database.

Uploading the WordPress files

In this section, you need to return to the folder on your computer where you unpacked the WordPress software that you downloaded earlier. You'll find all of the files you need (shown in Figure 6-3) in a folder called /wordpress.

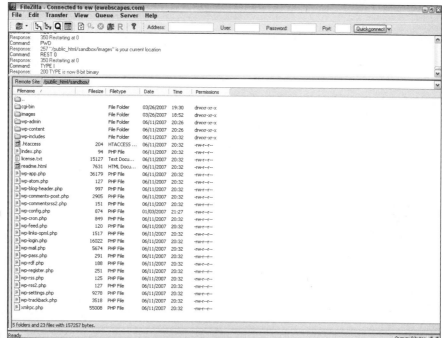

Using your FTP client, connect to your Web server and upload all of these files to your hosting account, into the root directory.

If you don't know what your root directory is, contact your hosting provider and ask the question, "What is my root directory for my account?" Every hosting provider is different. On my Web server, my root directory is the `public_html` folder; some of my clients have a root directory in a folder called `httpdocs` — it really depends on what type of setup your hosting provider has. When in doubt, ask!

Upload the *contents* of the `/wordpress` folder to your Web server — not the folder itself. Most FTP client software lets you select all of the files and drag 'n' drop them to your Web server. Other programs have you highlight the files and click a Transfer button.

File transfers via FTP have two different forms: ASCII and binary. Most FTP clients are configured to auto-detect the transfer mode. However, it's important to understand the difference, as it pertains to this WordPress installation, to be able to troubleshoot any problems you have later. *Binary transfer mode* is how images (such as `.jpg`, `.gif`, `.bmp`, and `.png` files) need to be transferred via FTP. *ASCII transfer mode* is for everything else (such as text files, PHP files, JavaScript, and so on). For the most part, it's a safe bet to make sure the transfer mode of your FTP client is set to Auto-Detect. But if you experience issues with how those files load on your site, you might want to go back and retransfer the files using the appropriate transfer mode.

You aren't required to transfer the files to the root directory of your Web server. You can make the choice to run WordPress on a subdomain, or in a different folder, on your account. For example, if you want your blog address to be `http://yourdomain.com/blog`, you would transfer the WordPress files into a folder named `/blog`.

File permissions are something you need to pay attention to when you're transferring files to your Web server. *File permissions* tell the Web server how these files can be handled on your server — whether they're files that can be written to. As a general rule, PHP files need to have a permission (`chmod`) of 666, whereas file folders need a permission of 755. Almost all FTP clients let you check and change the permissions on the files, if you need to.

Some hosting providers run their PHP software in a more secure format called *safe mode*. If this is the case with your host, you need to set the PHP files to 644. If you're unsure, you can ask your hosting provider what permissions you need to set for PHP files.

Typically, you can find the option to change file permissions within the menu options of your FTP client.

Last step! Running the install script

This is the final step in the installation procedure for WordPress. This is the part where you connect the WordPress software you uploaded to the MySQL database.

Type this URL in the address window of your browser, replacing *your domain.com* with your own domain name: `http://yourdomain.com/wp-admin/install.php`.

If you chose to install WordPress in a different folder than the root directory of your account, make sure you indicate that in the URL for the install script. For example, if you transferred the WordPress software files to a folder called `/blog`, you would point your browser to the following URL in order to run the installation: `http://yourdomain.com/blog/wp-admin/install.php`.

Assuming you did everything correctly (see Table 6-1, later in this chapter, for help with common installation problems), you see the message shown in Figure 6-4.

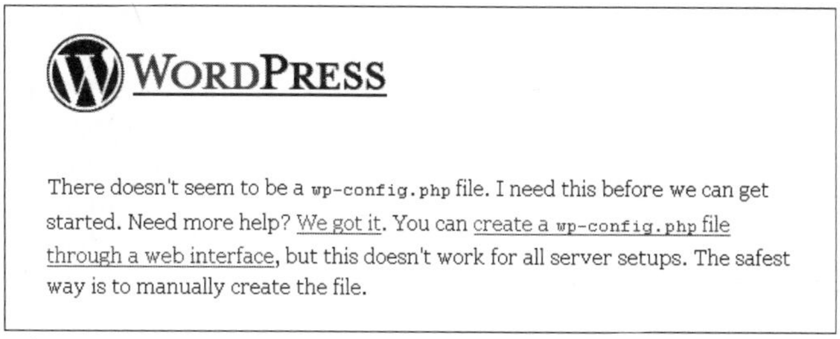

Figure 6-4:
The first
time you
run the
installation
script for
WordPress,
you see this
message.

There doesn't seem to be a `wp-config.php` file. I need this before we can get started. Need more help? We got it. You can create a wp-config.php file through a web interface, but this doesn't work for all server setups. The safest way is to manually create the file.

Click the You Can Create a `wp-config.php` File through a Web Interface link. The next page that opens is a Welcome to WordPress message, which gives you the information you need to proceed with the installation.

Next, click the Let's Go link. Remember the database name, username, and password that you saved earlier? Dig it out and use it to fill in the following fields, shown in Figure 6-5:

✔ **Database Name:** Type the database name you used when you created the MySQL database prior to this installation. Because hosts differ in configurations, you need to enter either the database name or the database name with your hosting account username appended.

For example, if you named your database *wordpress,* you would enter that in this text box. Or if your host requires you to append the database name with your hosting account username, you enter username_*wordpress,* substituting your hosting username for *username.* My username is *lisasabin,* so I enter *lisasabin_wordpress.*

✔ **User Name:** Type the username you used when you created the MySQL database prior to this installation. Depending on what your host requires, you might need to append this username with you hosting account username.

✔ **Password:** Type in the password you used when you set up the MySQL database. No need to append the password with your hosting account username here.

✔ **Database Host:** Ninety-nine percent of the time, you'll leave this as localhost. Some hosts, depending on their configuration, will have a different host set for the MySQL database server. If localhost doesn't work, you need to contact your hosting provider to find out the MySQL database host.

✔ **Table Prefix:** Leave this set as wp_.

Figure 6-5:
At this
step of the
WordPress
installation
phase, you
need to
enter the
database
name,
username,
and
password.

When you have all that information filled in, click the Submit button. You see a message that says, "All right, sparky! You've made it through this part of the installation. WordPress can now communicate with your database. If you're ready, time now to run the install!"

Go ahead, Sparky — click the Run the Install link and you'll see another `Welcome to WordPress` message. Click the First Step link.

Here, you need to enter or possibly change some information:

- ✔ **Weblog Title:** Enter the title you want to give your weblog (blog). This isn't written in stone; you can change this at a later date, if you'd like.

- ✔ **Your E-Mail Address:** Enter the e-mail address you want to use to be notified of administrative information about your blog. This, also, can be changed at a later date.

- ✔ **I Would Like My Blog To Appear in Search Engines Like Google and Technorati:** By default, this check box is selected, which allows the search engines to index the content of your blog and include your blog in search results. To keep your blog out of the search engines, deselect this check box.

When you're done, click the Continue to Second Step button.

Here's where the WordPress installation machine works its magic and creates all the tables within the database that contain the default data for your blog. On this screen (shown in Figure 6-6), WordPress gives you the login information you need to access the WordPress Administration panel (which I discuss in Chapter 7). Make note of this username and password before you leave this page. You should either scribble it down on a piece of paper or copy it into a text editor, such as Notepad.

After you click the Continue to Second Step button, you're sent an e-mail with the login information and login URL. This is handy if you're called away during this part of the installation process. So go ahead and let the dog out, answer the phone, brew a cup of coffee, or take a 15-minute power nap. If you somehow get distracted away from this page, the e-mail sent to you contains the information you need to successfully log in to your WordPress blog.

Do you have that username and password saved somewhere? Great! Click the `wp-login.php` link.

Figure 6-6:
This step of the installation process assigns a username and password. Be sure to keep them handy!

Second Step

Now we're going to create the database tables and fill them with some default data.

Finished!

Now you can log in with the **username** "admin" and **password** "bc0713".

Note that password carefully! It is a *random* password that was generated just for you. If you lose it, you will have to delete the tables from the database yourself, and re-install WordPress. So to review:

Username
    admin
Password
    bc0713
Login address
    wp-login.php

Were you expecting more steps? Sorry to disappoint. All done! :)

WordPress, personal publishing platform.

If you happen to lose this page prior to clicking the `wp-login.php` link, you can always find your way to the login page by entering your domain followed by the call to the login file. For example: `http://yourdomain.com/wp-login.php`.

You know you're finished with the installation process when you see the login page, as shown in Figure 6-7. Check out Table 6-1 if you experience any problems during this installation process; it covers some of the common problems users run into.

Figure 6-7:
You know
you've run a
successful
WordPress
installation
when you
see the
login page.

So, do tell — how much time does your watch show for the installation? Was it five minutes? Stop by my blog sometime (`http://ewebscapes.com/designblog`) and let me know if WordPress stood up to its famous five-minute-installation reputation. I'm a curious sort.

The good news is — you're done! Were you expecting a marching band? WordPress isn't that fancy . . . yet. Give them time, though; if anyone can produce it, the folks at WordPress can.

Table 6-1	Common WordPress Installation Problems	
Error Message	**Common Cause**	**Solution**
Error Connecting to the Database	The database name, user name, password, or host was entered incorrectly.	Revisit your MySQL database to obtain the database name, user-name, and password and reenter that information.

Error Message	Common Cause	Solution
Headers Already Sent Error Messages	A syntax error occurred in the `wp-config.php` file.	Open the `wp-config.php` file in a text editor. The first line should contain only this line: `<?php`. The very last line should contain only this line: `?>`. Make sure there's nothing else on those lines, not even white space. Save the file changes.
500: Internal Server Error	Permissions on PHP files are set incorrectly.	Try setting the permissions (`chmod`) on the PHP files to 666. If that doesn't work, set them to 644. Each Web server has different settings for how it allows PHP to execute on its servers.
404: Page Not Found	The URL for the login page is incorrect.	Double-check that the URL you're using to get to the login page is the same as the location of your WordPress installation (such as `http://yourdomain.com/wp-login.php`).
403: Forbidden Access	An `index.html` or `index.htm` file exists in the WordPress installation directory.	WordPress is a PHP application, so the default home page is `index.php`. Look in the WordPress installation folder on your Web server. If there is an `index.html` or `index.htm` file in there, delete it.

Let me be the first to congratulate you on your newly installed WordPress blog! When you're ready, log in and familiarize yourself with the Administration panel, which I describe in Chapter 7.

Chapter 7

Understanding the WordPress.org Administration Panel

. . . .

In This Chapter

▶ Logging in and finding the Administration panel

▶ Personalizing your settings

. . . .

*W*ith WordPress successfully installed, you can explore your new blogging software. This chapter guides you through the preliminary setup of your new WordPress blog using the Administration panel. When you blog with WordPress, you spend a lot of time in the Administration panel, which is where you make all the exciting, behind-the-scenes stuff happen. In the Administration panel, you find all the different settings and options that enable you to set your blog up just the way you want it. (If you still need to install and configure WordPress, check out Chapter 6.)

Feeling comfortable with the Administration panel sets you up for successful entrance into the WordPress blogging world. You will tweak your WordPress settings several times throughout the life of your blog. As I go through the various sections, settings, options, and configurations available to you, understand that nothing is set in stone. You can set options today and then change them at any time.

Logging In and Finding the Administration Panel

I find that the direct approach (also known as jumping in) works best when I want to get familiar with a new software tool. To that end, just follow these steps to log in to WordPress and take a look at the guts of the Administration panel.

1. **Open your Web browser and type the WordPress login page address (or URL) in the address box.**

   The login page address looks something like this:

   `http://www.yourdomain.com/wp-login.php.`

   If you install WordPress in its own folder, you include that folder name in the login URL. For example, if you install WordPress in a folder ingeniously named `wordpress`, the login URL becomes `http://www.yourdomain.com/wordpress/wp-login.php`.

2. **Type your username in the Username text box and your password in the Password text box. (See Figure 7-1.)**

   In case you forget your password, WordPress has you covered. Click the Lost Your Password? link (located near the bottom of the page), enter your username and e-mail address, and then click the Submit button. WordPress resets your password and e-mails it to you.

   After you request a password, you'll receive two e-mails from your WordPress blog. The first e-mail contains a link that you click to verify that you requested the password. After you've verified your intentions, you'll receive an e-mail containing your new password.

3. **Select the Remember Me check box if you want WordPress to place a cookie in your browser.**

   The cookie tells WordPress to remember your login credentials the next time you show up. The cookie set by WordPress is harmless and stores your WordPress login on your computer. Because of the cookie, WordPress remembers you the next time you visit.

   Note: You do need to make sure your browser is configured to allow cookies. (If you aren't sure how to do this, check the help documentation of the Internet browser you're using.)

4. **Click the Login button.**

After you've successfully logged in to your WordPress Administration panel, you see the Dashboard page. Consider the Dashboard page, along with the rest of the WordPress Administration panel, to be the mothership, and you're Captain Kirk (of the original "Star Trek" series, for the younger crowd) at the helm of all the controls that enable you to launch your blog into orbit — or, in this case, into the blogosphere. All the controls you need to bring your new WordPress blog to life exist within the Administration panel, starting with the Dashboard page, as shown in Figure 7-2.

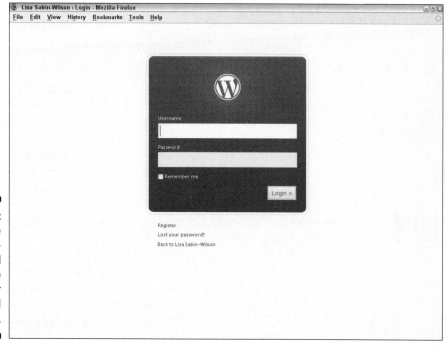

Figure 7-1:
Log in to the
Administra-
tion panel
to manage
your
options and
settings.

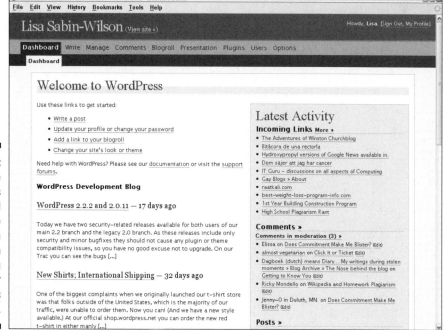

Figure 7-2:
The
WordPress
Dashboard
page is the
screen you
see when
you log
in to your
WordPress
blog.

Welcome to WordPress

The Welcome to WordPress Dashboard page takes you right to the meat of your WordPress blog. The underlined phrases (refer to Figure 7-2) are hyperlinks that give you access to various WordPress functions, as follows:

- **Write a Post:** Takes you to the page where you can write a blog post. (I present more information about writing posts in Chapter 8.)

- **Update Your Profile Or Change Your Password:** Leads you directly to the page where you can update your personal profile information and modify your user password. (Check out the "Personalizing Your Profile Settings" section later in this chapter for more about personalizing your profile and modifying your password.)

- **Add a Link to Your Blogroll:** Launches you into the blogroll (link list) manager of your WordPress Administration panel, where you can manage your blogroll by adding new links, editing old links, and deleting existing links. (Find out more information about managing your blogroll in Chapter 8.)

- **Change Your Site's Look Or Theme:** Displays the Themes page for changing your WordPress template design options. With these options, you can modify your current theme or change to an entirely new theme. (Details about managing your theme and design show up in Chapters 9 and 11.)

Also included on the Welcome to WordPress page of the Dashboard page are two *very* important and helpful links:

- **Documentation:** Loads the WordPress Codex, which is a portal of helpful information and resources that provides some great resources on the WordPress software and how to use it. The Codex is maintained by volunteer document writers who are part of the WordPress community of users at `http://codex.wordpress.org`.

- **Support Forum:** Takes you to a discussion group of WordPress community members helping one another (at `http://wordpress.org/support`). If you have pressing questions about using WordPress, you can post them in the forum. WordPress has a large user base of people who, by and large, are very willing to share what they've learned in their travels within WordPress.

Tracking blog activity

The Latest Activity section on the right side of the Dashboard page provides links to the following essential statistical information about the current state of your blog:

✔ **Incoming Links:** Click these links to visit those *very smart* fellow blog-gers who've placed a link on their blog to your blog. Click the More link and access Technorati.com (Figure 7-3), where you see exactly how many other sites have linked to yours. Technorati gathers information on who is linking to whom, and the WordPress Dashboard compiles that infor-mation, as it relates to your blog, and displays it under the Incoming Links header. And you can link back (see Chapter 8 for information about adding links to your blog) and visit those sites.

✔ **Comments:** These links lead to the most recent comments that were left on your blog. Click links to visit the commenter's Web site, revisit the actual post on your site, and respond to a commenter, if you wish. Click the arrow next to Comments to access the Administration panel, where you can manage your comments by moderating, editing, or deleting them. (See Chapter 8 for more information.)

✔ **Posts:** These are links to the most recent posts you've made to your blog. Click the arrow to the right of Posts and you access the Administration panel, where you can manage your current posts by editing or deleting them. (See Chapter 8 for more information on editing and deleting posts.)

✔ **Blog Stats:** This area gives you information about how many posts, com-ments, and categories are currently on your blog, at a glance.

Figure 7-3: Technorati shows you information about incoming links (or blog reactions) to your site and information on how many people have linked to your site.

Getting the latest news on WordPress development

On the left side of the Welcome to WordPress page, you see the WordPress Development Blog section. Here, you can find the last three posts from the WordPress Development blog, located at http://wordpress.org/ development. WordPress developers maintain this blog, posting important information about WordPress (such as new version releases, security patches, and the latest WordPress news). The developers update this blog as new information becomes available, so bookmark it or subscribe to the RSS feed.

Obtaining other WordPress news

The bottom section of the Welcome to WordPress page, the Other WordPress News section, links to many of the brand-new toys, bells, and whistles that are released for WordPress.

You see several boxes in this section, with each box containing a link to a recent post made on a blog owned and operated by a WordPress developer — or a WordPress user who frequently posts relevant and useful information about WordPress. Whenever a new plugin or theme is developed and released, you'll usually find information about it in this Other WordPress News section. (You can find more information about WordPress plugins and themes in Chapters 9, 10, and 11.)

Click the Read More link to go to WordPress Planet (at http://planet.word press.org), which is a collection of important WordPress news gathered from several different WordPress resources found throughout the blogosphere. The blogs listed here include those of the many developers involved in the creation, development, and release of the WordPress software — including Matt Mullenweg, Ryan Boren, and Alex King, to name just a few.

Personalizing Your Profile Settings

After you've installed the WordPress software and logged in to your Word-Press Administration panel, you can put your own stamp on your blog by giving it a title and description, setting your contact e-mail address, and identifying yourself as the author of the blog. You take care of these and other settings on the General Options page and the User page, as described in the following sections.

Setting your General options

To begin personalizing your settings, follow these steps:

1. **Click the Options tab on the WordPress Administration panel.**

   The General Options page appears. (See Figure 7-4.)

2. **Enter the name of your blog in the Blog Title text box.**

   The title you enter here is the one that you've given to your blog to iden-tify it as your own. For example, the title of my blog is Lisa Sabin-Wilson, which appears on the blog as well as in the title bar of the browser, as shown in Figure 7-4. I chose to title my blog using my name to identify it as mine. Mine! MINE! And with it, I shall rule the world! Ahem.

   Give your blog an interesting and identifiable name. For example, you might use Fried Green Tomatoes if you're blogging about that topic, or the movie, or even anything remotely related to the lovely southern dish.

Administration panel

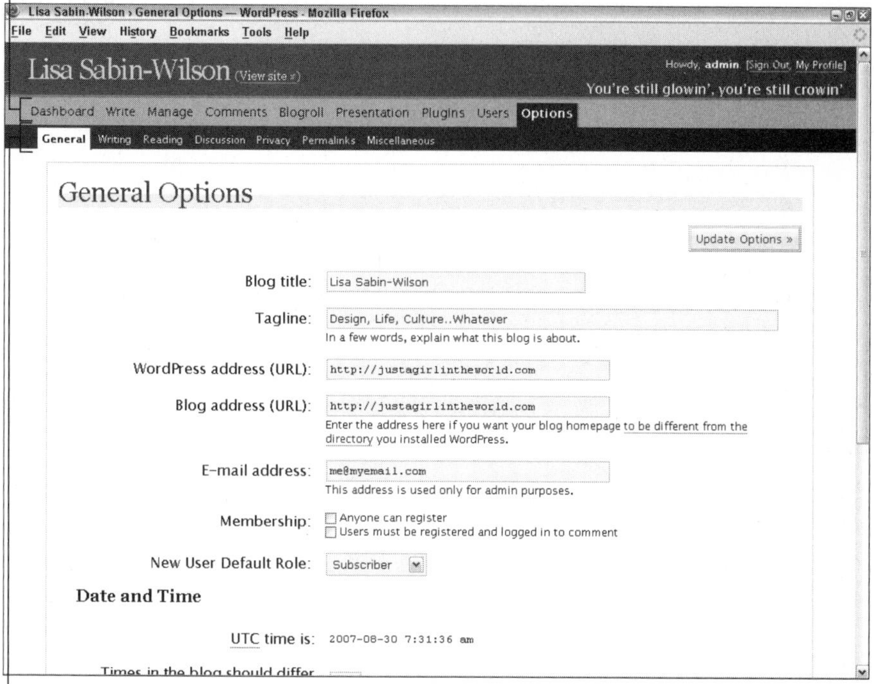

Figure 7-4:
Personalize
the settings
of your
WordPress
blog on the
General
Options
page.

Lisa Sabin-Wilson › General Options — WordPress - Mozilla Firefox

File Edit View History Bookmarks Tools Help

Lisa Sabin-Wilson (View site ≥)

Howdy, **admin**. [Sign Out, My Profile]
You're still glowin', you're still crowin'

Dashboard Write Manage Comments Blogroll Presentation Plugins Users **Options**

General Writing Reading Discussion Privacy Permalinks Miscellaneous

General Options

Update Options »

Blog title: Lisa Sabin-Wilson

Tagline: Design, Life, Culture..Whatever
In a few words, explain what this blog is about.

WordPress address (URL): http://justagirlintheworld.com

Blog address (URL): http://justagirlintheworld.com
Enter the address here if you want your blog homepage to be different from the directory you installed WordPress.

E-mail address: me@myemail.com
This address is used only for admin purposes.

Membership: ☐ Anyone can register
☐ Users must be registered and logged in to comment

New User Default Role: Subscriber

Date and Time

UTC time is: 2007-08-30 7:31:36 am

Times in the blog should differ

Administration subpanel

3. **In the Tagline text box, enter a five- to ten-word phrase that describes your blog.**

   In Figure 7-4, you can see that my tagline is Design, Life, Culture . . . Whatever — which is what I blog about on any given day.

   The general Internet-surfing public can view your blog title and tagline, which various search engines (such as Google, Yahoo!, MSN, and so on) grab for indexing. So choose your words with this in mind. (You can find more information about search engine optimization, or SEO, in Chapter 16.)

4. **In the WordPress Address (URL) text box, enter the location where you've installed your WordPress blog software.**

   Be sure to include the `http://` portion of the URL and the entire path to your WordPress installation. In Figure 7-4, you can see that my WordPress software is installed at `http://justagirlintheworld.com`. If you've installed WordPress in a folder in your directory — for example, a folder called `wordpress` — you need to make sure to include that here. If I had installed WordPress into a folder called `wordpress`, my WordPress Address would be `http://justagirlintheworld.com/wordpress`.

5. **In the Blog Address (URL) text box, enter the Web address where people can find your blog using their Web browsers.**

   Typically, what you enter here is the same as your domain name. In Figure 7-4, my blog address is `http://justagirlintheworld.com` because that's the Web address anyone can type in to find my blog on the Internet. However, if you install WordPress in a subdirectory of your site, the WordPress installation URL is different than the blog URL. For instance, if you've installed WordPress at `http://yourdomain.com/wordpress/` (WordPress URL), you need to tell WordPress that you want the blog to appear at `http://yourdomain.com` (blog URL).

6. **Enter your e-mail address in the E-Mail Address text box.**

   WordPress sends messages about the details of your blog to this e-mail address. For instance, when a new user registers for your blog, WordPress sends you an e-mail alert.

7. **Choose one of the options for Membership:**

   - Select the Anyone Can Register check box to allow any visitor to your site to register for a user account on your blog.

   - Select the Users Must Be Registered and Logged In to Comment check box to allow only registered users to leave comments on your blog. This option can be helpful in combating what is known as the dreadful *comment spam*. (See Chapters 2 and 8 for more about comment spam.)

8. **From the New User Default Role drop-down list, select the role that you want new users to have when they register for user accounts on your blog.**

You need to understand the differences among the user roles because each user role is assigned different levels of access on your blog, as follows:

- *Subscriber:* The default role. It's a good idea to maintain this as the role assigned to new users, particularly if you don't know who's registering. Subscribers are given access to the Dashboard page, and they can view and change the options within their profiles on the Your Profile and Personal Options page (they don't have access to your account settings, however). Each user can change his username, e-mail address, password, bio, and other descriptors found in a user profile. Subscribers' profile information is stored in the WordPress database, and your blog remembers them each time they visit — so they don't have to complete the profile information each time they leave comments on your blog.

- *Contributor:* In addition to the access Subscribers have, Contributors can upload files and write, edit, and manage their own posts. Contributors can write posts; however, they can't publish the posts — the administrator reviews all Contributor posts and decides whether to publish them. This is a nice way to moderate content written by new authors.

- *Author:* In addition to the access Contributors have, Authors can publish and edit their own posts.

- *Editor:* In addition to the access Authors have, Editors can moderate comments, manage categories, manage links, edit pages, and edit other Authors' posts.

- *Administrator:* Administrators can edit all of the options and settings within the WordPress blog.

9. In the Date and Time section of the General options page, enter the format in which you want the date and time displayed on your blog, through the following options:

- *Times in the Weblog Should Differ By:* Refers to the number of hours that your local time differs from the Coordinated Universal Time (UTC) displayed directly above this option. This makes sure that all of your blog posts and comments left on your blog are time stamped with the correct time. For example, if you're lucky enough, like me, to live in the frozen tundra of Wisconsin, which is in the Central time zone (CST), you would enter **–6** in this box. If you're unsure what your UTC time is, you can find it at the Greenwich Mean Time (`wwp.greenwichmeantime.com`) Web site. (GMT is, essentially, the same thing as UTC.)

- *Default Date Format:* Determines the style of the date display. The default format is already inserted for you: F d, Y (F = the full month name; d = the two-digit day; Y = the four-digit year), which gives you the date output. This default date format displays the date like this: January 1, 2007. You can change this with your own display options; find out how at `http://codex.wordpress.org/Formatting_Date_and_Time`.

- *Default Time Format:* Determines the style of the time display. The default time format is already inserted for you: g:i a, (g = two-digit, 12-hour format of the hour; I = two-digit format of the minutes; a = 2 lowercase ante meridiem and post meridiem — that is, am or pm), which gives you the time output: 12:00 p.m. You can change this with your own time display options; find out how at `http://code x.wordpress.org/Formatting_Date_and_Time`.

- *Weeks in the Calendar Should Start On:* The display of the calendar in the sidebar of your blog is optional. If you choose to display the calendar, you can select the day of the week you want your calendar to start on.

Creating your profile

The next place to visit in your WordPress Administration panel to continue personalizing your settings is your own user profile. Click the Users tab on the Administration panel and then click the Your Profile subtab, and WordPress opens the Your Profile page. (See Figure 7-5.)

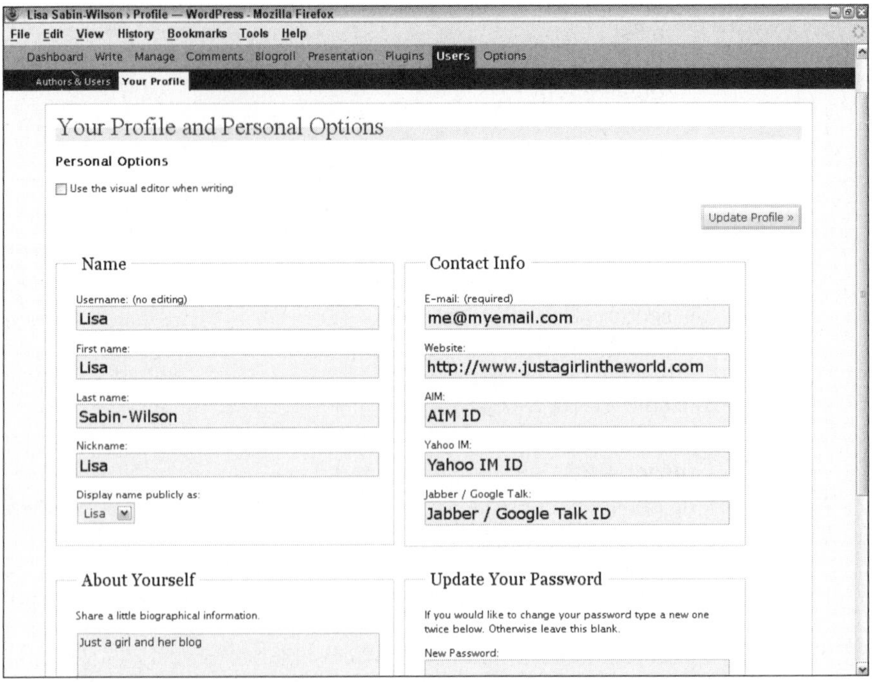

Figure 7-5:
Establish your profile details here.

The next sections guide you through identifying yourself to the blogging world.

Name

In the Name section of the Your Profile page, you can't edit the Username field. This is the username you use to log in to your WordPress blog and was assigned to you during the installation process. (See Chapter 6.)

To fill out this section of your profile, follow these steps:

1. **Enter your first name in the First Name text box and your last name in the Last Name text box.**

   You're using your real first and last names here, but these aren't published publicly on your blog.

2. **Enter the nickname of your choice in the Nickname text box.**

   The name that you enter here is published publicly to your blog; it's the name the blog world knows you by.

3. **From the Display Name Publicly As drop-down list, choose the name you want to appear on your blog.**

   WordPress takes all the names you've entered in Steps 1 and 2 and creates a list of possible names for you to choose from. For example, if I enter my first and last names in Step 1 and just my first name in Step 2, the drop-down list creates options that include each of those fields. This step allows you to further define (and in the future, easily change) the name that is displayed publicly on your blog.

About Yourself

The About Yourself section is where you enter a short biography or a description of your blog. WordPress doesn't limit you on word or character count in this section. However, the field is meant for a brief bio. Some WordPress themes are coded to display this short bio in the sidebar of the theme. For themes that do this, it's helpful to know that search engines will pick up the text in this bio, so that's something to keep in mind when creating it.

Contact Info

This section gives you the opportunity to share your contact information, including your e-mail, Web site, and various Instant Messenger identities. You can display this contact information on your blog if you want — but you may not want all of your contact information displayed to just anyone who happens along. Alternatively, you can let your contact information appear only for other registered users to view within the Administration panel on the Users page after they are logged in. To include your contact information, follow these steps:

1. **Enter your e-mail address in the Email Address text box.**

   This field is required but doesn't have to be the same as the Administrator e-mail that you entered in the General Options area. (Refer to Figure 7-4.) WordPress will use this e-mail address to notify you of new comments and for other administrative reasons. This e-mail address doesn't appear on your site, nor is it shared with anyone without login access to your WordPress Administration panel.

2. **(Optional) Enter your Web site address in the Website Address text box**.

   If you leave this blank, this field defaults to just `http://`.

   Some templates use this field to provide a hyperlink on your blog wherever your name appears. (For instance, underneath my blog post title it might say something like Posted by Lisa, and when you click my name, it takes you to back to the main page of my blog.)

3. **(Optional) Enter your AOL Instant Messenger (AIM) ID.**

   Some WordPress templates display the author's AOL Instant Messenger ID using a tag that looks like this: `<?php the_author_aim(); ?>`. (See Chapter 9 for more in-depth information about WordPress template tags.)

4. **(Optional) Enter your Yahoo! Instant Messenger (Yahoo! IM) ID.**

   Some WordPress templates display the author's Yahoo! Instant Messenger ID using a tag that looks like this: `<?php the_author_yim(); ?>`.

5. **(Optional) Enter your Jabber/Google Talk ID.**

   Some plugins use this data field, but there aren't any easy template tags to display the author's Jabber/Google Talk ID in your blog template at this time. With some fancy work, you could include it in the WordPress Loop for display on your blog. Visit the `http://codex.wordpress.org/Author_Templates#Using_Author_Information` page of the WordPress Codex to find out how to insert your Jabber/Google Talk ID in your blog using the `$curauth->jabber;` tag.

Update Your Password

The Update Your Password section lets you change the password you use to log in to your WordPress blog. This is purely a security measure to help protect your blog from malicious behavior that sometimes happens in an Internet environment. Are there mean people who would try to access your blog without your permission? You bet! It's a good idea to protect yourself by changing your password regularly. Set yourself a monthly reminder to do it — just don't forget your new password!

To update your password, follow these steps:

1. **Enter your new password in the New Password text box.**

2. **Enter the new password in the Type It One More Time text box.**

When you're done setting the options on this page, click the Update Profile button at the bottom of the page. Not doing so will result in catastrophic events and natural disasters in your local area, causing the people around you to run through the streets screaming in fear.

Not really. Just click the button to make sure your options are updated and the changes take effect; otherwise, you'll have to do it all over again.

You may have noticed, in Figure 7-5, the Use the Visual Editor When Writing text box near the top-left corner of the page. The Visual Editor refers to the formatting options you find on the Write Post page (discussed in detail in Chapter 8). By default, the box is selected, which means that the Visual Editor is on. To turn it off, deselect the box.

Options Galore

Within the WordPress Administration panel, there are several other options you can set, according to your own preferences. Remember that when you log in to your WordPress account, you see the following tabs on the Administration panel across the top of the page: Dashboard, Write, Manage, Comments, Blogroll, Presentation, Plugins, Users, and Options. Earlier in the chapter, I discuss some of the settings you can find when clicking the Dashboard, Users, and Options tabs. In the sections that follow, I highlight some of the things you can do with the remaining tabs.

I cover these areas of the WordPress Administration panel in other chapters, but they're worth a mention here so that you know what you're looking at. (Each section contains a cross-reference telling you where you can find more in-depth information on that topic in this book.)

Write

Click the Write tab in the Administration panel and you find two subtabs: Write Post and Write Page. Each of these subtabs gives you the tools you need to publish content to your blog:

  ✔ **Write Post:** Just as the title of the subtab indicates, this is where you write your blog posts, set the options for each post (such as assigning a post to a category, making it a private or public post, and others), and publish the posts to your blog. (You can find more information on writing posts in Chapter 8.)

✔ **Write Page:** This is where you write a *page,* which is a post that appears on its own page rather than the page that displays all of your blog posts. This is called a *static page,* and the content you publish here does not get published to your blog content, but rather serves as a page on your site containing content that does not change often, such as an "About Me" or a "Contact Me" page. (Chapter 16 gives you information on how to publish a static page as the main/front page on your site.)

Table 7-1 illustrates the differences between a WordPress *post* and a WordPress *page.*

Table 7-1	The Differences between a Post and a Page	
WordPress Options	*Page*	*Post*
Appears in blog post listings	No	Yes
Appears as a static page	Yes	No
Appears in category archives	No	Yes
Appears in monthly archives	No	Yes
Appears in Recent Posts listings	No	Yes
Appears in search results	No	Yes

Manage

Click the Manage tab on the Administration panel and you see the following subtabs below it: Posts, Pages, Uploads, Categories, Files, Import, and Export. From the Posts, Pages, Uploads, and Categories subtabs, you can manage your posts, pages, file uploads, and categories. Check out Chapter 8 for all the details on that. Or continue in this chapter for information on the Files, Import, and Export subtabs.

When you click the Files subtab, you see the Editing page. This is where you can edit some core WordPress files.

Changes you make in the Manage/Files area are saved immediately, with no backups of the original files. So proceed with caution, and *only* if you're confident in what you're doing. This isn't an area for "OOOooo, I wonder what happens if I pull *this* lever" type of experimentation. For example, incorrect changes to the .htaccess file can render your site completely useless. This type of boo-boo isn't permanent; you can fix it. But it requires you to directly re-edit the file you messed up. Your best bet? Plan on not touching anything here unless you know what you're doing — or have someone who does to help you.

There are several editable files contained within a WordPress installation. Listed on the right side of File Editing page, under the Recent header, are the last five most recent files that you've viewed in this section. Underneath that section is the Common header, which lists the three most commonly edited files in a WordPress installation. Those include the following:

- **Main Index Template:** This is the `index.php` file found in the main WordPress installation directory. Typically, you will never need to edit this file.

- `.htaccess`**:** This file contains, among other things, rules pertaining to the permalink URLs that serve as permanent Web addresses for the information that your visitors can find on your blog. You can find more specific information about this file in Chapter 8.

- `my-hacks.php`**:** Some people use this file to add some hacks and modifications to their WordPress blog settings. These hacks have typically been replaced by WordPress plugin functionality, but the real hard-core geek types still use them. (More information about such geek activity can be found in Chapter 10, where I cover more about WordPress plugins.)

Moving further along the subpanel, you see the Import and Export subtabs. This is where you can import data and archives from another blogging platform (such as Blogger, Movable Type, and so on) into your WordPress blog and/or export your current WordPress blog information. Check out Chapter 15 for lots more details on the Import and Export features.

Comments

When you click the Comments tab on the Administration panel, you see the following subtabs: Comments, Awaiting Moderation, and Akismet Spam. Under these subtabs, you can view comments left on your blog, view and deal with comments that are awaiting moderation, and view comments that have been caught by the Akismet Spam filter.

You can find information about the use and purpose of comments on blogs in Chapter 2, and I give you the details on how to use this section of your WordPress Administration panel in Chapter 8.

Blogroll

Clicking the Blogroll tab on the Administration panel displays the following subtabs:

   ✔ **Manage Blogroll:** You can edit or delete existing links in this section.

   ✔ **Add Link:** Add new links to your blogroll here.

   ✔ **Import Links:** Import links from other blogroll applications (such as blogrolling.com).

   ✔ **Categories:** Create new blogrolls and categorize them by topic here.

I tell you all about building and managing your blogroll in Chapter 8.

Presentation

When you click the Presentation tab on the Administration panel, you see these subtabs: Themes, Widgets, and Theme Editor. Within these subpages you can:

   ✔ Select the theme for your blog.

   ✔ Edit the template of your theme.

   ✔ Use sidebar widgets.

I tell you all about managing the presentation of your blog with template tags and themes in Chapter 9, and I give information on how to use widgets in Chapter 10.

Users

WordPress guarantees you at least one user for every WordPress blog, and in the WordPress.org version, that user is you. Find the Users section by clicking the Users tab on the Administration panel.

The two subtabs here are Authors & Users and Your Profile. A really super feature of WordPress is that you can have as many authors as you want, and you can run a multi-author blog, in case that is something that trips your trigger. In this section of the WordPress Administration panel, you manage your authors and users.

The Users page lists all the users on your blog, their roles on the blog, and the number of posts each user has made. Click the Edit link to the far right of a username and you find that you can edit the profile details (such as e-mail address and password) for a user. You can also click the View Posts link to view all of the posts made by that author. At the bottom of this page, you can add new users to your blog by entering their e-mail addresses, assigning a User Role to each, and clicking the Add User button.

Options

Click the Options tab on the Administration panel and you find, well — a whole lot of options! On the Administration subpanel, you see the following subtabs: General, Writing, Reading, Discussion, Privacy, Permalinks, and Miscellaneous.

If the General subtab sounds familiar to you, it might be because I cover it earlier in this chapter, in the "Setting your General options" section.

The next subtab to the right is Writing. It's where you set some basic options for writing your posts. Table 7-2 gives you some information on choosing how your posts look and how WordPress handles some specific conditions. After you set your options here, be sure to click the Update Options button, or else the changes won't take effect.

Table 7-2	General Writing Options	
Option	*Default*	*Function*
Size of Post Box	10 lines	Determines the size of the text edit box on the Write Post page. The bigger the number, the taller the box.
Formatting	Convert emoticons to graphics and correct invalidly nested XHTML	Determines whether WordPress converts emoticons — such as :-) and :-P — to graphics. Determines whether WordPress corrects invalidly nested XHTML automatically. In general, I recommend selecting this option. (You can find more information about valid XHTML code at http:// validator.w3.org/docs/ #docs_all.)
Default Post Category	Uncategorized	Lets you choose the category that WordPress defaults to any time you forget to choose a category when you publish a post.

(continued)

Table 7-2 (continued)

Option	Default	Function
Default Link Category	Blogroll	Lets you choose the category that WordPress defaults to any time you forget to categorize a link.
Post via E-Mail	N/A	Allows you publish blog posts from your e-mail.
Update Services	`http://rpc.ping omatic.com`	Lets you indicate which ping service you'd like to use in order to notify the world that you've made updates, or new posts, to your blog. These update services include blogrolling.com and weblogs.com. The default, rpc.pingomatic.com, was created by Automattic and updates all the popular services simultaneously.

Go to `http://codex.wordpress.org/Update_Services` for comprehensive information on update services.

The third subtab on the Options tab is Reading, where you can set the following options:

- **Front Page:** Choose what you want displayed on the front page of your blog: your latest posts or a static page. You can find detailed information on using a static page for your front page in Chapter 16.

- **Blog Pages:** Enter the number of posts you want to display on each blog page.

- **Syndication Feeds:** In the Show Most Recent Box, enter the number of posts you want shown in your RSS feed; then, next to the For Each Article, Show section, select either Full Text or Summary. Full Text publishes the entire post to your RSS Feed, whereas Summary publishes only a short excerpt. (Check out Chapter 8 for more information on WordPress RSS Feeds.)

- **Encoding for Pages and Feeds:** UTF-8 is the default, and recommended, character encoding for your blog. *Character encoding* is code that handles the storage and transmission of the text from your blog through the Internet connection. Your safest bet is to leave the default in place because it is the most commonly accepted character encoding and supports a wide range of languages.

✔ **WordPress Should Compress Articles (gzip) If Browsers Ask for Them:** By default, this box is not selected. Gzip is a method of compression that occurs if a visitor's browser is configured to ask for it. Select this box to compress your blog posts (articles). Compressed files can potentially save you on the bandwidth used by your blog. (See Chapter 6 for information about bandwidth.)

When you're done setting these options, don't forget to click the Update Options button. Doing so reloads the Reading Options page with your settings saved.

The fourth subtab on the Options tab is Discussion, whose sections let you set the options for how you handle comments and the publishing of posts on your blog.

The Usual Settings for an Article section contains the following options:

✔ **Attempt to Notify Any Weblogs Linked to from the Article (Slows Down Posting):** By default, this box is selected, and your blog sends out a notification (or ping) to any site you have linked to in your blog posts. This is also commonly referred to as a trackback (I discuss trackbacks in Chapter 2). Deselect this box if you don't want these notifications sent.

✔ **Allow Link Notifications from Other Weblogs (Pingbacks and Trackbacks):** By default, this box is selected, and your blog is open to be notified via a ping or trackback from another blog that has linked to yours. Any trackbacks or pings sent to your blog are listed on your site in the comments section of the blog post. If you deselect this box, your blog won't accept pingbacks or trackbacks from other blogs.

✔ **Allow People to Post Comments on the Article:** By default, this box is selected, and people can leave comments on your blog posts. If you deselect this box, no one can leave comments on your blog.

The E-mail Me Whenever section of the Discussion tab has the following two options:

✔ **Anyone Posts a Comment:** Enabled by default, this option lets you receive an e-mail notification whenever anyone leaves a comment on your blog. Deselect the box if you do not want to be notified by e-mail about every new comment.

✔ **A Comment Is Held for Moderation:** Enabled by default, this option lets you receive an e-mail notification whenever a comment is awaiting your approval in the comment moderation queue. (See Chapter 8 for more information about the comment moderation queue.) You need to deselect this option if you don't want this notification.

The three options in the next section, Before a Comment Appears, tell WordPress how you want comments to be handled before they appear on your blog, as follows:

✔ **An Administrator Must Always Approve the Comment:** Disabled by default, this option keeps every single comment left on your in the moderation queue until you, the administrator, log in and approve it. Select this box to enable this option.

✔ **Comment Author Must Fill Out Name and E-mail:** Enabled by default, this option requires all commenters on your blog to fill out the Name and E-mail field when leaving a comment. This option is very helpful in combating comment spam (See Chapters 2 and 10 for information on comment spam.) Deselect this box to disable this option.

✔ **Comment Author Must Have Previously Approved Comment:** Enabled by default, this option requires all first-time commenters on your blog to be sent to the comment moderation queue for approval by the administrator of the blog. After comment authors have been approved for the first time, they remain approved for every comment thereafter. WordPress stores their e-mail address in the database, and any future comments that match any stored e-mails are automatically approved. This is another measure that WordPress has built in to combat comment spam.

The Comment Moderation section of the Discussion tab is useful because comment spammers try to spam your blog with a *ton* of links in hopes of promoting their own sites using your comment form. You can type a number in the text box in this section to set the number of links that are allowed in a comment before it is tossed into the moderation queue to await approval. The default is 2. Give that a try, and if you find that you're getting lots of spam comments with multiple links, you may want to revisit this page and increase that number.

The large text box underneath the link setting lets you type in keywords, URLS, e-mail addresses, and IP addresses in comments that you want held in moderation for your approval.

In contrast to the Comment Moderation list, the Comment Blacklist is a listing of words, URLs, e-mail addresses, and/or IP addresses that appear in comments that you just want to flat-out ban from your blog. Items placed here don't even make it into your comment moderation queue — they are filtered as spam by the system and completely disregarded.

Let me just say that the words I have placed in my Blacklist are not family friendly and have no place in a nice book like this.

The next subtab of the Options tab is Privacy, which contains two options for you to choose between concerning how you want to deal with publicity on your blog:

✔ **I Would Like My Blog to Appear in Search Engines Like Google, Sphere and Technorati and Archivers:** This is the default setting and means that you are freely allowing search engines to visit your blog and then list you in their search results, and allowing your site to get indexed in blog archive services such as Technorati.

✔ **I Would Like to Block Search Engines, but Allow Normal Visitors:** If you are one of those rare bloggers who does *not* want that type of exposure for your blog, but you do want to allow normal (read: no search engines) visitors, select this option.

Be sure to click the Update Options button after you've set all of your options on the Discussion page to make the changes take effect.

The next subtab of the Options tab is Permalinks. Each of the posts you make on your blog has a unique URL called a *permalink,* which is permanent link (URL) for all your blog posts, pages, and archives. I provide more details on permalink options in Chapter 8.

The final subtab of the Options tab is Miscellaneous, which has the following three options:

✔ **Uploading:** Type the server path to the folder that you want your entire file uploads to be stored in on your Web server. The default is `wp-content/uploads`. You can, however, specify any folder you'd like; just be sure that the folder you specify has permissions (chmod) of 755 so that it is writeable. (See Chapter 6 for more information on setting file permissions.) The box underneath the Uploading option, Organize My Uploads into Month- and Year-Based Folders, is not selected by default. Select that box if you want your uploaded files to be organized in folders by month and by year.

For example, files you upload in January of 2008 will exist in the following folder: `/wp-content/uploads/2008/01/`. Likewise, files you upload in February 2008 will exist in the following folder: `/wp-content/uploads/20087/02/`.

✔ **Track Bookmarks Update Time:** Select this box to have WordPress track the update times on links that you have listed in your blogroll. The key here is that the blogs you have listed in your blogroll need to ping (or notify) and update services, such as blogrolling.com, in order for this to work. WordPress can be configured to display special notations for updated links in your blogroll, such as with an asterisk.

✔ **Use Legacy my-hacks.php File Support:** In the "Manage" section, earlier in this chapter, I gave some information about the `my-hacks.php` file. Select this box only if you are using the file. If you don't know whether you are using the `my-hacks.php` file, then you probably aren't and are safe to leave it alone.

In Chapter 8, I get you started on writing and publishing blog posts, managing your categories, creating your blogroll, and exploring WordPress themes.

Chapter 8

Establishing Your Blog Routine

*W*ordPress is a powerful publishing tool, especially when you use the full range of options available. With the basic settings configured (which you do in Chapter 7), now is the time to go forth and blog! You can, at this point, skip forward to the "Blog It! Writing Your First Entry" section in this chapter and jump right into creating new posts to your blog. Or, you can stay right here with me and discover some of the options you can set to make your blog a bit more organized and logical from the get go.

A blog can become unwieldy and disorganized, requiring you to revisit these next few features sometime in the near future so that you can get the beast under control. So why not do a little planning and get it over with now? I promise it won't take that long, and you'll thank me for it later.

Staying On Topic with Categories

In WordPress, a *category* is what you determine to be the main topic of a blog post. Through the use of categories, you can file your blog posts into topics, by subject. To improve your readers' experience in navigating through your blog, WordPress organizes posts by the category you assign to each one. Visitors can click the categories they're interested in to see the blog posts you've written on those particular topics. You should know ahead of time that the list of categories you set up is displayed on your blog in a few different places, including the following:

✔ **Body of the post:** In most WordPress themes, you see the title followed by a statement such as Filed In: *Category 1, Category 2.* The reader can click the category name to go to a page that lists all of the posts you've made in that particular category. You can assign a single post to more than one category.

✔ **Sidebar of your blog theme:** You can see a full list of category titles in the sidebar. (Figure 8-1 shows the category list on my blog.) A reader can click any category to see a list of posts you've made in that particular category.

Subcategories (also known as category children) are used to further refine the main category topic by listing specific topics related to the main, or parent, category. In your WordPress Administration panel, on the Manage Categories page, subcategories are listed directly beneath the main, or Parent, category. Here's an example, where Books I Enjoy is the Parent category and the topics listed underneath are subcategories, or child categories:

✔ Books I Enjoy

- Fiction

- Nonfiction

- Trashy romance

- Biographies

- For Dummies

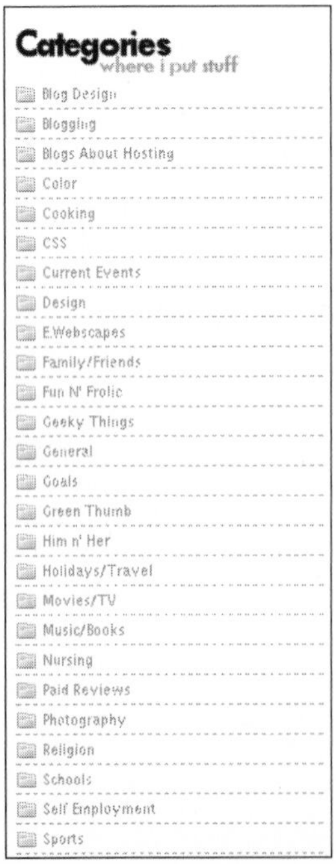

Figure 8-1:
The list of category titles on my blog. Clicking any title takes you to the posts I've made in that category.

Categories
where i put stuff

- Blog Design
- Blogging
- Blogs About Hosting
- Color
- Cooking
- CSS
- Current Events
- Design
- E-Webscapes
- Family/Friends
- Fun N' Frolic
- Geeky Things
- General
- Goals
- Green Thumb
- Him n' Her
- Holidays/Travel
- Movies/TV
- Music/Books
- Nursing
- Paid Reviews
- Photography
- Religion
- Schools
- Self Employment
- Sports

Upon installation, WordPress gives you one default category called Uncategorized. Notice that it sounds pretty generic. Go ahead and change that category name to one that's more specific to you. (On my blog, I changed it to Life in General. Although that's still a bit on the generic side, it doesn't sound quite so, well . . . uncategorized.)

Notice that the Uncategorized category (or whatever you decide to rename it) is marked as Default under the Actions column. Any post you publish to your blog for which you have not chosen a category is automatically filed under this default category.

Changing the name of a category

You definitely will want to change the name of that default category so that you have an interesting topic to publish your very first post to. So, how do you change the name of that default category? When you're logged in to your account, just follow these steps:

1. **On the Administration panel, click the Manage tab. Then click the Categories subtab on the Administration subpanel.**

   You see the Manage Categories page, which contains all the tools you need to set up and edit category titles for your blog. (Part of this page is shown in Figure 8-2.)

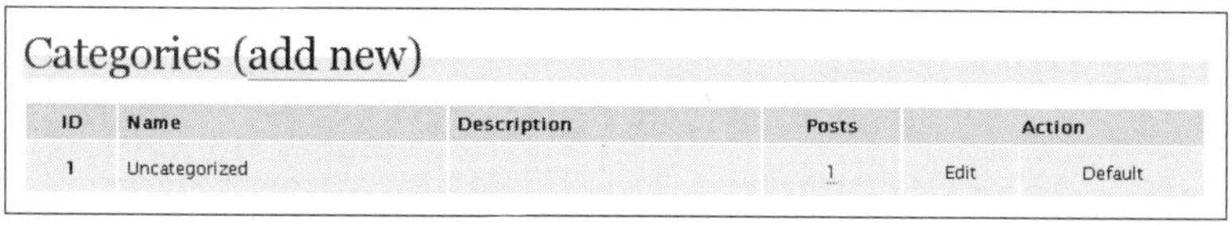

Figure 8-2:
The tools needed to create categories for your blog.

ID	Name	Description	Posts	Action	
1	Uncategorized		1	Edit	Default

Categories (add new)

2. **Click the Edit link to the far right of the category name.**

   This takes you to the Edit Category Page (as shown in Figure 8-3), where you can change the name, slug, parent, and description of the category (as shown in Table 8-1).

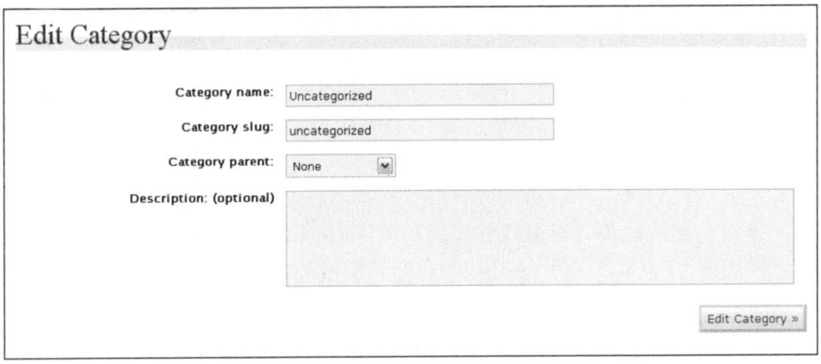

Figure 8-3:
Editing a
category in
WordPress.

3. **Type the new name for the category in the Category Name text box.**

4. **Type the new slug in the Category Slug text box.**

   If your new Category Name is Books, for example, the category slug should be *books*.

5. **Select None from the Category Parent drop-down menu.**

   Choose None because you want this category to be a main category, not a subcategory (see the explanation of subcategories earlier in this section if you need more help with this).

6. **Click the Edit Category button.**

   This saves the information you just edited and reloads the category page.

Table 8-1 gives a description of the options in this area. You can use this table as a reference later, as you're creating more categories on your blog.

Table 8-1	Edit Category Options	
Item	*Action*	*Result*
Category Name	Assigns the name to your category that you type in the Category Name text box.	Creates the category with the title you've chosen for it.
Category Slug	Creates a link to the page that lists all posts in a category when you type a name in the Category Slug text box.	Creates a link based on what you type in the Category Slug text box. Typing **General**, for example, results in this link: http://yourdomain. com/category/general

Item	Action	Result
Category Parent	Creates a subcategory (or child) if you select the category's parent from the Category Parent drop-down menu. Selecting None creates a parent category.	Determines whether a category is a parent (main) category or a child (subcategory of an existing parent category).

Creating new categories

Today, tomorrow, next month, next year — as your blog grows in size and age, you will continue adding new categories to help further define and archive the history of your blog posts. You aren't limited in the number of categories and subcategories you can create on your blog.

Creating a new category on your blog is as easy as these steps:

1. **On the Administration panel, click the Manage tab. Then click the Categories subtab on the Administration subpanel.**

2. **Click Add New.**

   This takes you to the Add Category section at the bottom of the page (see Figure 8-4).

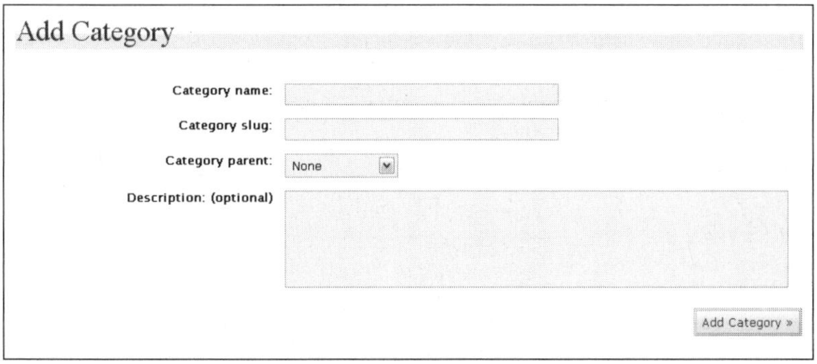

Figure 8-4:
Create a new category on your blog using the tool shown here.

Add Category

Category name:

Category slug:

Category parent: None

Description: (optional)

Add Category »

3. **Type the name of your new category in Category Name text box.**

   Say you want to create a category where you file all your posts about the books you read. In the Category Name text box, type something like **Books I Enjoy**.

4. **Type a name in the Category Slug text box.**

   As mentioned in Table 8-1, the Category Slug creates the link to the category page that lists all the posts you've made in this category. If you leave this field blank, it automatically creates a slug based on the category name. Using *Books I Enjoy* as the example, WordPress automatically creates a Category Slug like this: `http://yourdomain.com/category/books-i-enjoy`. However, if you want to shorten it, you can! Type the word **books** in the Category Slug field and the link to the category becomes this: `http://yourdomain.com/category/books`.

5. **Select the category's parent from the Category Parent drop-down list.**

   Select None if you want this new category to be a parent category.

6. **(Optional) Type the description of the category in the Description text box.**

   This is optional; however, some WordPress templates are set up to actually display the category description directly beneath the category name (see Chapter 9). Providing a description helps you to further define the category intent for your readers. The description can be as short or as long as you like.

7. **Click the Add Category button.**

   That's it! You've added a new category to your blog. Armed with this information, you can add an unlimited number of categories to your blog.

Deleting a category does not delete the posts and links in that category. Instead, posts in the deleted category are assigned to the Uncategorized category (or whatever you've named the default category).

For those of you with an established WordPress blog who already have categories created, you can, if you want, convert some or all of your categories to tags. To do so, scroll to the bottom of the Categories page in the WordPress Administration panel and click the Selectively Convert Categories to Tags link.

Blogrolls: Sharing Your Favorite Sites

A blogroll is a list of links to other Web sites and blogs that you've collected and want to share with your readers. The blogroll is displayed on your blog, usually located either in the sidebar or on its own dedicated page of links. Bloggers use their blogrolls in various ways, such as to

✔ Share links with other blogs who have linked to your blog

✔ Provide additional resources to sites and blogs you find and think your readers will find useful

✔ Provide links to other sites you own, if any

Organizing your blogroll

As with posts, you can create multiple categories for your links in the Word-Press administration panel if you want to have more than one link list. For example, sometimes having a large list of links under the heading of "Blogroll" is just too generic, and you may want to separate your list of links under different headings that will further define the links you've added to your blog. You can do this by creating blogroll categories in the Administration panel and then assigning links to the appropriate category as you add them. You can create blogroll categories by following these steps:

1. **In the Administration panel, click the Blogroll tab.**
2. **Click the Categories subtab.**

   The Categories page appears.

3. **Click the Add New link at the top of the page.**
4. **Type the name of the category in the Category Name box.**
5. **Type the slug of the category in the Category Slug box.**

   This is the same as the Category Slug described in Table 8-1, earlier in this chapter.

6. **(Optional) Type a description of the category in the Category Description box.**

   Although this step is optional, some WordPress templates are set up to actually display the category description directly beneath the category name (see Chapter 9). Providing a description helps you to further define the category intent for your readers. The description can be as short or as long as you like.

7. **Click the Add Category button.**

   This refreshes the Blogroll Category page with your new category saved.

Adding new link loves

You've created your blogroll categories; now you just need to add some links! Click the Blogroll tab on the Administration panel, as shown in Figure 8-5.

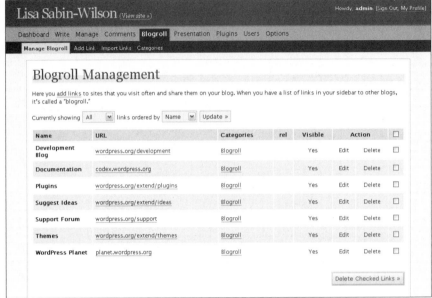

Figure 8-5:
Click the
Blogroll tab
and manage
your link
lists.

To add a new link to the blogroll, follow these easy steps:

1. **Click the Add Link subtab.**

   You see the Add Link page, where you can add a new link and adjust some settings for that link, which I explain in the sections that follow this one.

2. **Type the name of the link in the Name box.**

   This is the actual name of the site that is displayed in your blogroll.

3. **Type the URL of the link in the Address box.**

   This is the destination you want your visitors to go to when they click the name of the site.

4. **(Optional) Type a description of the site in the Description box.**

   Although this step is optional, some WordPress templates are set up to display the link description directly beneath the link name (see Chapter 9). Some templates are not set up for this. It depends on what code the theme developer has placed in the template file. Providing a description helps you further define the site for your readers. This can be as short or as long as you like.

5. **In the Categories area to the right, click to check the box next to the Blogroll category you want your link assigned to (see Figure 8-6).**

   To display the Categories box, click the plus sign shown in the upper-right corner. After you click it, the box drops down, the plus sign turns into a minus sign, and you see a list of the blogroll categories you created ear-lier. You can click the minus sign to close that Categories box after you are done using it. (This method of opening the box also applies to the next two steps in this list.)

Figure 8-6:
You can assign a link to a category already listed or add a new category here.

In Figure 8-6, you see the list of blogroll categories I created on my blog. I've chosen the Designer Favorites category, as evidenced by the check-mark in the box to the left of the category name.

6. **Under the Target header (see Figure 8-6), select a target for your link.**

   The target tells your browser how you want this link to load in your visitor's browser window after the visitor has clicked it. You have three choices. Select the radio button next to one of the following:

   - *_blank:* Loads the link in a new browser window

   - *_top:* Loads the link in the top frame (if your site is designed with frames)

   - *None:* Loads in the same browser window

   The third option — None — is my personal preference and recommen-dation here. I like to let my visitors decide if they want a bunch of new browser windows opening every time they click a link on my site. Visitors have that choice, anyway, by simply right-clicking the link and choosing Open in New Window (or new tab, if you're using tabbed browsing in a browser such as Firefox).

7. **Under the Visible header (see Figure 8-6), select the Yes or No radio button.**

   This option determines whether you want the link to be displayed on your site. Yes is the default. By selecting No, the link still exists in your blogroll category but is not displayed on your site. You might want to choose No if a particular site you've linked to is temporarily unavailable and you want to temporarily hide it in your blogroll until it is back up again. You can return to this section and change the Visible option at any time in the future.

8. **Click the Add Link button.**

This saves the link you just added and reloads the Add Link page so that it is ready for you to add another link.

You can set two other areas of options when managing your links shown on this page: Link Relationship (XFN) and Advanced. Read on to find out more.

Friend of a friend of a friend

The Link Relationship (XFN) is kind of a silly bookmark-type of assignment that allows you to indicate how well you know the person you're linking to by defining your relationship with them. Table 8-2 gives you definitions of the different relationships you can assign to your links.

When you define the relationships for your links, WordPress automatically embeds a `rel` attribute in the HTML tag for the link. For example, if you're linking to me at my blog, without the XFN Link Relationship, the HTML code looks like this:

```
<a href="http://justagirlintheworld.com">Lisa Sabin-
        Wilson</a>
```

If you were to indicate me as a friend by using the XFN Link Relationship options (see Table 8-2), the HTML code then becomes

```
<a href="http://http://justagirlintheowrld.com"
        rel="friend">Lisa Sabin-Wilson</a>
```

In the second example, you see that the attribute `rel="friend"` is added to the code. This tells the browser that it is a tag added by the author and is used by some programs (such as search engines, RSS feed readers, and link directories) to build a *tagged Web* (that is, linking sites together that have similar tags).

You can find more information on XFN at `http://gmpg.org/xfn`.

Table 8-2	Link Relationships (XFN) Defined
Link Relationship	**Description**
Identity	Select this check box if the link is to a Web site you own.

Link Relationship	*Description*
Friendship	Select the option (Contact, Acquaintance, Friend, or None) that most closely identifies that friendship, if any.
Physical	Select this check box if you've met the person you're linking to face-to-face. Sharing pictures over the Internet doesn't count here. This selection identifies a person you've physically met with.
Professional	Select one of these check boxes if the person you're linking to is a co-worker or colleague.
Geographical	Select Co-Resident if the person you're linking to lives with you. Or select Neighbor or None, depending on which options applies to your relationship with the person you're linking to.
Family	If the blogger you're linking to is a family member, select the option that tells how the person is related to you.
Romantic	Select the option that applies to the type of romantic relationship you have with the person you're linking to. Do you have a crush on her or him? Is he or she your creative muse? Someone you consider a sweetheart? Select the one that most closely identifies the romantic relationship, if any.

Advanced link options

This section gives you more options to configure for your links, such as assigning an image to a link, providing the RSS feed, and assigning ratings. Figure 8-7 shows you what the advanced link options section looks like in your WordPress administration panel.

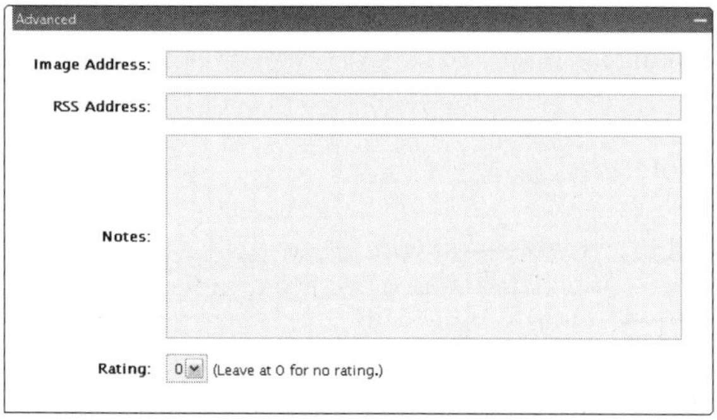

Figure 8-7:
Advanced link options give you settings to further manage the individual links in your blogroll.

Advanced

Image Address:

RSS Address:

Notes:

Rating: 0 ⌄ (Leave at 0 for no rating.)

These options are, well . . . optional. You can set them using the following steps:

1. **Type the URL of the picture that you'd like to appear next to the link in your blogroll in the Image Address field.**

   This associates an image with the link, and some WordPress themes accommodate that by displaying the image on your site, along with the link. For this, you need to know the direct URL to the image source (for example: `http://yourdomain.com/images/image.jpg`).

    To find out what the URL is for an image displayed on a Web site, right-click the image and choose Properties. Copy and paste all the text in the Address (URL) field into the Image Address box in the advanced link options.

2. **Type the RSS URL for the blog you're linking to in the RSS Address field.**

   WordPress displays the link to the site's RSS feed alongside the link that appears on your site. Not all WordPress themes accommodate this feature.

    To find the RSS URL of the site you're linking to, visit that site and locate the RSS link. (It's usually listed in the sidebar or footer of the site.) Right-click the link and choose Copy Shortcut, in Internet Explorer (select Copy Link Location in Mozilla Firefox) and paste the link in the RSS Address field.

3. **Type your notes in the Notes field.**

   These notes aren't displayed on your site, so feel free to leave whatever notes you need to further define the details of this link. A month from now, you may not remember who this person is or why you linked him, so here is where you can add notes to remind yourself.

4. **Use the Rating drop-down menu to rate this link from 0–10, 0 being the worst, 10 being the best.**

   Some WordPress themes will display your blogroll in the order you've rated your links here — from best to worst.

Revisit the Blogroll Management page any time you want to add a new link, edit an old link, or delete an existing link. You can create an unlimited amount of blogroll categories in order to sort your blogrolls by topics. I know one blogger who has 50 different categories for his links. So the options are really limitless.

 By default, WordPress provides you with a bunch of links already installed in your blogroll. You see them when you click the Blogroll tab for the first time. These are links to some very helpful Web sites that contain information and resources for the use of the WordPress software. You can delete them if you'd like, but you may want to save them for future reference.

Examining a Blog Post's Address

Each blog post is assigned its own Web page, and the address to that page is called a *permalink*. Posts that you see on WordPress blogs usually have the post permalink in four typical areas:

- ✔ The title of the blog post
- ✔ The Comments link underneath the post
- ✔ A Permalink link that appears (in most themes) under the post
- ✔ The titles of posts appearing in a Recent Posts sidebar

Permalinks are meant to be *permanent links,* which fully explains the *perma* part of that word, in case you're wondering. Other bloggers can use a post permalink to refer to that particular blog post. So the permalink of a post ideally never changes. WordPress creates the permalink automatically when you publish a new post.

By default, this is how a blog post permalink in WordPress looks:

```
http://yourdomain.com/?p=100/
```

The p stands for *post* and 100 is the ID assigned to the individual post. You can leave the permalinks in this format, if you don't mind letting WordPress associate each post with an ID number.

However, WordPress lets you take your permalinks to the beauty salon for a bit of makeover, where you can create pretty permalinks. I'll bet you didn't know permalinks can be pretty, did you? They certainly can. Allow me to explain.

Giving Your Post Links a Makeover

Pretty permalinks are links that are more pleasing to the eye and, ultimately, more pleasing to search engine spiders. (See Chapter 16 for an explanation of why search engines like pretty permalinks.) Pretty permalinks look something like this:

```
http://yourdomain/2007/02/01/pretty-permalinks/
```

Break down that URL and you can see the date that the post was made, in the year/month/day format. You can also see the topic of the post.

To choose how your permalinks will look, click the Options tab in the Administration panel and then click the Permalinks subtab.

Listed here (as shown in Figure 8-8), you find the options that are available for creating permalinks:

- **Default** (ugly permalinks): WordPress assigns an ID number to each blog post and creates the URL in this format: `http://yourdomain.com/?p=100`.

- **Date and Name Based** (pretty permalinks): WordPress generates a permalink URL for each post that includes the date and name of the post.

- **Numeric** (not so pretty): WordPress assigns a numerical value to the permalink. The URL is created in this format: `http://yourdomain.com/archives/123`.

- **Custom:** WordPress creates permalinks in the format you choose. You can create a custom permalink structure using the tags, or variables, shown in Table 8-3.

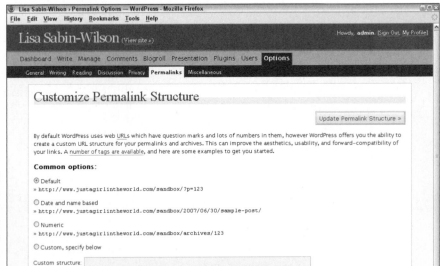

Figure 8-8:
Make your permalinks pretty in this section.

To create the pretty permalink structure, select the Date and Name Based radio button and then click the Update Permalink Structure button at the top.

Table 8-3	Create Custom Permalinks Using These Tags
Permalink Tag	*Results*
`%year%`	4-digit year (such as `2007`)
`%monthnum%`	2-digit month (such as `02` for February)
`%day%`	2-digit day (such as `30`)
`%hour%`	2-digit hour of the day (such as `15` for 3 p.m.)
`%minute%`	2-digit minute (such as `45`)
`%second%`	2-digit second (such as `10`)
`%postname%`	Text separated by dashes; usually the post name (such as `making-pretty-permalinks`)
`%post_id%`	The unique, numerical ID of the post (such as `344`)
`%category%`	The text of the category name that you filed the post in (such as `books-i-read`)
`%author%`	Text of the post author's name (such as `lisa-sabin-wilson`)

A *custom permalink structure* is one that allows you to define which variables you'd like to see in your permalinks, using the tags in Table 8-3. For example, if you want your permalink to show the year, month, day, category, and post name, you'd choose the Custom option on the Customize Permalink Structure page and type the following tags in the Custom Structure text box:

```
/%year%/%monthnum%/%day%/%category%/%postname%/
```

Using this permalink format, the link for a post made on February 1, 2007, called "WordPress For Dummies," and filed in the Books I Read category would look like this:

```
http://yourdomain/com/2007/02/01/books-i-read/wordpress-for-dummies/
```

Be sure to include the slashes at the beginning of the tags, between tags, and at the very end of the string of tags. This ensures that WordPress creates correct, working permalinks using the correct `re_write` rules found in the `.htaccess` file for your site. (See the following section for more information on `re_write` rules and `.htaccess` files.)

Changing the structure of your permalinks in the future will affect the permalinks for all posts on your blogs . . . new and old. Keep this in mind if you ever decide to change the permalink structure. This is especially important to know because the search engines (such as Google and Yahoo!) have indexed the posts on your site by their permalinks, and changing the permalink structure makes all of those indexed links obsolete.

Making sure your permalinks work with your server

This is a brief introduction to a file called .htaccess — what it means, what it does, and why you need to know about it. First, you need to determine two things:

✔ Does your Web server configuration use and give you access to the .htaccess file?

✔ Does your Web server run Apache with the mod_rewrite module?

If you don't already know the answer to these two questions, contact your hosting provider to find out.

If the answer to those two questions is yes, go ahead and proceed with the next section. If the answer is no, skip to the later section, "Working with servers that don't use Apache mod_rewrite."

Understanding and creating .htaccess files

You and WordPress work together in glorious harmony to create the .htaccess file necessary to use a pretty permalink structure on your blog. It works like this:

1. You create the .htaccess file and upload it to your Web server. (Sometimes, the .htaccess file already exists on your server. Check that out first so that you know whether you need to create one).

2. You create the permalink structure on the Customize Permalink Structure page in your WordPress Administration panel.

3. WordPress inserts the specific rules to the .htaccess file necessary for making the permalink structure functional on your blog.

See? Perfect harmony and a solid partnership are formed between you and WordPress, working together to create correct functionality.

More than likely, your Web server runs a software program called Apache. The .htaccess (which stands for Hypertext Access) file is Apache's directory-level configuration file. In other words, this file provides directions on how visitors are able to access your Web site (that is, whether they need a password to access your site, what type of browsers can access your site, and so on).

I could delve deeply into .htaccess and all of the things you can do with this file. However, I'm restricting this section to how it applies to WordPress permalink structures only. If you'd like to unlock more mysteries about .htaccess, check out "A Comprehensive Guide to .htaccess" at http://javascriptkit.com/howto/htaccess.shtml.

After you set the format for the permalinks for your site using any options other than the default, WordPress writes specific rules, or directives, to the .htaccess file on your Web sever. The .htaccess file, in turn, communicates to your Web server how it should serve up the permalinks, according to the permalink structure you've chosen to use.

If the .htaccess already exists, you can find it in the root of your directory on your Web server — that is, the same directory where you find your wp-config.php file.

Some FTP clients (see Chapter 6 for information about FTP) don't show the .htaccess in the directory structure. In that case, try changing the options of your FTP client to show hidden files. (Because the .htaccess file starts with a dot [.], it may not be visible until you configure your FTP client to show hidden files.)

If the .htaccess file doesn't exist, you'll need to create one with the instructions I give you next. If it does exist, you can skip these instructions completely.

Create an .htaccess file by following these steps:

1. **Create a blank text file on your computer using a text editor such as Notepad.**

2. **Save the text file with the name** htaccess.txt.

3. **Open your FTP client and connect it to your Web server.**

4. **Upload the** htaccess.txt **file to the same directory as your WordPress installation.**

5. **Set the permissions of the** htaccess.txt **file to 666.**

   (See Chapter 6 if you need more information about setting permissions for files on your Web server.)

6. **Rename the file** .htaccess.

   This step names the file correctly. Your FTP client will, most likely, ask you to confirm your actions.

7. **Click OK (or Yes, depending on the FTP client you're using).**

If you've followed these steps correctly, you have an `.htaccess` file on your Web server that has the correct permissions set so that WordPress can write the correct rules to it. Your pretty permalink structure works flawlessly. Kudos!

Working with servers that don't use Apache mod_rewrite

Using permalink structures requires that your Web hosting provider have a specific Apache Module option activated on their servers called mod_rewrite. If your Web hosting provider doesn't have this item activated on its servers, or if you're hosting your site on a Windows server, the custom permalinks will work only if you type **index.php** in front of any custom permalink tags.

For example, create the custom permalink tags like this:

```
/index.php/%year%/%month%/%date%/%postname%/
```

This creates a permalink that looks like this:

```
http://yourdomain.com/index.php/2007/02/01/wordpress-for-
dummies
```

You don't need an `.htaccess` file to use this permalink structure.

Discovering the Many WordPress RSS Options

In Chapter 2, you can read about RSS feed technology and why it's an important part of publishing your blog. Allow me to quote myself from that chapter: In order for your blog readers to stay updated with the latest and greatest content you've posted to your site, they do need to subscribe to your RSS feed.

RSS feeds come in different flavors: RSS 0.91, RSS 1.0, RSS 2.0, and Atom. The differences among them lie within the base code that makes up the functionality of the syndication feed. What's important to note is that WordPress supports all versions of RSS — which means anyone can subscribe to your RSS feed with any type of feed reader available.

I mention many times throughout this book that WordPress is very intuitive, and this section is a shining example of that. WordPress has a built-in feed generator that works behind the scenes to create feeds for you. This feed generator creates feeds from your posts, comments, and even categories.

The RSS feed for your blog posts is auto-discoverable. This means that almost all RSS feed readers and even some browsers (Firefox, Internet Explorer 7, and Safari, for example) automatically detect the RSS feed URL for a WordPress blog. The feeds for your categories and comments, on the other hand, aren't auto-discoverable. The information in Table 8-4 gives you some good guidelines on how to find the RSS feed URLs for the different sections of your blog.

Table 8-4	URLs for Built-In WordPress Feeds
Feed Type	*Example Feed URL*
RSS 0.92 Feed	`http://yourdomain.com/wp-rss.php` or `http://yourdomain.com/?feed=rss`
RDF/RSS 1.0 Feed	`http://yourdomain.com/wp-rss2.php` or `http://yourdomain.com/?feed=rdf`
RSS 2.0 Feed	`http://yourdomain.com/wp-rss2.php` or `http://yourdomain.com/?feed=rss2`
Atom Feed	`http://yourdomain.com/wp-atom.php` or `http://yourdomain.com/?feed=atom`
Comments RSS Feed	`http://yourdomain.com/?feed=rss&p=50` Where `p` stands for *post,* and `50` is the post ID. You can find the Post ID in the Administration panel by clicking the Manage tab. The post ID is listed immediately to the left of the post title.
Category RSS Feed	`http://yourdomain.com/wp-rss2.php?cat=50 cat` stands for *category,* and `50` is the category ID. You can find the category ID in the Administration panel by clicking the Manage tab and then the Categories subtab. The category ID is listed immediately to the left of the category title.

If you're using custom permalinks (see the "Giving Your Post Links a Makeover" section, earlier in this chapter) you can simply add `/feed` to the end of any URL on your blog to find the RSS feed. For example some of your links will look similar to these:

- `http://yourdomain.com/feed` —Your main RSS feed

- `http://yourdomain.com/comments/feed` — Your comments RSS feed

- `http://yourdomain.com/category/cat-name/feed` — RSS feed for a category

Try it with any URL on your site. Add /feed at the end of it and you'll have the RSS feed for that page.

RSS feeds are a very important part of the delivery of content from your blog to your readers. RSS feeds are expected these days, so the fact that WordPress has this taken care of for you, is compliant with all RSS formats, and offers so many internal feeds gives the software a huge advantage over any of the other blog software platforms.

Blog It! Writing Your First Entry

It's finally time to write your first post in your new WordPress blog! The topic you choose to write about and the writing techniques you use to get your message across are all on you — I have my hands full writing this book! However, I can tell you how to write the wonderful passages that could bring you blog fame. Ready?

Posting a text-only message

Typing a blog post is a lot like typing an e-mail: You give it a title, you write the message, and you click a button to send your words out into the world. Here are the details:

1. **Click the Write tab in the WordPress Administration panel.**

   You see the Write Post page, as shown in Figure 8-9.

2. **Type the title of your post in the Title field.**

3. **Type the content of your post in the Post field.**

4. **Type your chosen tags in the Tags field.**

   Tags are a way to archive your posts in specific topics without having to create new categories for them. Be sure to separate each tag with a comma so that WordPress knows where the tag begins and ends. For example, "Cats, Kittens, Feline" are three different tags, but without the commas, WordPress would consider those three words all one tag.

5. **Click the Save and Continue Editing button.**

   WordPress actually gives you three options for saving your post: Save and Continue Editing, Save, and Publish. I discuss these three options in the next section; for now, clicking the Save and Continue Editing button saves your post and allows you to continue editing it.

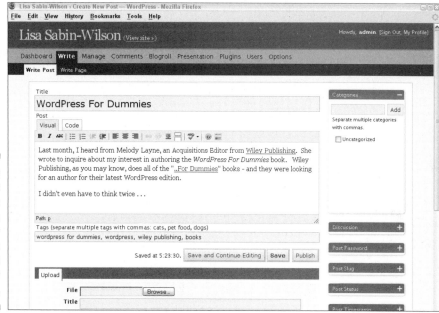

Figure 8-9:
This is the
text area
where you
give your
blog post a
title and
write your
post body.

As I mention in Step 4, WordPress gives you three options when you have finished writing your post:

- ✔ **Save and Continue Editing:** Saves your post but doesn't publish it. This allows you to continue editing it immediately or at a later time.

- ✔ **Save:** Saves your post as a draft but doesn't publish it to your blog yet.

- ✔ **Publish:** Saves your post and publishes it to your blog.

After you click Publish, visit the front page of your blog and make sure the post you just made has, indeed, been published successfully. If it has, you'll see it there, in all its glory! (See Figure 8-10 for an example of a successfully published post.)

If the post doesn't publish, there could be a few reasons. First, go back to your Administration panel and click the Manage tab. Then click the Edit link to the right of the entry you just made. Make sure that the Post Status is set to Published and check that the Timestamp is set to the current date and time (just to make sure you didn't put a timestamp on that post for sometime in the future).

In Figure 8-9, shown earlier, you can see the Visual Text Editor — the row of text-editing buttons above the box that you type your post in. If you've ever used a word processing program, such as Microsoft Word, you'll recognize these buttons. In WordPress, they let you *format* the text (apply bold, align right, apply italics, and so on) without having to know how to embed the HTML code that creates that formatting. This Visual Text Editor, also called Rich Editing, is also referred to as a WYSIWYG (What You See Is What You Get) editor. When using this editor, you just need to highlight (select) the text that you want to apply the formatting to, click the button, and violà! Change happens, and the world is a better place with beautifully formatted text.

On the Write Post page (and in Figure 8-9, shown previously), under the Title box, you see the row of buttons; they are, from left to right, as follows:

- **Bold:** Embeds the `<strong> </strong>` HTML tag to emphasize the text in bold. Example: **Bold Text**.

- **Italics:** Embeds the `<em> </em>` HTML tag to emphasis the text in italics. Example: *Italics Text*.

- **Strikethrough:** Embeds the `<strike> </strike>` HTML tag that puts a line through your text. Example: ~~Strikethrough Text~~.

- **Unordered List:** Embeds the `<ul><li> </li></ul>` HTML tags that create an unordered, or bulleted, list.

- ✔ **Ordered List:** This embeds the `<ol><li> </li></ul>` HTML tags that create an ordered, or numbered, list.

- ✔ **Outdent:** Moves the paragraph, or section of text you have selected, to the left.

- ✔ **Indent:** Inserts the `<blockquote> </blockquote>` HTML tags that move the paragraph, or section of text you have selected, to the right.

- ✔ **Align Left:** Inserts the `<p align="left"> </p>` HTML tags that position the paragraph, or section of text you have selected, along the left margin.

- ✔ **Align Center:** Inserts the `<p align="center"> </p>` HTML tags that position the paragraph, or section of text you have selected, in the center of the page.

- ✔ **Align Right:** Inserts the `<p align="right"> </p>` HTML tags that position the paragraph, or section of text you have selected, along the right margin.

- ✔ **Insert/Edit Link:** Inserts the `<a href=" "> </a>` HTML tags around the text you have selected to create a hyperlink to a URL.

- ✔ **Unlink:** Removes the URL (hyperlink) from the selected text if it has been previously linked.

- ✔ **Insert/Edit Image:** Lets you insert an image in your post by using the image URL. You can set options for this image by setting the alignment, dimensions, borders, and spacing around the image here.

- ✔ **Split Post with More Tag:** Inserts the `<!--more-->` tag, allowing you to split the display on your blog page. It publishes the text written above this tag with a link to "Read More," which takes the user to a page with the full post. This is good for really long posts.

- ✔ **Toggle Spellchecker:** Perfect for the typo enthusiasts! Checking your spelling before you post is always a good idea.

- ✔ **Help:** Opens a new browser window, where you see the Rich Editing Basics page containing helpful information on Rich Editing.

- ✔ **Show Advanced Toolbar:** Drops down even more options for formatting the text in your posts, such as underlining, font color, special characters, and more.

For those users who are familiar with HTML code for formatting, click the Code tab and you see the posting area stripped of the visual editing options. You can use code and the Quicktag buttons there to format various aspects of your post.

Across all versions of its software, WordPress has a nifty Auto-Save option built in. What does this do for you? Well, while you're typing and editing a new post, WordPress is working for you, behind the scenes, by auto-saving your post. You don't even know it's happening. So, if your browser crashes while you're writing or if you accidentally close your browser window before you've saved your post, it will be waiting for you when you get back, shown as a draft post when you click Manage in your WordPress Administration panel. Those WordPress folks are so thoughtful!

Uploading and using images in your post

Pictures can greatly enhance the text content of a post. To use a picture in a blog post, you transfer the image to your Web server from your computer by using the image upload feature that appears on the Write Post page.

While creating a new blog post, follow these steps to upload an image:

1. **In the area below the Save and Continue button, make sure the Upload tab is selected.**

2. **To the right of the File text box, click the Browse button.**

   This opens a window that allows you to navigate the files saved on your system.

3. **Double-click the image file you'd like to upload.**

   The window closes, returning you to the Write Post page.

4. **Click in the Title text box and type the title.**

5. **Click in the Description text box and type the description.**

6. **Click the Upload button.**

   This takes you to the Browse tab (see Figure 8-11) that lets you set parameters for how that image is displayed within your blog post.

   Here you have a few decisions to make on how you want to display the image and whether you want to link that image to another source.

Figure 8-11:
Set the options for the image you've uploaded.

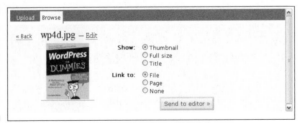

7. **In the Show area, click one of the three radio buttons to choose how you'd like to display the image in your blog post.**

   • *Thumbnail:* Display a smaller-sized version of the original.

   • *Full Size:* Display the full-sized image.

   • *Title:* Display the image's title, hyperlinked to the image on another page.

   Your next decision is how you would like to handle whether the image is linked to another source.

8. **In the Link To area, click one of the three radio buttons to choose how you'd like to link the image.**

   • *File:* Links the image to the original file location on your server. After it's published, when a visitor clicks the image, the file opens in its own browser window.

   • *Page:* Links the image to a formatted page within your blog — with a unique permalink (URL).

   • *None:* Does exactly what you'd expect. Nothing. The image isn't linked at all.

9. **Click the Send to Editor button.**

   This embeds the necessary HTML code to make sure the image appears in your post when you publish it to your blog.

10. **Click the Publish button.**

    Click this only when you're done composing your post. This step publishes your new post to your blog and reloads the Write Post page.

You can view and manage all the images that you upload to your blog by clicking the Manage tab on the Administration panel and then clicking the Uploads subtab. This page shows thumbnails of all the images you've uploaded. Click one of the images, and you can change the options for that single image, including the ability to edit the URL, title, and description of the image.

Applying optional post settings

On the Write Post page underneath the image uploader, you see a few extra options you can set for your post before you publish it. Table 8-5 explains those options in further detail.

Table 8-5	Additional Post Settings
Setting	*Description*
Optional Excerpt	An *excerpt* is a condensed summary, or description, of the blog post content. Bloggers handle the excerpt in different ways. You can put the first few paragraphs of your post in the Optional Excerpt text box and allow that to introduce your post. Or you can write a description of the post to give visitors an idea of what they can expect to read in the full post. Also, if your RSS feed is set to display excerpts only, you can control what those excerpts show by using the Optional Excerpt text box.
Trackbacks	I define and discuss *trackbacks* in Chapter 2. So if you're looking at this section with that wide-eyed stare of a deer caught in headlights, you may want to head over to Chapter 2 and read about trackbacks — what they are and how they function. To send a trackback to another site, you can grab the trackback URL from the site and copy it in the Send Trackbacks To text box. When you click the Save button, your blog communicates with the other blog — and then, well . . . you can do lunch!
Custom Fields	There are an infinite amount of things that can be done with custom fields; it's impossible for me to cover them all in this section. Seriously, it would take another book, or at the very least a minihandbook, to cover the possibilities. A short explanation is that the Custom Fields option lets you add data to your blog posts — things like My Current Mood or Listening To. It's called *meta data,* and you can find more information about using custom fields in the WordPress Codex at `http://codex.wordpress.org/Using_Custom_Fields`.

Categorize, privatize, and accessorize

At the beginning of this chapter, you find out how to set up categories for your blog posts. This section shows you how to put those categories to work.

When you think you might be done writing your post — you have a title and maybe you've added an image or two — WordPress gives you several more options to further optimize your blog posts. You find these options, described in the following sections, to the right of the text box where you write your post. You can set these configurations on a post-by-post basis, so never let it be said that all posts must be the same! Read on to find out more.

Categories

To display the Categories box on the right side of the Write Post page, click the plus sign shown in the upper right of the box. After you've clicked it, the box drops down, the plus sign turns into a minus sign, and you see a list of the categories you created earlier. (Figure 8-11 shows the Categories box expanded with the minus sign in the right corner.) You can file one or more of your posts in categories to organize them by subject matter. You can also add new categories to your blog by typing the name of the category in the Categories text box and clicking Add. To choose the category that you want to file your post in, select the check box next to the category name (as shown in Figure 8-12).

Figure 8-12:
Assign your post to a category.

Discussion

Make a decision on whether you'd like to allow readers to submit their feedback to one or more of your blog posts and whether you want to allow your posts to be open for pings and trackbacks by selecting or deselecting the check boxes. (You can find information on pings and trackbacks in Chapter 2.)

Post Password

To protect your post, create a password for it in the Post Password text box. After you do this, you can share the password with only the readers you want reading that post — everyone else is simply left guessing. This is perfect for those times when you'd love to make a blog post about all the stupid things your boss did today, but don't want your boss to see it — and you don't want search engines to see the post so that anyone can find it! (You have heard about bloggers getting fired for blogging about the company they work for in a negative way, haven't you? It happens more often than you'd think.) Some things just aren't meant for mass consumption.

If you don't want to password protect the post, leave this box blank.

Post Slug

In journalism, a *slug* is also referred to as a *catch line,* which is a short phrase or title that indicates the content of the story. In the case of writing a post in your WordPress blog, a slug refers to a portion of the permalink URL of your post. Every post on your blog has its own URL (also referred to as a *permalink,* meaning the permanent link to that individual post).

The Post Slug function strips the title of your post of all spaces and punctuation, creating an extension of the post URL made up of alphanumerical characters. Why is this important, really? First, you can create nice, short URLs for your post. For example, if you create a post entitled Five Weddings, Three Funerals, and a Bar Mitzvah on the Weekend, WordPress automatically creates the post URL based on the words in the title of your post, as well as the date. So, by default, the URL of the post about your weekend would be this:

```
http://yourdomain.com/2007/01/15/five-weddings-three-
        funerals-and-a-bar-mitzvah-on-the-weekend
```

If you want to shorten it, you can enter your desired post slug in the Post Slug box. For instance, to shorten it, you can type something like **my weekend plans** in the Post Slug box, and then your URL would look like this:

```
http://yourdomain.com/2007/01/15/my-weekend-plans
```

Post Status

With this option, you can set the status option of your post. You set this option by clicking the radio button to the left of the option you want.

- ✔ **Published:** Indicates the post is to be published publicly to your blog.

- ✔ **Pending Review:** Sets the post status as Pending and makes the post show up in your list of Drafts next to a Pending Review header. This allows the administrator of the blog to know that contributors have entered posts that are waiting for administrator review and approval (which is helpful if you have multiple authors on your blog.)

- ✔ **Draft:** Saves the post as a draft, which isn't published for public consumption until you change the status to Published.

- ✔ **Private:** Allows you to publish the post to your site; however, only you can see the post.

    This is different than password protecting a post. In that case, you share the password with your readers, if you wish. You can share a private post with others only when you change the status to Published.

Post Timestamp

When you edit the timestamp of your post, you can have WordPress publish it at a later time. This is especially helpful if you want to make a future post. For example, if today is 01/01/07 and your birthday is a week from now on 01/07/07, you can write a post announcing your birthday today — but schedule it to post publicly in a week by using the Post Timestamp feature. Select the Edit Timestamp check box and then set the date you wish to publish your post. Likewise, you can use the timestamp option to publish a post in the past using the same technique.

You are your own editor

While I write this book, I have editors looking over my shoulder, making their recommendations, correcting my typos and spelling errors, and helping me out by telling me when I get too long-winded; you, on the other hand, are your own editor and have full control over what you write, when you write it, and how you write it. You can always go back and edit previous posts to correct those typos, spelling errors, or incorrect facts by following these few steps:

1. **Click the Manage tab on the Administration panel.**

   This shows you a page with all of your blog posts listed chronologically. Sometimes, however, this method makes it difficult to find the exact post you're looking for. In that case, you can use the Search feature, shown in Step 2.

2. **(Optional) Click in the Search text box and type the keywords from the post you're searching for. Then click the Search button (or press the Enter key).**

   This shows you a list of posts that contain the keyword(s) you just searched for.

3. **When you find the post you need, click the Edit link on the right.**

   This opens a window where you can edit the post or any of its options.

4. **Edit your post and then click the Save button.**

   This saves your changes and takes you back to the list of posts you saw in Step 1 or 2, depending on which method you used to locate your post.

If you'd like to edit posts with a status of Draft, go to the Manage tab, where you can find the posts that you've saved as drafts listed at the very top. To edit those posts, just click the post title, and it opens the post edit window. From there, click the Publish button.

Look Who's Talking on Your Blog

The most popular feature that really catapulted blogging into the limelight is Comments, which lets visitors interact with the author of the blog. I cover the concept of blog comments and trackbacks in Chapter 2. There, I discuss the importance and fun of having comments available on your blog. They provide a great way for readers to interact with the site owner, and vice versa.

Managing comments and trackbacks

Click the Comments tab on the Administration panel to find and manage the comments that people have left on your blog. (See Figure 8-13.)

Here, you can edit or delete comments and/or trackbacks. Use the links beneath each item to manage your feedback.

- **Edit:** Clicking this loads the comment in a new page where you're able to edit it by fixing any typos, grammatical errors, and so on.

- **Delete:** Clicking this permanently removes the comment from your blog.

- **Unapprove:** Places the comment in the *moderation queue,* which you can get to by clicking the Comments tab in the Administration panel and then clicking the Awaiting Moderation subtab. The moderation queue is kind of a holding area for comments that haven't yet been published to your blog. (See the following section for more on the moderation queue.)

- **Spam:** Marks the comment as spam, which is an illegitimate comment left on your blog.

- **View Post:** Lets you look at the post the comment is associated with.

Moderating comments and trackbacks

If you have your comments options set so that comments aren't published on your blog until you approve them, you can approve comments in this section, as well. Just click the Awaiting Moderation subtab, and you're taken to the Moderation Queue page. If you have comments and/or trackbacks awaiting moderation, you'll see them here. (See Figure 8-14.)

Figure 8-13:
Clicking the
Comments
tab shows
you a page
with all the
comments
and
trackbacks
on your
blog.

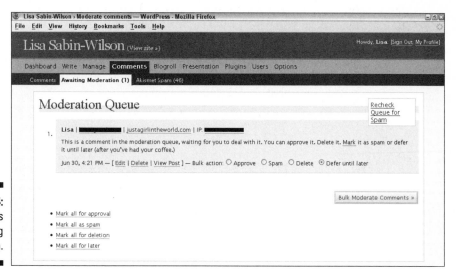

Figure 8-14:
Comments
awaiting
moderation.

The radio buttons beneath the comments give you different actions for handling options for each comment:

- ✓ **Approve:** Click this, and the comment is published to your blog.
- ✓ **Spam:** Marks the comment as spam, or illegitimate, and removes the comment from your blog. (If you're using the Akismet plugin, this action marks this comment as spam. If this user ever tries to leave a comment on your blog again, Akismet won't allow it. See Chapter 10 for further discussion about Akismet.)
- ✓ **Delete:** Click this, and the comment is permanently removed from your blog.
- ✓ **Defer Until Later:** Keep the comment in the queue and decide later what to do with it.

Click the Bulk Moderate Comments button to apply these actions. When several comments are in the moderation queue, WordPress gives you the option to Mark All with one action. At the bottom, you see the Mark All For: Approval, Spam, Deletion, or Later options. Clicking one of these links applies that action to all of the comments/trackbacks in the moderation queue.

Many WordPress themes have an Edit This link next to the comment on the page where the post is published. Only the logged-in administrator (you!) can see this link. Its purpose is to provide you with an easy way to get to the Comment Manager in the Administration panel to make quick edits to comments. Bonus: Many themes have this in place for posts, as well, by providing a quick Edit Post link (which usually appears next to the title) that only you can see. Clicking that link takes you to the interface in the Administration panel, where you can make quick edits to your post.

Chapter 9

Typing Up Templates

*T*here are those among us who like to get their hands dirty (present company included!). If that's the case with you, this is the chapter you need to read. WordPress users interested in creating their own theme do so in the interest of

✔ **Individuality:** Having a theme that no one else has (using one of the free themes available, you can pretty much count on the fact that at *least* a dozen other WordPress bloggers have the same look as your blog).

✔ **Creativity:** Displaying your own personal flair and style.

✔ **Control:** Creating the theme means that you have full control over how it looks, acts, and delivers your content.

Many of you aren't at all interested in creating your own templates for your WordPress blog. Sometimes, it's just easier to leave it to the professionals and hire an experienced WordPress designer to create an individual look for your blog (check out Chapter 11) or use one of the thousands of themes provided for free from WordPress designers. (In Chapter 17, I tell you where you can get ten free WordPress themes.)

Creating themes does require that you step into the code of the templates, which can be a scary place sometimes — especially if you don't really know what you're looking at. A good place to start is to first understand the structure of a WordPress blog and all its different pieces and parts. Separately, those pieces and parts won't do you any good. But when you put them together, that's where the real magic begins! This chapter covers the basics of doing just that, and near the end of the chapter, you find the specific steps to follow to put your own theme together.

WordPress Themes — The Basics

A quick word about terminology: A *WordPress theme* is a collection of Word-Press templates made up of WordPress template tags. When I refer to a *WordPress theme,* I'm talking about the group of templates that makes up the theme. When I talk about a *WordPress template,* I am referring to only one of the template files that contains WordPress template tags. WordPress template tags make all the templates work together as a theme (more about this later in the chapter).

Theme structure: An overview

The rest of this chapter provides you with important information about the steps to take when building a WordPress theme, but here is a brief overview of the templates that make up a WordPress theme, and where you find them; both on your server and within your WordPress administration panel:

1. **Connect to your Web server via FTP and have a look at the existing WordPress themes on your server.**

   The correct location is the `/wp-content/themes/` folder found in the WordPress installation on your Web server (see Figure 9-1). When you open this folder, you find two default theme folders: Default and Classic. It's important to know that if a theme is uploaded in any other folder other than `/wp-content/themes`, it will not work.

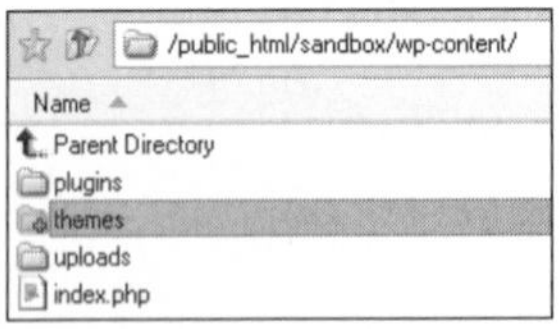

Figure 9-1:
WordPress themes in the /wp-content/ themes folder on your Web server.

2. **Open the folder for the Default Theme (`/wp-content/themes/ default`) and have a look at the template files inside. (See the section "Including the Five Required Templates," later in this chapter.)**

   At a minimum, you will find these five templates in the Default theme (the filenames are standard — the same — in every WordPress theme):

   - *Stylesheet* (`style.css`)

   - *Header template* (`header.php`)

- *Main Index* (`index.php`)
- *Sidebar template* (`sidebar.php`)
- *Footer template* (`footer.php`)

You see all five of these files in any WordPress theme. You may see other template files, but these five are the *minimum* requirements.

3. **Click the Presentation tab on the WordPress Administration panel to look at and eventually edit the template files within a theme.**

This shows you a page with the available themes installed on your WordPress blog. If this is a new installation, you see the Default and Classic themes listed with a screenshot of each. The very top of the page lists the current theme, which is the active one currently showing on your live blog.

4. **Click the Theme Editor subtab on the Presentation page.**

This page lists the various templates available within the active theme. (Figure 9-2 shows the templates available in the default Kubrick theme.) A text box displays the contents of each template, and this is also where you can edit the template file(s). Here, you can view and edit the different template files by clicking the template name in the list that appears on the right side of the page. You'll use the Select Theme to Edit drop-down menu at the top of this page to select the theme you wish to view and edit. After you make your edits, click the Update File button to save your changes.

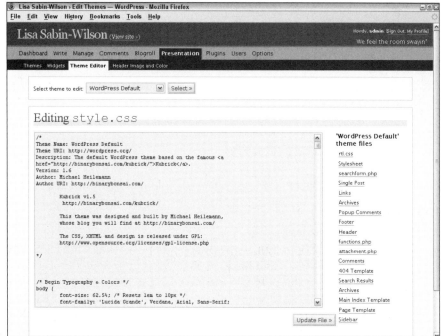

Figure 9-2:
A list of templates available in the default, Kubrick WordPress theme.

In Step 4, you see the template tags within the template file. These tags make all the WordPress magic happen on your blog; these tags also connect all the WordPress templates to form a WordPress theme. The next section of this chapter goes into detail about these template tags, what they mean, and how they function. After that, you find the section that gives you the steps to put them all together to create your own WordPress theme (or edit an existing theme).

Connecting templates

Remember as I've stated before, these template files won't work alone — they need each other for the theme to function as one. To tie them all together as one working entity, you use template tags to pull the information from each of these templates — Header, Sidebar, and Footer — into the Main Index. I refer to this as *calling* one template into another. (You can find more information later, in the section "Getting Familiar with the Four Main Templates.")

I stand by my statement that you don't need to know HTML to use WordPress. However, if you plan to create and design WordPress themes and templates, you do need some basic knowledge of HTML and CSS. For assistance with HTML, check out *HTML 4 For Dummies,* 5th Edition, by Ed Tittel and Mary Burmeister, or *HTML, XML, and CSS Bible,* 3rd Edition, by Bryan Pfaffenberger, Steven M. Schafer, Chuck White, and Bill Karow (both published by Wiley).

Contemplating the Structure of a WordPress Blog

Looking at a WordPress blog in its very basic form, you can see four main areas (labeled in Figure 9-3).

These four main areas appear in the default theme that comes in every version of WordPress:

- ✔ **Header:** This area usually contains the name of the site along with the site tagline or slogan. Sometimes, the header also contains a graphic or image.
- ✔ **Body:** This is where your blog posts appear in chronological order.
- ✔ **Sidebar:** This is where you find lists of blog-related elements, such as the blogroll, the archives, a list of recent posts, and so on.
- ✔ **Footer:** This is the area at the very bottom of the blog that often contains links to further information about the blog, such as who designed it, which company provides hosting for the blog, copyright information, and so on.

Header

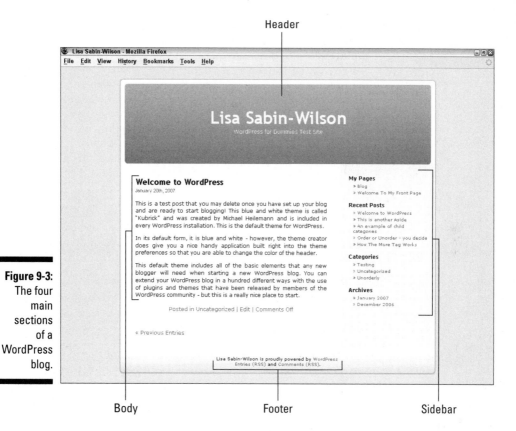

Figure 9-3:
The four
main
sections
of a
WordPress
blog.

Body   Footer   Sidebar

These four areas are the absolute bare bones of a basic WordPress blog template. Of course, it's possible to extend these areas and create new sections that carry more information; however, for the purpose of this chapter, I'm focusing on the basics.

The default WordPress theme is called Kubrick, and in my opinion, it isn't the best theme to use as an example for people who are brand new to template creation. It's kind of like teaching your teenager to drive using a brand new Lamborghini — there's just a little too much power under the hood for a beginner, you know? However, because this is the default theme available in all WordPress installations (including your new blog), it makes perfect sense to use something that you can reference while reading this chapter. I don't cover all the tags and templates that the Kubrick theme includes; rather, I touch on the basics to get you on your way to understanding templates and template tags for WordPress.

There've been many themes developed for WordPress that are free for public use; I strongly recommend finding one that you like and downloading it. Use the free themes as a jumping off place to get you started in your own theme development. Really, why reinvent the wheel? With the free themes available today, most of the work has already been completed for you, and you may find it easier to use one of these themes rather than start a theme from scratch.

You may find a template that is easier than the default Kubrick to work with, depending on your own skill level. Each free theme that is available for download is different, depending on what the theme developer has included in the theme (such as CSS styling, display options, format, and layout). So experimenting with a few different themes is fun and is a great way to learn more about the development of WordPress themes. A great place to find free WordPress themes is at the WordPress Theme Viewer site located at `http://themes.wordpress.net`.

Including the Five Required Templates

To accomplish the task of building a basic WordPress theme that covers the four areas discussed in the preceding bullet list, you need these five templates:

- ✔ `header.php`
- ✔ `index.php`
- ✔ `sidebar.php`
- ✔ `footer.php`
- ✔ `style.css`

The Stylesheet (`style.css`) drives the formatting and layout of your blog template in terms of where the elements are positioned on the page, what the font looks like, what colors your hyperlinks will be, and so on. As you may have already figured out, you don't use CSS to put content on your site; rather, you use CSS to style the content that's already there.

All WordPress themes come with a Stylesheet. Because this chapter covers the actual template tags, there isn't enough room here for a lesson on CSS. Instead, Table 9-1 gives you some excellent CSS resources on the Web that you may find helpful when it comes to editing or creating the Stylesheet for your theme. Or you may want to pick up a copy of *CSS Web Design For Dummies,* by Richard Mansfield (published by Wiley).

Right now, I'm covering only the basics; at the end of this chapter, however, I provide you with some ideas on how you can use various templates to further extend your blog functionality — using templates for categories, archives, static pages, multiple sidebars, and so on. After you build the basics, you can spread your wings and step into more advanced themes.

Table 9-1	CSS Resources on the Web
Resource Name	*Resource Location*
WestCiv's CSS Guide	`www.westciv.com`
CSS Crib Sheet	`www.mezzoblue.com/css/cribsheet`
CSS Tips	`http://websitetips.com/css/`
CSS: An Interactive Tutorial for Beginners	`www.davesite.com/web station/css`
W3Schools CSS Tutorial	`www.w3schools.com/css`

Examining the Anatomy of a Template Tag

Before starting to play around with template tags in your WordPress templates, it's important to understand what makes up a template tag and why.

WordPress is a program based in PHP (which is a scripting language for creating Web pages) and uses PHP commands to pull information from the MySQL database. Every tag begins with the function to start PHP and ends with a function to stop PHP. In the middle of those two commands lives the request to the database telling WordPress to grab the data and display it.

A typical template tag looks like this:

```
<?php get_info(); ?>.
```

The command to start PHP looks like this:

```
<?php
```

The command to stop PHP looks like this:

```
?>
```

This entire example tells WordPress to do three things:

- ✔ Start PHP (`<?php`).
- ✔ Use PHP to get information from the MySQL database and deliver it to your blog (`get_info();`).
- ✔ Stop PHP (`?>`).

In this case, `get_info` is the actual tag function and grabs information from the database to deliver it to your blog. What information is retrieved depends on what tag function appears between the two PHP commands. As you may notice, there's a lot of starting and stopping of PHP throughout the WordPress templates. It seems like it would be resource intensive, if not exhaustive — but it really isn't.

It's important to emphasize that for every PHP command you start, you need a stop command. Every time you see a command beginning with `<?php`, somewhere later in the code you need to see the closing command `?>`. PHP commands that aren't properly structured will cause really ugly errors on your site, and they've been known to send programmers, developers, and hosting providers into loud screaming fits.

Getting Familiar with the Four Main Templates

In the following sections, I cover some of the template tags that pull in the information you want to include in your blog. For the purpose of keeping this chapter under a thousand pages, I focus on the four main templates that get you going on either creating your own theme or editing and understanding the template tags found in the theme you're currently using. Here are those four main templates:

- ✔ Header
- ✔ Main Index
- ✔ Sidebar
- ✔ Footer

The Header template

The Header template for your WordPress themes is the starting point for every WordPress theme because it tells the browsers the following:

- ✔ The title of your blog
- ✔ The location of the Cascading Stylesheet (CSS)
- ✔ The location of the RSS feed URL
- ✔ The URL of the blog
- ✔ The tagline (or description) of the blog

Every page on the Web has to start with a few pieces of code in order for it to function. In every `header.php` file in any WordPress theme, you'll find these bits of code at the top of the file. They are the DOCTYPE, `html` tag, and `head` tag. The DOCTYPE (which stands for document type declaration) tells the browser which type of XHTML standards you're using. The `head` tag tells the browser that the information contained within the tag shouldn't be displayed on the site; rather, it's information about the document. The `html` tag (which stands for HyperText Markup Language) tells the browser which language you're using to write your Web page. In a WordPress Header template, these bits of code look like this, and you should always leave them intact:

```
<!DOCTYPE html PUBLIC "-//W3C//DTD XHTML 1.0
        Transitional//EN"
        "http://www.w3.org/TR/xhtml1/DTD/xhtml1-
        transitional.dtd">
<html xmlns="http://www.w3.org/1999/xhtml" <?php
        language_attributes(); ?>>
<head profile="http://gmpg.org/xfn/11">
```

The `head` and `html` tags need to be closed at the end of the Header template, which looks like this: `</head>`. You also need to include a fourth tag, the `body` tag, which tells the browser where the information you want to display begins. Both the `body` and `html` tags need to be closed at the end of the template, like this: `</body></html>`.

Using bloginfo parameters

Interestingly enough, all the information that I just listed about your blog is included in the Header template through the use of one single WordPress tag: `bloginfo();`.

What differentiates the type of information that one tag pulls in is something called a *parameter*. Parameters are placed inside the parentheses of the tag, enclosed in single quotes. For the most part, these parameters pull information from the settings you have in place under the Options tab and the General subtab on your WordPress Administration panel. For example, the template tag to get your blog title looks like this:

```
<?php bloginfo('name'); ?>
```

Table 9-2 gives you the various parameters that you need to be aware of for the `bloginfo();` tag and shows you what the template tag looks like, all put together.

Table 9-2	Tag Values for bloginfo(); in the Default Kubrick Template header.php	
The Parameter	*The Information*	*The Tag*
`Name`	Blog title set in Options/General	`<?php bloginfo ('name'); ?>`
`Description`	Tagline for your blog set in Options/General	`<?php bloginfo('des cription'); ?>`
`url`	Your blog's Web address set in Options/General	`<?php bloginfo ('url'); ?>`
`stylesheet _url`	URL for primary CSS file	`<?php bloginfo('style sheet url'); ?>`
`Version`	Your version of WordPress Found in `/wp-includes/ version.php`	`<?php bloginfo('ver sion'); ?>`
`rss2_url`	URL of your RSS 2.0 feed	`<?php bloginfo('rss 2_url'); ?>`
`stylesheet _directory`	URL to your theme directory	`<?php bloginfo('style sheet_directory'); ?>`

Creating title tags and popular characters

Here's a useful tip about your blog title tag, which is the piece(s) of code that lives in the Header template between these two tag markers: `<title></title>`. In the default Kubrick theme, this bit of code looks like this:

```
<title><?php bloginfo('name'); ?> <?php if ( is_single() )
        { ?> &raquo; Blog Archive <?php } ?> <?php
        wp_title(); ?></title>
```

It may help for me to put this into plain English. First, the `<title></title>` tags are simple HTML tags that tell the browser to display the title of your Web site in the title bar of the browser. Figure 9-4 shows you where the title of my personal blog sits in the title bar of my browser window. (The *title bar* is the very top bar in your browser. In Figure 9-4, it says Lisa Sabin-Wilson — Design, Life, Culture . . . Whatever.)

Search engines love the title bar — and the more you can tweak that title to provide detailed descriptions of your site, the more the search engines will love you. They'll show that love by giving you higher rankings in their search engine results. For more information and tips on search engine optimization (SEO) with WordPress, see Chapter 16.

The title bar displays your site name

To deconstruct the rest of the code between those title tags, refer to Table 9-1 and follow along with me. The first part of the code calls in the name of your blog:

```
<?php bloginfo('name'); ?>
```

The second part of the code tells WordPress this: If this is a single post page, display the following:

```
<?php if ( is_single() ) { ?>
```

Which, then, brings us to the third part of the code:

```
&raquo; Blog Archive <?php } ?> <?php wp_title(); ?>
```

If your reader is on a single blog post page, this tells WordPress to display your blog name followed by the name of the post. This is great for search engines because the name of your post provides some rich keyword content that search engines just eat up like candy.

So, in short, the title bar of the browser window always displays your blog name, unless you're on a single post page. In that case, it displays your blog title plus the title of the post on that page.

Within some of the WordPress template tags, such as the title tag in the previous example, you may notice some weird characters that look like a foreign language. For example, you may be wondering what » is. It isn't a part of any PHP function or CSS styling. Rather, it's called a *character entity* and is actually a kind of code that enables you to display a special character in your blog. The » character entity, for example, displays a double, right-angle quotation mark. (See Table 9-3 for examples of common character entities.)

Table 9-3	Popular Character Entities	
The Code	*The Description*	*The Display*
&raquo;	A double, right-angle quote	»
&laquo;	A double, left-angle quote	«
&bull;	A bullet	•
&hearts;	A black heart	♥
&diams;	A black diamond	♦
&clubs;	A black shamrock	♣
&spades;	A black spade	♠
&lt;	A single left arrow	<
&gt;	A single right arrow	>

Displaying your blog name and tagline

In the default Kubrick theme header (refer to Figure 9-3), you see that my blog name and tagline are displayed:

- ✔ **Blog name:** Lisa-Wilson Sabin
- ✔ **Blog tagline:** WordPress For Dummies Test Site

You can use the bloginfo(); tag plus a little HTML code to display your blog name and tagline. Most blogs have what is commonly referred to as a title that's *clickable,* which is a site title that takes you back to the main page when it's clicked. No matter where your visitors are on your site, they can always go back home by clicking the title of your site in the header.

To create the clickable title, use the following code:

```
<a href="<?php bloginfo('url'); ?>"><?php
        bloginfo('name'); ?></a>
```

If you refer to Table 9-2, you can see that the bloginfo('url'); tag is the URL for your main blog Internet address, and the bloginfo('name'); tag is the name of your blog. So the code creates a link that looks something like this:

```
<a href="http://yourdomain.com">Your Blog Name</a>
```

In the default Kubrick theme, the link to the home page looks a little different from the one I've described here. The link back home in Kubrick looks like this:

```
<?php echo get_option('home'); ?>
```

It's basically the same function as `<?php bloginfo('url'); ?>` with a slightly different way of getting from point A to point B. I used the `blog info();` tag in my example for reasons of congruity.

The tagline generally isn't linked back home. You can display it using the following tag:

```
<?php bloginfo('description'); ?>
```

This pulls the tagline directly from the one that you've set up in the Options tab and General subtab on the WordPress Administration panel.

This is an example of what I mean when I say that WordPress is intuitive and user friendly — you can do things such as changing the blog name and tagline with a few keystrokes within the WordPress Administration panel. Changing it in your options there creates the change on every page of your site — no coding experience is required. Beautiful, isn't it?

In the Kubrick template, you can see that these tags are surrounded by tags that look like these: `<h1></h1>` or `<h2></h2>`. These are header tags, which define the look and layout of the blog name and tagline in the Cascading Stylesheet (CSS) of your theme.

The Main Index template

It's within the Main Index Template that your blog posts are dragged out of the MySQL database and inserted into your blog. The Main Index template is to your blog what the dance floor is to a nightclub — it's where all the action happens.

The filename for the Main Index template is `index.php`. You can find it in the `/wp-content/themes/` folder.

The first template tag in the Main Index template calls in the Header template, meaning that it pulls the information from the Header template into the Main Index template:

```
<?php get_header(); ?>
```

This single line of code pulls all the information that's included in the Header template into your blog. Your theme will work without calling in the Header template; however, it'll be missing several essential pieces, such as the CSS and the blog name and tagline, for starters. Without the call to the Header template, your blog will resemble the image shown in Figure 9-5.

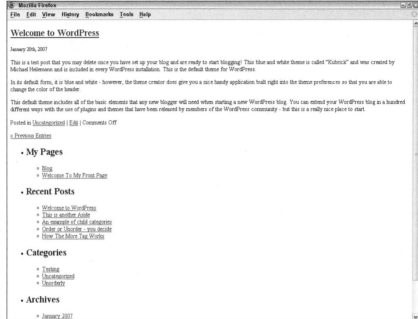

Figure 9-5:
A
WordPress
blog missing
the call to
the header.
It's naked!

The Loop

I'm not talking about America's second largest downtown business district, originating at the corner of State and Madison streets in Chicago. I could write about some interesting experiences I have had there . . . but that would be a different book.

The Loop, in this case, is a function that WordPress uses to display the posts on your blog. The Loop has a starting point and an ending point — anything placed in between is used and displayed for each post. This includes any HTML, PHP, or CSS tags and codes.

In your travels as a WordPress user, you may run across plugins or scripts with instructions that say something like this: "This must be placed within The Loop." That's The Loop that I discuss in this section, so pay particular attention. Understanding The Loop arms you with the knowledge you need for tackling and understanding your WordPress themes.

There are actually quite a few variations of the WordPress Loop. However, I'm covering the most common use in this section. When you understand the common use, you can then begin to push the envelope a bit further and use different variations to suit your individual needs. This common use displays your posts in chronological order, starting with your most recent post on top, followed by the less recent posts, ordered by date.

First, take a look at how The Loop starts. It begins with this code (which you see inside the Main Index template of the default Kubrick theme):

```
<?php while (have_posts()) : the_post(); ?>
```

Several lines later, you see the code that ends The Loop:

```
<?php endwhile; ?>
```

Earlier in this chapter, I mention that each template tag begins with a function to start PHP and ends with a function to stop PHP. The Loop is no different. Take a look at the code for The Loop — the start of The Loop begins with PHP and then makes a request. The request is, basically, "While there are posts in my blog, display them on this page." This PHP function tells WordPress to grab the blog post information from the database and return it to the blog page. The end of The Loop is like a traffic cop with a big red stop sign telling WordPress to stop the function completely.

Remember, you can set the number of posts displayed per page on the Options menu of your WordPress Administration panel by clicking the Reading subtab on the Administration subpanel. The Loop abides by this rule and displays only the number of posts per page that you've set in your options.

The big if

PHP functions in a pretty simple, logical manner. Breaking it down, it functions by doing what you and I do on a daily basis — we make decisions based on questions and answers. PHP deals with three basic variables:

- if
- then
- else

The basic idea here is this: IF this, THEN that, or ELSE this.

The code directly above the start of The Loop looks like this:

```
<?php if (have_posts()) : ?>
```

This if statement asks the question, "Does this blog have posts?"

If the answer is yes, WordPress proceeds with The Loop, starting with the piece of code that looks like this:

```
<?php while (have_posts()) : the_post(); ?>
```

This code tells WordPress to grab the posts from the MySQL database and display them on your blog page.

Then, The Loop closes with this tag:

```
<?php endwhile; ?>
```

However, if the answer to the `if` question ("Does this blog have posts?") is no, WordPress skips The Loop entirely and displays a message that no posts exist. This is accomplished through the `else` statement you see directly beneath the end of The Loop:

```
<?php else : ?>
        <h2 class="center">Not Found</h2>
<p class="center">Sorry, but you are looking for something
        that isn't here.</p>
<?php include (TEMPLATEPATH . "/searchform.php"); ?>
```

Remember I said that every good PHP function has to come to an end? The `if` statement is ended in the next line of code:

```
<?php endif; ?>
```

Following the `if`, `then`, `else` logic, Table 9-4 breaks it down in a way that I hope is easy to understand. In the "Customizing Your Blog Posts with Template Tags," section, I get into the fun part of providing all the different template tags that you can include within The Loop.

Table 9-4	Deconstructing The Loop
The Code	*What It Means*
`<?php if (have_ posts()) : ?>`	Poses the question: "Does this blog have posts?"
`<?php while (have_ posts()) : the_ post(); ?>`	If the answer is yes, this piece of code tells WordPress to retrieve the blog posts from the database and display them on the page.
`<?php endwhile; ?>`	Ends the display of blog posts, ending the loop.
`<?php else : ?>` `<h2 class="center">` `Not Found</h2>` `<p class="center">` `Sorry, but you are` `looking for something` `that isn't here.</p>` `<?php include (TEMP LATEPATH . "/search form.php"); ?>`	If the answer is no, the blog doesn't have posts, WordPress displays the title "Not Found," followed by the statement "Sorry, but you are looking for something that isn't here," followed by the template tag to include a search box that allows users to search your blog for more information.
`<?php endif; ?>`	Ends the `if` question.

If, then, and else

In our daily lives, we deal with if, then, else situations every day, as in these examples:

✔ **IF** I have a dollar, **THEN** I'll buy coffee, or **ELSE** I'll drink water.

✔ **IF** it's warm outside, **THEN** I'll take a walk, or **ELSE** I'll stay in.

✔ **IF** I understand this code, **THEN** I'll be happy, or **ELSE** I'll rip my hair out.

The Sidebar template

The filename for the Sidebar template is `sidebar.php`. Typically, the sidebar is displayed on the right or left side of your WordPress template. In the default Kubrick theme, the sidebar is displayed on the right side of the template (refer to Figure 9-3).

Similarly to the Header template in the previous section, the Sidebar template is called into the Main Index template with this function:

```
<?php get_sidebar(): ?>
```

This calls the Sidebar and all the information contained within it into your blog page. Chapter 16 addresses some additional ways you can call in the Sidebar template, including having multiple Sidebar templates and using an `include` statement to pull them into the Main Index Template.

Later in this chapter, in the section "Using Tags with Parameters for Sidebars," you find information on template tags to use in the sidebar in order to display the usual sidebar elements, such as a list of the most recent posts or a list of categories.

The Footer template

The filename for the Footer template is `footer.php`. Usually, the footer sits at the very bottom of your site (as shown in Figure 9-3) and contains brief information on the site, such as copyright statements, credits to the theme designer or hosting company, or even a list of links to other pages within the site.

The default Kubrick theme shows site ownership information and RSS feed links for the blog. You can, however, use the footer to include all sorts of information for your site. You don't have to restrict it to only small bits of information. For the purpose of this chapter, however, I cover the typical footer that you see in the default Kubrick theme.

Fat footers have become very popular, and I happen to use one on my business blog, which you can see in Figure 9-6. This is called a *fat footer* because it's, well . . . fat. It's larger than your typical footer and actually comprises a whole other section of your site, containing several bits of information.

Figure 9-6:
An example
of a fat
footer.

Similarly to the Header and Sidebar, the Footer gets called into the Main Index Template through the use of this bit of code:

```
<?php get_footer(); ?>
```

This calls the Footer and all the information contained within it into your blog page.

Other templates

There are other templates that you see in the default Kubrick theme that I don't list here. But it's a good idea for you to have at least a basic under- standing of them. The ones I list here give you that good, solid kick in the pants you need to get started with understanding WordPress templates. When you have that licked, you can move on to learning the rest.

Some of these other (optional) templates include

✔ **Comments template** (`comments.php`): Later, in Table 9-11, you find some useful template tags for WordPress. The Comments template is required if you plan to host comments on your blog, and it provides all the template tags you need to display those comments. The template tag used to call the comments into the template is `<?php comments_template(); ?>`.

✔ **Single Post template** (`single.php`): When your visitors click the title or permalink of a post you've published to your blog, they're taken to that post's individual page. There, they can read the entire post and, if you have comments enabled on your blog, they will see the comments form and can leave comments (as shown in Figure 9-7).

✔ **Page template** (page.php)**:** You can use a Page template for static pages within your WordPress site.

✔ **Search Results** (search.php)**:** You can use this template to create a custom display of search results on your blog. For example, when someone uses the search feature to search your site for specific key-words, this template formats the return of those results.

✔ **404 template** (404.php)**:** Use this template to create a custom 404 page. That's the page visitors get when the browser cannot find the page requested and returns that ugly 404 Page Cannot Be Found error.

As I mentioned, the templates in the preceding list are optional. If these templates don't exist within your WordPress themes folder, it won't break anything. The Main Index template handles the display of these items (including the single post page, the search results page, and so on). The only exception to this is the Comments template. If you want to display comments on your site, you must have that template.

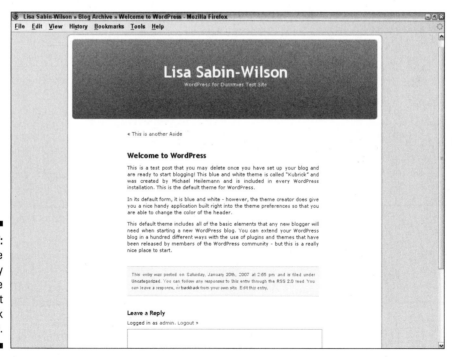

Figure 9-7:
The single post display with the default Kubrick theme.

Customizing Your Blog Posts with Template Tags

This section covers the template tags that you use to display the body of each blog post you publish. The body of a blog post includes information such as the post date, post time, post title, post author name, post category, and post content. Table 9-5 provides the common template tags that you can use and that you'll also find in the default Kubrick theme to display your blog posts.

Table 9-5	Template Tags for Blog Posts
The Tag	*The Function*
`<?php the_date(); ?>`	Displays the date of the post.
`<?php the_time(); ?>`	Displays the time of the post.
`<?php the_title(); ?>`	Displays the title of the post.
`<?php the_permalink(); ?>`	The permalink (URL) of the post.
`<?php the_author(); ?>`	Displays the post author's name.
`<?php the_author_link(); ?>`	Displays the URL to the post authors site.
`<?php the_content('Read More...'); ?>`	Displays the content of the post. (If you use an excerpt [below], the words Read More appear and are linked to the individual post page.)
`<?php the_excerpt(); ?>`	Displays a short excerpt (snippet) of the post.
`<?php the_category (','); ?>`	Displays the category(ies) assigned to the post. (If the post is assigned to multiple categories, they'll be separated by commas.)
`<?php comments_popup_link ('No Comments', 'Comment (1)', 'Comments(%)'); ?>`	Displays a link to the comments, along with the comment count for the post in parentheses. (If there are no comments, it displays a No Comments message.)
`<?php next_posts_link('&la quo; Previous Entries') ?>`	Displays the words Previous Entries hyperlinked to the previous page of blog entries.*

The Tag	The Function
`<?php previous_posts_link ('Next Entries &raquo;') ?>`	Displays the words Next Entries hyper-linked to the next page of blog entries.*

* The tags in Table 9-5 work only if you place them within The Loop. (See the earlier section titled "The Loop.") The two tags marked with an asterisk, however, aren't like the others. You don't place these tags within The Loop; instead, you insert them after The Loop but before the `if` *statement ends. Here's an example:*

```
<?php endwhile; ?>
<?php next_posts_link('&laquo; Previous Entries') ?>
<?php previous_posts_link('Next Entries &raquo;') ?>
<?php endif; ?>
```

Putting It All Together

In this section, you put together the guts of a Main Index template by using the information on templates and tags I've provided so far in this chapter. You create a new WordPress theme, using some of the basic templates included in the default Kubrick theme. The first steps in pulling everything together are as follows:

1. **Connect to your Web server via FTP, click the** `wp-content` **folder, and then click the** `themes` **folder.**

   These folders are the themes currently installed on your WordPress blog. (See Chapter 6 if you need more information on FTP.)

2. **Create a new folder and call it** `mytheme`.

   In most FTP programs, you can right-click and choose New Folder. (If you aren't sure how to create a folder, refer to your FTP program help files.)

3. **Upload the following files from the default Kubrick theme:**

   - `sidebar.php`
   - `footer.php`
   - `header.php`
   - `style.css`
   - `comments.php`
   - The `images` folder

   You find the default Kubrick theme files in the original WordPress files you downloaded from the WordPress Web site. *Do not upload the* `index. php` *file.* In the next section, you create a new `index.php` file to try out your new mastery of WordPress template tags.

Using the tags provided in Table 9-5, along with the information on The Loop and the calls to the Header, Sidebar, and Footer templates given in earlier sections, you can follow the next step list for a very bare-bones example of what the Main Index template look likes when you put the tags together.

To create a Main Index template to work with the other templates in your WordPress theme, open a new window in a text editor program, such as Notepad, and follow these steps. (Type the text in each of these steps on its own line. Press the Enter key after typing each line so that each tag starts on a new line.)

1. **Type** `<?php get_header(); ?>`.

   This template tag pulls in the information contained within the Header template of your WordPress theme.

2. **Type** `<?php if (have_posts()) : ?>`.

   This template tag is an `if` statement and asks the question, "Does this blog have posts?" If yes, it grabs the post content information from your MySQL database and displays the posts on your blog.

3. **Type** `<?php while (have_posts()) : the_post(); ?>`.

   This template tag starts The Loop. (See "The Loop" section of this chapter for more information.)

4. **Type** `<a href="<?php the_permalink(); ?>"><?php the_title(); ?></a>`.

   This tag tells your blog to display the title of a post that's clickable (hyperlinked) to the post permalink.

5. **Type** `Posted on <?php the_date(); ?> at <?php the_time(); ?>`.

   This template tag displays the date and time the post was made. With these template tags, the date and time format are determined by the format you've set under the Date and Time section on the General Options page in your WordPress Administration panel.

6. **Type** `Posted in <?php the_category(); ?>`.

   This template tag displays a comma-separated list of the categories you've assigned the post to in this manner: *Posted in: category 1, category 2.*

7. **Type** `<?php the_content('Read More..'); ?>`.

   This template tag displays the actual content of the blog post. The `'Read More..'` portion of this tag tells WordPress to display the words `Read More`, which are clickable (hyperlinked) to the post's permalink, where the reader can read the rest of the post in its entirety. This tag applies when you're displaying a post excerpt, as determined by the actual post configuration in your WordPress Administration panel.

8. Type `Posted by: <?php the_author(); ?>`.

This template tag displays the author of the post in this manner: *Posted by: Lisa Sabin-Wilson.*

9. Type `<?php comments_popup_link('No Comments', '1 Comment', '% Comments'); ?>`.

This template tag displays the link to the comments for this post, along with the comment count (number of comments) for the post.

10. Type `<?php comments_template(); ?>`.

This template tag calls in the comments template (`comments.php`). Any and all code and information in the comments template is pulled into the Main Index template at this point. However, the comments template is displayed only on the single post page, not on the front page of your blog site.

11. Type `<?php endwhile; ?>`.

This template tag ends The Loop and tells WordPress to stop displaying blog posts here. WordPress knows exactly how many times The Loop needs to work, based on the setting in your WordPress Administration panel under the Options tab and the Reading subtab — where you've set the number of posts you would like displayed on your front page. That's exactly how many times WordPress will execute The Loop.

12. Type `<?php next_posts_link('&laquo; Previous Entries'); ?>`.

This template tag displays a clickable link to the previous page of blog entries, if any.

13. Type `<?php previous posts link('&raquo; Next Entries'); ?>`.

This template tag displays a clickable link to the next page of blog entries, if any.

14. Type `<?php else : ?>`.

This template tag refers to the `if` question asked in Step 2. This is the `else` statement if the answer to the question in Step 2 is no. For example: If this blog has posts, then list them here (Step 2 and Step 3) or else display the following message.

15. Type `Not Found. Sorry, but you are looking for something that isn't here.`

This is the message followed by the template tag that is displayed after the `else` statement from Step 14. You can, actually, reword this statement to have it say whatever you want; for now, type the message as it appears in this step.

16. Type `<?php endif; ?>`.

This template tag ends the `if` statement from Step 2.

17. Type `<?php get_sidebar(); ?>`.

This template tag calls in the Sidebar template and all the information contained within and pulls that information into the display of the Main Index template. (See "The Sidebar template" section, earlier in this chapter, for more information about this template, and see the "Using Tags with Parameters for Sidebars" section, later in this chapter, for further descriptions about tags for this template.)

18. Type `<?php get_footer(); ?>`.

This template tag calls in the Footer template and all the information contained within and pulls that information into the display of the Main Index template. (See "The Footer template" section of this chapter for more information about this template.)

19. Type </body>. Then type `</html>`.

This closes the `body` and `html` tags that were opened in the Header template. (See "The Header template" section for more information.)

When typing out templates, be sure to use a text editor such as Notepad or TextMate. Using a word processing program such as Microsoft Word opens a whole slew of problems in your code. Word processing programs insert hidden characters and format double quotation and single quotation marks in a way that WordPress can't read.

When you're done, the display of the Main Index template code should look like this:

```
<?php get_header(); ?>
<?php if (have_posts()) : ?>

    <?php while (have_posts()) : the_post(); ?>

    <a href="<?php the_permalink(); ?>"><?php the_title();
        ?></a>
    Posted on: <?php the_date(); ?> at <?php the_time();
        ?>
    Posted in: <?php the_category(','); ?>

    <?php the_content('Read More..'); ?>

    Posted by: <?php the_author(); ?> | <?php
        comments_popup_link('No Comments', '1 Comment',
        '% Comments'); ?>
<?php comments_template(); ?>
    <?php endwhile; ?>
<?php next_posts_link('&laquo; Previous Entries') ?>
<?php previous_posts_link('Next Entries &raquo;') ?>
```

```
<?php else : ?>
    Not Found
    Sorry, but you are looking for something that isn't
        here.

<?php endif; ?>

<?php get_sidebar(); ?>
<?php get_footer(); ?>
</body>
</html>
```

When you're finished and feel confident that you've followed all of these steps perfectly, save this file as `index.php` and upload it to the `mythemes` folder you created earlier in the chapter. (In Notepad, you can save it by choosing File➪Save As. Type the name of the file in the File Name text box and click Save.) Activate the theme in your WordPress Administration panel and view your blog to see your handiwork in action!

Using Tags with Parameters for Sidebars

If you've been following along with me in this chapter as I've covered the Header and Main Index templates and tags, you actually have a functional WordPress blog with blog posts and various meta data displayed in each post.

In this section, I give you the template tags for the items commonly placed in the sidebar of a blog. I say "commonly placed" because it's possible to get creative with these template tags and place them in other locations on your blog (as in the Footer template, for example). To keep this introduction to sidebar template tags simple and clear, I stick with the most common usage and leave the creative and uncommon uses up to you to try when you're comfortable with building the basics.

This section also introduces *tag parameters,* which are additional options you can include within the tag to control some of the display properties of the tag. Not all template tags have parameters. You place tag parameters inside the parentheses of the tag. Many of the parameters found in this section were obtained from the WordPress software documentation found in the WordPress Codex at `http://codex.wordpress.org`.

Table 9-6 helps you understand the three variations of parameters used by WordPress.

Identifying some blog post meta data

Meta data is simply data about data. In WordPress, meta data refers to the data about each blog post, including:

✔ The post author name

✔ The category(ies) the post is assigned to

✔ The date and time of the post

✔ The comments link and number of comments for the post

Table 9-6	Three Variations of Template Parameters
Variation	**Description**
Tags without parameters	These tags have no additional options available. Tags without parameters have nothing within the parentheses.
Tags with PHP function-style parameters	These tags have a comma-separated list of values placed within the tag parentheses.
Tags with query-string parameters	These types of tags generally have several available parameters. This tag style enables you to change the value for each parameter without being required to provide values for all available parameters for the tag.

The WordPress Codex, located at `http://codex.wordpress.org`, has every conceivable template tag and possible parameters known to the WordPress software. The tags and parameters that I share with you in this chapter are the ones used most often.

The Calendar

The `calendar` tag displays a calendar that highlights each day of the week on which you've posted a blog. Those days are also hyperlinked to the original blog post.

Here's the tag to use to display the calendar:

```php
<?php get_calendar(); ?>
```

The `calendar` tag has only one parameter, and it's Boolean. (See the "Types of parameters in WordPress" sidebar if you need to know what a Boolean parameter is.) Set this parameter to `true`, and it displays the day of the week with one letter. (For example, Friday = F.) Set this parameter to `false`, and it displays the day of the week as a three-letter abbreviation. (For instance, Friday = Fri.)

Here are examples of the template tag used to display the calendar on your WordPress blog:

```
<?php get_calendar(true); ?>
<?php get_calendar(false); ?>
```

List pages

The `<?php wp_list_pages(); ?>` tag displays a list of the static pages you've created on your WordPress site (such as About Me or Contact pages). Displaying a link to the static pages makes them available so that readers can click the links and read the content you've provided on those pages.

`List` tag parameters use the string style. (See the "Types of parameters in WordPress" sidebar if you need to know what a string parameter is.) Table 9-7 provides the most common parameters used for the `wp_list_pages` template tag.

Table 9-7	Most Common Parameters (Query-String) for wp_list_pages();	
Parameter	**Type**	**Description and Values**
child_of	integer	Displays only the subpages of the page; uses the numeric ID for a page as the value. Defaults to 0 (display all pages).
sort_column	string	Sorts pages with one of the following options: `'post_title'` — Sorts alphabetically by page title (default). `'menu_order'` — Sorts by page order (the order they appear in your WordPress Administration panel under the Manage tab and Pages subtab). `'post_date'` — Sorts by the date on which pages were created. `'post_modified'` — Sorts by the time page was last modified. `'post_author'` — Sorts by author, according to the author ID #. `'post_name'` — Sorts alphabetically by the post slug.
exclude	string	Lists the numeric page ID numbers, separated by commas, that you want excluded from the page list display (for example, `'exclude=10, 20, 30'`). There is no default value.

(continued)

Table 9-7 *(continued)*

Parameter	Type	Description and Values
Depth	integer	Uses a numeric value for how many levels of pages are displayed in the list of pages. Possible options: 0 — Displays all pages, including main and sub-pages (default). –1 — Shows subpages but doesn't indent them in the list display. 1 — Shows only main pages (no subpages).
show_date	string	Displays the date the page was created or last modified. Possible options: ' ' — Displays no date (default). 'modified' — Displays the date the page was last modified. 'created' — Displays the date the page was first created.
date_format	string	Sets the format of the date to be displayed. It defaults to the date format configured in your WordPress Administration panel under the Options tab and General subtab.
title_li	string	Types in text for the heading of the page list. Defaults to display the text: "Pages". If value is empty (''), no heading is displayed; for example, 'title_li=My Pages" displays the heading My Pages above the page list.

Page lists are displayed in an *unordered list* (you may know it by the term *bulleted list)*. Whichever term you use, it's a list with bullet points in front of every page link.

Types of parameters in WordPress

These are the three types of parameters you need to know:

✔ **String:** A line of text that can be anything from a single letter to a long list of words. A string is placed between single quotation marks and sets an option for the parameter or is displayed as text.

✔ **Integer:** A numeric parameter that's either a positive or negative number. Integers are placed within the parentheses and either in or out of single quotation marks. Either way, they'll be processed correctly.

✔ **Boolean:** Sets the parameter options to either true or false. This can be numeric, where 0=false and 1=true, or textual, by using false or true. Boolean parameters aren't placed within any quotation marks.

The following tag and query string displays a list of pages without the text heading `"Pages"`. In otherwords, it displays no title at all at the top of the pages link list:

```
<?php wp_list_pages('title_li='); ?>
```

The next tag and query string displays the list of pages sorted by the date they were created; the date is also displayed along with the page name:

```
<?php wp_list_pages('sort_column=post_date&show_date='created'); ?>
```

Take a look at the way query-string parameters are written:

```
'parameter1=value&parameter2=value&parameter3=value'
```

The entire string is surrounded by single quotation marks, and there is no white space within the query string. Each parameter is joined to its value by the = character. When you use multiple parameters/values, you separate them with the & character. You can think of the string like this: parameter1= value**AND**parameter2=value**AND**parameter3=value. Keep this convention in mind for the remaining template tags and parameters in this chapter.

Displaying bookmarks (blogroll)

In the WordPress Administration panel, you can manage your links from the Blogroll tab. Before I forge ahead and dig into the template tag for the display of the blogroll, I want to clear up a little terminology.

A *blogroll* is a list of links that you add to the Blogroll area in the WordPress Administration panel. However, the specific template tag used to call those links into your template refers to *bookmarks*. So, this begs the question: Are they links, or are they bookmarks? The answer is *both*. It's a matter of semantics, really, and for purposes of simplicity and to ensure that you and I are on the same wavelength, I refer to them the same way half the planet does — as links.

Here is the tag used to display your blogroll:

```
<?php wp_list_bookmarks(); ?>
```

In Chapter 8, I show you how to add links to your blogroll and also discuss all the different options you can set for each link. The parameters for this tag give you control over how the links are displayed and put some of the options to work. (Table 9-8 shows the most common parameters used for the wp_list_ bookmarks template tag.)

In the Possible Values column of Table 9-8, values that appear in bold are the default values set by WordPress. Keep this convention in mind for all parameter values in the rest of this chapter.

Table 9-8	Most Common Parameters (Query-String) for wp_list_bookmarks();	
Parameter and Type	*Possible Values*	*Example*
`Categorize` (Boolean) Displays links within the assigned category.	**1 (True)** 0 (False)	`<?php wp_list_book marks('categorize= 0'); ?>` Returns the list of links not grouped into the categories.
`Category` (string) Displays only the link categories specified; if none are specified, all link categories are shown.	Category ID numbers separated by commas	`<?php wp_list_book marks('category= 10, 20, 30'); ?>` Displays the list of links from the categories with ID numbers 10, 20, and 30.
`category_name` (string) Displays only the link categories specified by name; if none are specified, all link categories are shown.	Text of the category names separated by commas.	`<?php wp_list_book marks('category_ name=books'); >` Displays only the links from the Books category.
`category_orderby` (string) Sorts the order in which links are displayed on your site.	**Name** id	`<?php wp_list_book marks('category_ orderby=name'); ?>` Displays the link categories alphabetically by name.
`title_li` (string) Text title appears above the link list.	**bookmarks** If left blank, no title is displayed.	`<?php wp_list_book marks('title_li =Links'); ?>` Displays the Links header. `<?php wp_list_book marks('title_li ='); ?>` Displays no heading at all.

Parameter and Type	*Possible Values*	*Example*
`title_before` (string) Formatting to appear before the category title — only if the `'categorize'` parameter is set to 1 (True).	**`<h2>`**	`<?php wp_list_book marks('title_before=' <strong>'); ?>` Inserts the `<strong>` HTML tag in front of the link category title.
`title_after` (string) Formatting to appear after the category title — only if the `'categorize'` parameter is set to 1 (True).	**`</h2>`**	`<?php wp_list_book marks('title_after= '</strong>'); ?>` Inserts the `</strong>` HTML tag after the link category title.
`Include` (string) Lists link ID numbers, separated by commas, to include in the display.	If no ID numbers are listed, displays all links.	`<?php wp_list_book marks('include= "1,2,3'); ?>` Displays only links with the IDs of 1, 2, and 3.
`Exclude` (string) List of link ID numbers, separated by commas, to exclude from the display	If no ID numbers are listed, all links are displayed.	`<?php wp_list_book marks('exclude= '4,5,6'); ?>` Displays all links except for the links with IDs of 4, 5, and 6.
`Orderby` (string) Tells WordPress how your link lists will be sorted.	**`name`** `id` `url` `target` `descriptions` `owner` `rating` `updated` `rel` (XFN) `notes` `length` `rand` (random)	`<?php wp_list_book marks('orderby= rand'); >` Displays the links in a random order. `<?php wp_list_book marks('orderby= 'id'); ?>` Displays the links in order by ID number.

(continued)

Table 9-8 *(continued)*

Parameter and Type	Possible Values	Example

`Before`
(string)
Formatting to appear before each link in the list.
	`<li>`	`<?php wp_list_book`
		`marks('before=`
		`<strong>'); ?>`
		Inserts the `<strong>` HTML tag before each link in the list.

`After`
(string)
Formatting to appear after each link in the list.
	`</li>`	`<?php wp_list_book`
		`marks('after=`
		`</strong>'); ?>`
		Inserts the `</strong>` HTML tag after each link in the list.

Here are a couple of examples of tags used to set a link list.

The following tag displays a list of links in the category ID of 2 and orders that list by the length of the link name (shortest to longest):

```
<?php wp_list_bookmarks('categorize=1&category=2&orderby=length'); ?>
```

This next tag displays only the list of links in a category (the Espresso category, in this example):

```
<?php wp_list_bookmarks('category_name=Espresso'); ?>
```

Displaying post archives

The `<?php wp_get_archives(); ?>` template tag displays the blog post archives in a number of different ways, using the available parameters and values shown in Table 9-9. Again, values that appear in bold are the default values set by WordPress. Here are just a few examples of what you can produce with this template tag:

- ✔ Display the titles of the last 15 posts you've made to your blog.
- ✔ Display the titles of the posts you've made in the last 10 days.
- ✔ Display a monthly list of archives.

Table 9-9	Most Common Parameters (Query-String) for wp_get_archives();	
Parameter and Type	*Possible Values*	*Example*
`type` (string) Determines the type of archive to display.	**monthly** `daily` `weekly` `postbypost`	`<?php wp_get_archives ('type=postby post'); ?>` Displays the titles of the most recent blog posts.
`format` (string) Formats the display of the links in the archive list.	**html** — Surrounds the links with `<li>` `</li>` tags. `option` — Places archive list in a drop-down menu format. `link` — Surrounds the links with `<link>` `</link>` tags. `custom` — Use your own HTML tags, using the before and after parameters.	`<?php wp_get_archives ('format=html'); ?>` Displays the list of archive links where each link is surrounded by the `<li>` `</li>` HTML tags.
`limit` (integer) Limits the number of archives to display.	If no value, **all are displayed.**	`<?php wp_get_archives ('limit=10'); ?>` Displays the last 10 archives in a list.
`before` (string) Places text or formatting before the link in the archive list when using the custom parameter.	No default.	`<?php wp_get_archives ('before= <strong>'); ?>` Inserts the `<strong>` HTML tag before each link in the archive link list.
`after` (string) Inserts text or formatting after the link in the archive list when using the custom parameter.	No default.	`<?php wp_get_archives ('after= </strong>'); ?>` Inserts the `</strong>` HTML tag after each link in the archive link list.

(continued)

Table 9-9 *(continued)*

Parameter and Type	Possible Values	Example
show_post_count (Boolean) This value displays the number of posts in the archive. You would use this if you use the 'type' of monthly.	true or 1 **false or 0**	<? wp_get_archives ('show_post_ count=1'); ?> Displays the number of posts in each archive after each archive link.

Here are a couple of examples of tags used to display blog post archives.

This tag displays a linked list of monthly archives (for example, January 2007, February 2007, and so on).

```
<?php wp_get_archives('type=monthly'); ?>
```

This next tag displays a linked list of the 15 most recent blog posts:

```
<?php wp_get_archives('type=postbypost&limit=15'); ?>
```

Displaying categories

WordPress lets you create categories and assign posts to a specific category (or multiple categories). This provides an organized navigation system for you and your readers to find posts you've made on certain topics.

The `<?php wp_list_categories(); ?>` template tag lets you display a list of your categories by using the available parameters and values. (Table 9-10 shows some of the most popular parameters.) Each category is linked to the appropriate category page that lists all the posts you've assigned to it. The values that appear in bold are the default values set by WordPress.

Table 9-10	Most Common Parameters (Query String) for wp_list_categories();	
Parameter and Type	***Possible Values***	***Example***
Orderby (string) Determines how the category list will be ordered.	**ID** name	`<?php wp_list_ categories ('orderby= name'); ?>` Displays the list of categories by name, alphabetically, as they appear in your WordPress Administration panel under the Manage tab and Categories subtab.
Style (string) Determines the format for the category list display.	**List** none	`<?php wp_list_ categories ('style=list'); ?>` Displays the list of category links where each link is surrounded by the `<li>` `</li>` HTML tags. `<?php wp_list_ categories ('style=none'); ?>` Displays the list of category links with a simple line break after each link.
show_count (Boolean) Determines whether to display the post count for each listed category.	true or 1 **false or 0**	`<?php wp_list_ categories ('show_count= 1'); ?>` Displays the post count, in parentheses, after each category list; for example, Espresso (10) means that there are ten posts within the Espresso category.
hide_empty (Boolean) Determines whether empty categories should be displayed in the list (meaning, a category with zero posts assigned to it).	**true or 1** false or 0	`<?php wp_list_ categories ('hide_empty=0'); ?>` Displays only those categories that currently have posts assigned to them.

(continued)

Table 9-10 *(continued)*

Parameter and Type	Possible Values	Example
Feed (string) Determines whether the RSS feed should be displayed for each category in the list.	rss **Default is no feeds displayed.**	`<?php wp_list_ categories ('feed=rss'); ?>` Displays category titles with an RSS hyperlink next to each one.
feed_image (string) Provides the path/ filename for an image for the feed.	No default.	`<?php wp_list_ categories('feed_ mage=/wp-content/ images/feed.gif'); ?>` Displays the `feed.gif` image for each category title. This image is linked to the RSS feed for that category.
hierarchical (Boolean) Determines whether the child categories should be displayed after each parent category in the category link list.	**true or 1** false or 0	`<?php wp_list_ categories ('hierarchical= 0'); ?>` Doesn't display the child categories after each parent category in the category list.

Here are a couple of examples of tags used to display a list of your categories.

This example, with its parameters, displays a list of categories sorted by name without showing the number of posts made in each category and displays the RSS feed for each category title:

```
<?php wp_list_categories('orderby=name&show_count=
        0&feed=RSS'); ?>
```

This example, with its parameters, displays a list of categories sorted by name with the post count showing and shows the subcategories listed underneath every parent category:

```
<?php wp_list_categories('orderby=name&show_count=
        1&hierarchical=1'); '>
```

Checking Out Miscellaneous but Useful Template Tags

In this chapter, I've picked out the template tags that are the most common, to get you started. You can find all the rest of the template tags in the WordPress Codex at this URL:

```
http://codex.wordpress.org/Template_Tags
```

There are a few miscellaneous tags that I didn't include in the preceding sections but want to briefly mention here because they're helpful and sometimes fun. Table 9-11 gives you some of these tags, the locations within the templates where they're commonly used, and their purposes.

Table 9-11	Some Useful Template Tags for WordPress
Tags Used in the Comments Template (`comments.php`)	
Tag	**Function**
`<?php comment_ author(); ?>`	Displays the comment author's name.
`<?php comment_ author_link(); ?>`	Displays the comment author's name, linked to the author's Web site if a URL was provided on the comment form.
`<?php comment_ text(); ?>`	Displays the text of a comment.
`<?php comment_> date() ?>`	Displays the date a comment was published.
`<?php comment_ time(); ?>`	Displays the time a comment was published.
Tags Used to Display RSS Feeds	
Tag	**Function**
`<?php bloginfo ('rss2_url'); ?>`	Displays the URL of the RSS feed for your blog. Usually surrounded by the `a href` HTML tag to provide a hyperlink to the RSS feed: `<a href=" <?php bloginfo ('rss2_url'); ?>">RSS Feed</a>`

(continued)

Table 9-11 *(continued)*

Tags Used in the Comments Template *(comments.php)*

`<?php bloginfo ('comments_ rss2_url'); ?>`	Displays the URL of the RSS feed for your comments. Usually surrounded by the `a href` HTML tag to provide a hyperlink to the comments RSS feed: `<a href=" ="<?php bloginfo ('comments_rss2_url'); ?>"> Comments RSS</a>`

Tags Used to Display Author Information

Tag	**Function**
`<?php the_author_ description(); ?>`	Pulls the information from the author bio located in the About Yourself section of your profile in the WordPress Administration panel under the Users tab and Your Profile subtab and displays that information on the blog.
`<?php the_author_ email(); ?>`	Pulls the author's e-mail address from the author profile in the WordPress Administration panel.

You can find additional hints, tips, and tricks on some creative uses of WordPress templates and template tags in Chapter 16.

Chapter 10

Making the Most of WordPress Plugins

. . . .

In This Chapter

▶ Plugging in to plugins

▶ Finding, downloading, and unpacking plugin files

▶ Uploading and installing a plugin

▶ Activating and managing plugins

▶ Using the plugins that come with WordPress

▶ Expressing yourself with different media

▶ Finding WordPress plugin resources

. . . .

*H*alf the fun of running a WordPress-powered blog is in playing with some of the hundreds of plugins that you can install to extend your blog's functions and options. WordPress plugins are like those really cool custom rims you put on your car: Although they don't come with the car, they're awesome accessories that make your car better than all the rest.

In this chapter, you find out what plugins are, how to find and install them, and how they enhance your blog in a way that makes your blog unique to you. You will find that using plugins can also greatly improve your readers' experiences on your blog by providing them with various tools to interact and participate — just the way you want them to!

This chapter assumes that you already have WordPress installed on your Web server. Installing plugins pertains only to the self-hosted version of the WordPress.org software (and the multiple-user solution of WordPress MU). If you're skipping around in the book and haven't yet installed WordPress on your Web server, you can find instructions in Chapter 6. Or if you want to find out about installing plugins for WordPress MU, see Chapter 13.

WordPress.com users can't install or configure plugins on their hosted blogs. WordPress.com doesn't allow it. I don't make the rules, so please don't kill the messenger.

What Are Plugins?

Plugins aren't a part of the core software; they also aren't software programs. They typically don't function as standalone software. They do require the host program (WordPress, in this case) in order to function — the plugin interacts with WordPress to provide some extensibility to the software.

Plugin developers are the people who write these gems and share them with the rest of us — usually, for free. Same as WordPress, plugins are free to use for anyone who wishes to further tailor and customize his site to his own specific needs.

Although plugins are written and developed by people who have the set of skills required to do so, I would say that the WordPress user community is also largely responsible for the ongoing development of plugins. It's the end users, ultimately, who put those plugins to the true test of the real world on their own blogs. It's also those same users who are the first to speak up and let the developers know when something isn't working right, helping the plugin developer troubleshoot and fine-tune the plugin. The most popular plugins are created by developers who encourage open communication with the user base. Overall, WordPress is really one of those great open source projects where the relationship between developers and users fosters a creative environment that keeps the project fresh and exciting every step of the way.

Literally thousands of different plugins are available for WordPress — certainly way too many for me to list in this chapter alone. I could, but then you'd need heavy machinery to lift this book off the shelf! So here are just a few examples of things that plugins allow you to add to your WordPress blog:

- ✔ **E-mail notification feature:** Your biggest fans can sign up to have an e-mail notification sent to them every time you update your blog.

- ✔ **Submit to social networking services feature:** Encourage and allow your readers to submit your blog posts to some of the more popular social networking services available, such as Digg, Technorati, and Del.icio.us.

- ✔ **Stats program:** Keep track of where your traffic is coming from, which posts on your blog are the most popular, and how much traffic is coming through your blog on a daily, monthly, and yearly basis.

When you start searching through all the possibilities in the plugin resources I provide for you at the end of this chapter, you'll be amazed at how much functionality you can add to your blog. And Chapter 18 gives you a peek at some of the more popular plugins on the scene today. In the meantime, this chapter takes you through the process of finding plugins, installing them on your WordPress blog, and managing and troubleshooting them.

Finding Plugins

The easy answer to the question, "Where can I find WordPress plugins?" is "Google it." In other words, visit the Google search engine at `http://google.com` and enter the keywords *WordPress plugins*. Will you find WordPress plugins with this method? Yes, you will. But other places on the Web have a focus on WordPress plugins and helping you, the end user, locate the ones you'd like to use for your blog.

One of the best places to learn about and download some of the most popular WordPress plugins is the WordPress Web site, which you see in Figure 10-1. By visiting this URL: `http://wordpress.org/extend/plugins`, you find a centralized repository for WordPress plugins in categories such as the following:

- Post plugins
- Comment plugins
- Sidebar Widget plugins
- Stats plugins
- Images plugins
- Anti-Spam plugins . . . and more

The plugin repository at the WordPress Web site is relatively new. It was launched to the WordPress community in March 2007.

Prior to the launch of this WordPress repository of plugins, we found our plugins at another site — the WordPress Plugin Database located at `http://wp-plugins.net`, which you see in Figure 10-2.

Figure 10-1:
Extend with plugins at WordPress. org.

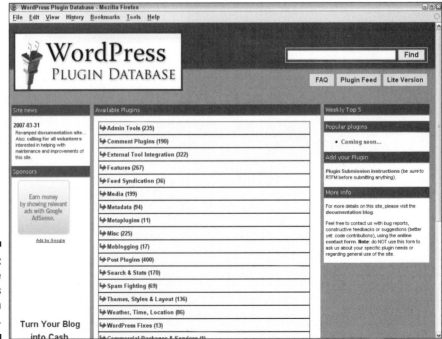

Figure 10-2:
The WordPress Plugin Database.

Other places where you can find WordPress plugins are given in Table 10-1.

Table 10-1	Where to Find More WordPress Plugins
Resource Name	*Site URL*
WordPress Web Site	`http://wordpress.org/extend/plugins`
WP Plugin Database	`http://wp-plugins.net`
WordPress Codex	`http://codex.wordpress.org/Plugins`
WordPress Plugin Repository	`http://dev.wp-plugins.org`
Blogging Pro	`www.bloggingpro.com/archives/ category/wordpress-plugins`

Installing a plugin: Just the basics

In this chapter, you can successfully install a plugin on your WordPress blog. Every plugin is different in the way you install it and set it up. However, there are three basic principles to every plugin installation that you need to know:

1. **Download and unpack the plugin files.**

   Visit the URL where the plugin files are located. Click the link to download the files to your computer. The files are usually in `.zip` format. Unzip the files and store them in a folder on your hard drive. (See Chapter 6 to brush up on information about handling zip files.) After you have the files unzipped, take a moment to read the documentation that comes with the plugin files. The documentation is usually in the form of a file called ReadMe; this file contains important information on how to install and use the plugin.

2. **Upload the plugin files.**

   Connect to your Web server account with your FTP client and transfer the files into the folder(s) that are indicated in the plugin instructions that you find either on the plugin Web site or within a `ReadMe.txt` file in the plugin zip file. (See Chapter 6 for more information on FTP.)

3. **Log in to your WordPress Administration panel, click the Plugins tab, and activate the plugin.**

   This step gives you a window with a list of all plugins that are located in your `/wp-content/plugins/` folder on your Web server. Locate the plugin you'd like to use and click the Activate link to the right. Doing so activates the plugin on your blog so that you can use it.

Considering the Materials and Mechanics

This section takes you through the motions you typically take when installing a plugin on your WordPress blog. I say "typically" because each plugin is different from the next. Each one has its own instructions and details when it comes to how you need to install the plugin, and the different tags you may, or may not, need to add to your WordPress blog template(s). (For some information on the anatomy of a template tag, please visit Chapter 9.)

Here is a list of things you will probably need in order to install a plugin on your WordPress blog:

- ✔ FTP client
- ✔ Decompression program (such as WinZip or WinRar)
- ✔ Connection details to your Web server (such as your username and password)
- ✔ Plain text editor (such as Notepad)

This chapter gives you a bonus: In addition to finding out how to install and use plugins, you see how to use the very popular Subscribe to Comments plugin developed by Mark Jaquith. I'm using the Subscribe to Comments plugin as a real-world example to take you through the mechanics involved in downloading, unpacking, uploading, activating, and using a plugin in WordPress.

Installing the Subscribe to Comments plugin takes you through the process, but remember that every plugin is different. So it's very important that you read the plugin description and installation instructions given to you for each plugin you want to install.

Downloading and Unpacking

The first step in using plugins is to locate the one you want to install (the plugin author gives you the download link on the plugin's home page). For example, you can find the Subscribe to Comments plugin at `http://txfx.net/code/wordpress/subscribe-to-comments`. Scroll down the page and find the Download heading, and you'll find the link to download the plugin underneath.

Subscribe to Comments is a very popular plugin for hundreds of WordPress users. It gives your readers the opportunity to subscribe to individual comment threads on your site so that they receive a notification, via e-mail, when a new comment has been left on the comment thread (or blog post) that they have chosen to subscribe to. This plugin helps keep lively discussions active on your blog.

Alternatively, you can find the download link for the Subscribe to Comments plugin at the WordPress.org Web site in the Extend Plugins section here: `http://wordpress.org/extend/plugins/subscribe-to-comments`.

If you're using the Internet Explorer browser, click the link and a dialog box opens, asking whether you want to open or save this file (as shown in Figure 10-3). Click the Save button to save the zip file to your hard drive, and *remember where you saved it.*

If you're using the Mozilla Firefox browser, click the link and a dialog box open and asks you, What should Firefox do with this file? (See Figure 10-4.) Click the Save to Disk radio button and then click the OK button to save it to your hard drive, and again, *remember where you saved it.*

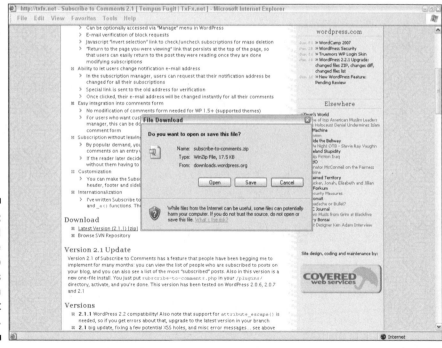

Figure 10-3: Download the Subscribe to Comments plugin in Internet Explorer.

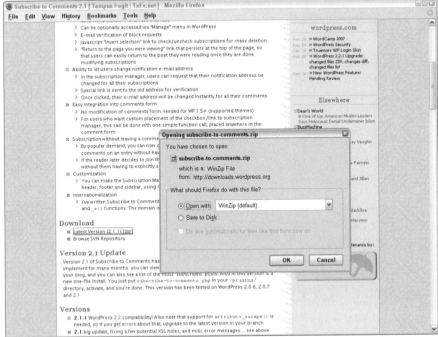

Figure 10-4:
Download
the
Subscribe to
Comments
plugin in
Firefox.

For other browser systems, follow the instructions for downloading in the dialog box given.

When you have the Subscribe to Comments plugin zip file safely tucked away on your computer, it's time to unpack and move on to the process of uploading and installing the plugin on your WordPress blog. Find the file on your hard drive and open it with your favorite decompression program (such as one of those in Table 10-2). If you're unsure of how to use a decompression program, please refer to the documentation available with the program.

Table 10-2	Decompression Programs Will Unpack Compressed Files
Program	**Where You Can Get It**
WinZip (for Windows)	`http://winzip.com`
WinRar (for Windows)	`www.rarlab.com`
StuffIt Expander (for Mac)	`www.stuffit.com/mac`

Using the decompression program of your choice, unpack the plugin files you downloaded for the Subscribe to Comments plugin.

Reading the Instructions

Frequently, the plugin developer includes a ReadMe file inside the zip file. Do what the title of the files says: Read it. Many times, it contains the exact documentation and instructions for use that you will find on the plugin developer's page.

Make sure that you read the instructions carefully and follow them correctly. Ninety-nine percent of WordPress plugins have great documentation and instructions from the plugin developer. If you don't correctly follow the instructions given by the plugin developer, at best, the plugin just won't work on your blog. At worst, the plugin will create all sorts of ugly errors, requiring you to start over from step one.

Every plugin is different in terms of where the plugin files are uploaded and the configurations and setup necessary to make the plugin work on your site. Make 100 percent sure that you read the plugin installation instructions *very carefully* and follow those instructions to the letter to correctly install the plugin on your site.

Uploading and Activating

Now you're ready to upload the plugin files to your Web server. Connect to your Web server via FTP. First, locate the plugin files you just unpacked on your hard drive. Second — and most important — refer to the plugin developer's page for specific instructions on how to install the plugin on your WordPress blog. Specifically, the documentation on the plugin developer's Web site should answer the following:

- ✔ What directory do I upload the plugin files to on my Web server?
- ✔ Do I need to change permissions on any of the plugin files after I have them uploaded to my Web server? (See Chapter 6 if you need information on changing file permissions.)
- ✔ Do I need to set specific configurations within the plugin file in order for it to work?
- ✔ Do I need to make any modifications to my theme template files in order to include the plugin's functions on my blog?

Installing the Subscribe to Comments plugin files

Mark Jaquith left some nice instructions for you in the plugin zip file. Look for the ReadMe.txt file inside the zip files you downloaded from his site.

You can open ReadMe.txt files in any text editor program, such as Notepad, WordPad on a PC, or TextMate for the Mac.

To install the Subscribe to Comments plugin, follow these easy steps:

1. **Double-click the** subscribe-to-comments **folder in the files you downloaded and unpacked onto your computer.**

   This opens the folder and shows you the contents inside of it. You see two files: subscribe-to-comments.php and readme.txt. (You also see another folder called extras. This folder contains the plugin installation instructions in two additional formats: HTML [readme.html] and PowerPoint [subscribe-to-comments.pot].)

   Figure 10-5 shows all the files and folders.

2. **Connect to your Web server via FTP and open the** /wp-content/
   plugins/ **folder.**

   You see that this folder contains all of the plugins that are currently
   installed on your WordPress blog.

3. **Upload the** subscribe-to-comments.php **file into the** /wp-
   content/plugins/ **folder.**

   Figure 10-6 shows the plugin files and where they should be located on
   your Web server. *Note:* The plugins on my Web server may differ from
   the ones you've chosen to install on yours. However, you can see where
   I've placed the subscribe-to-comments.php file.

   If you follow the directions in this chapter correctly, the plugin should
   be located in the same directory as mine: /wp-content/plugins/
   subscribe-to-comments.php. If not, back up and start over again. If so,
   move on . . . you're almost there!

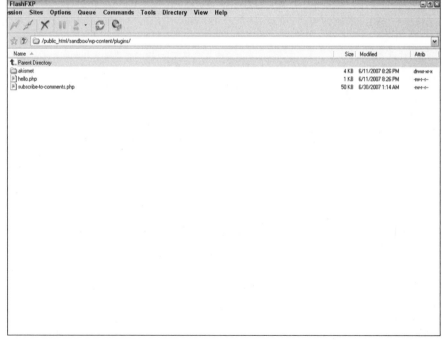

Figure 10-6:
Correct
location for
Subscribe to
Comments
plugin on
your Web
server.

Activating the Subscribe to Comments plugin

When you have the plugin files uploaded to their correct location on your Web server, open your browser and log in to your WordPress Administration panel. After you log in, head to the Plugin Management page to activate the Subscribe to Comments plugin:

1. **Click the Plugins tab on the Administration panel.**

   This displays the Plugin Management page, which lists all plugins installed on your WordPress blog.

2. **Locate the Subscribe to Comments plugin.**

   All activated plugins are highlighted with a green background color. Deactivated plugins don't have the green background color. Because you have not activated the Subscribe to Comments plugin yet, it won't have the green background highlight.

3. **Click the Activate link on the right.**

   This reloads the Plugins page, and you, once again, see the list of plugins installed on your WordPress blog. The Subscribe to Comments plugin now has the green background color, indicating that you've successfully activated it on your blog.

Setting plugin options

Some, but not all, WordPress plugins give you a plugin administration page where you can configure the settings that are specific to that particular plugin. Typically, you can find the plugin administration page on the Options tab of your WordPress Administration panel. However — you *knew* that was coming! — not all plugins are created equal. This means you may have to hunt for it. If you don't find it under the Options tab, check under the Manage tab; if it isn't there, check under the Plugins tab.

For the Subscribe to Comments plugin, you'll find the plugin administration page on the Options tab of the Administration panel. Click that and you see a Subscribe to Comments subtab — click that and you see the Subscribe to Comments Administration Options page (as shown in Figure 10-7).

You can find full documentation on how to set up and use the plugin on the developer's Web site and/or in the ReadMe file.

Installing the Subscribe to Comments plugin took you through the mechanics of finding, downloading, unpacking, uploading, activating, and using a plugin for WordPress. Just keep in mind that while the *mechanics* are the same for every plugin, the *process* and instructions differ from plugin to plugin.

After going through the process of installing the Subscribe to Comments plugin, you can see that the developer has provided some very clean and clear instructions on how to accomplish the installation, configuration, and use of the plugin right there on his Web site. This is how all plugin documentation should be and usually is. Ideally, the plugin developer also provides a comprehensive ReadMe text file within the files you've downloaded from his site.

Managing Your Plugins

In the previous section, you visit the Plugin Management page in the WordPress Administration panel when you activate the Subscribe to Comments plugin. I want to revisit that section once again and give you a more complete explanation of the different pieces of information that will help you with managing your plugins now and in the future.

Exploring the Plugin Management page

Go back and find the Plugin Management page by logging in to your WordPress Administration panel and clicking the Plugins tab. Figure 10-8 shows you the layout and different sections of information available for your plugins.

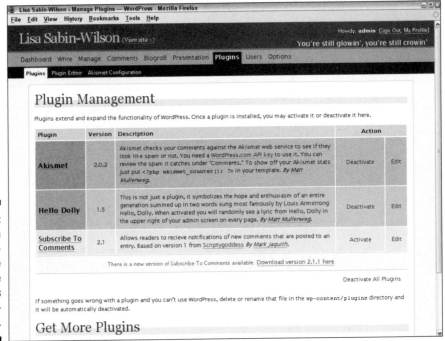

Figure 10-8:
The Plugin Management page in the WordPress Administration panel.

Upon first glance at the screen shown in Figure 10-8, you see a few very obvious things:

- ✔ Every plugin you've uploaded to your Web server is shown on the Plugin Management page.

- ✔ Some plugins are shown with a light-green background. These are the plugins that are currently activated and in use. The other plugins, while installed, aren't activated.

- ✔ In Figure 10-8, you see an alert box under the Subscribe to Comments plugin. This alert box will appear under any plugin that has a new upgrade available, along with a link to download the new version.

The Plugin Management page shows you the plugins listed in a table with five columns; this table gives you some details available for each plugin:

- ✔ **Plugin:** The plugin name, listed alphabetically, so you can easily find it when browsing the Plugin Management page. The name of the plugin is, usually, also linked to the Web site of the plugin author or the page where you can find additional information and details about the plugin.

- ✔ **Version:** The version release number of the plugin. Sometimes, a plugin author will release an update and change the version number on the plugin Web site. You want to periodically check the plugin developer's Web site to make sure the version number you have corresponds to the current version number displayed by the plugin author. This will tell you if you need to upgrade the plugin.

- ✔ **Description:** The description for the plugin. Sometimes, depending on the plugin, it also gives you some brief instructions on using the plugin.

- ✔ **Activate/Deactivate:** This is the link you click to either activate or deactivate a plugin. Activated plugins are highlighted with a green-colored background, whereas deactivated plugins aren't.

- ✔ **Edit:** Click this link to bring up the plugin file in a text edit window where you can make changes to it, if needed. Editing a plugin file is recommended only when the plugin author makes that a part of the plugin instructions. If the plugin instructions tell you to edit a portion of the plugin file, you can accomplish that here.

You can find a very nice feature of WordPress at the bottom of the Plugin Management page. It's a link that says Deactivate All Plugins. This is especially helpful when you're upgrading your WordPress installation. Because not all plugins were created equal, you may find that one or two (or more) of the plugins you have installed don't work with a newer version of WordPress. Deactivating all plugins at once before you upgrade ensures that you don't have any problems with the upgrade. After completing the upgrade, you can go in and reactivate them one by one and make sure they work. If you find that the new version of WordPress stops working after you've reactivated one particular plugin, at least you know which one is the culprit. This feature takes the guesswork away!

Having the ability to edit the actual plugin file within your WordPress Administration panel is really handy. You see the Edit link to the far right of each listed plugin. Clicking that opens a text edit window with the plugin file you wish to edit. However, let's be honest here — not everyone is code savvy and for some of you, editing plugin code is downright dangerous! Another really super feature of WordPress is that it won't let you make code mistakes when editing the plugin file. If you make an edit that could potentially cause a malfunction with the plugin, WordPress rejects your edit(s) and restores the plugin file to its original state, before you started tinkering with it. Talk about dummy proof!

Uninstalling a plugin

All this talk about installing and activating plugins — what happens if you run into a situation where you've installed the plugin, activated it, and then, at some point, just decide it isn't what you want?

Don't worry — you aren't forever stuck with a plugin that you don't want. WordPress allows you to be fickle and finicky in your plugin choices! Uninstalling a WordPress plugin is so much easier than installing one; check it out:

1. **Click the Plugins tab on the Administration panel.**

   This shows you the Plugin Management page, with a list of all the plugins that are installed on your WordPress blog.

2. **Locate the plugin you want to deactivate.**

   Plugins are listed in alphabetical order on this page. The activated plugins are highlighted in light green.

3. **Click the Deactivate link to the right.**

   This reloads the plugin listing and the dark-green highlighting is now gone for the plugin you've just deactivated. You'll note that the link to the right no longer says Deactivate; it now says Activate, indicating that this isn't a plugin that's activated yet. You're now done with the plugin deactivation steps that you need to do in the WordPress Administration panel.

4. **Open your FTP program and connect it to your Web server.**

5. **Open the** `/wp-content/plugins/` **folder in the WordPress installation files.**

   This folder contains all of the plugins you currently have installed in your WordPress setup. Locate the file(s) for the plugin you just deactivated in the steps above, and delete those files from your Web server.

Bang! You're done — that's all it takes. Don't forget that if there were any bits of code that you needed to add to your theme templates for that particular plugin, you'll need to remove those, or they'll cause ugly error messages to be displayed on your blog.

Getting the Most out of Plugins Included with WordPress

WordPress, at the time of this writing, packages three plugins within the installation files:

- ✔ Akismet
- ✔ Hello Dolly
- ✔ Widgets

The first plugin is absolutely essential, while the second plugin is just a little WordPress foolery to add some extra fun to your blog. Finally, the third plugin, Widgets, is also optional — but very useful and popular among WordPress users.

Akismet

I touch on Akismet a few times throughout this book. Why so much? Only because it's this author's humble opinion that Akismet is the mother of all plugins, and no WordPress blog is, or should be, complete without a fully activated version of Akismet running on the blog.

Apparently, WordPress agrees because the plugin is packaged in every WordPress software release — and has been since version 2.0. Akismet was created by the folks at Automattic, the same folks who bring you the Sidebar Widgets plugin. Automattic also works with of some of the original developers of the WordPress software platform.

Akismet is the answer to combating comment and trackback spam. Matt Mullenweg, of Automattic, says that Akismet is a "collaborative effort to make comment and trackback spam a non-issue and restore innocence to blogging, so you never have to worry about spam again" (from the Akismet Web site at `http://akismet.com`).

To use the plugin, simply click the Activate link to the right of the plugin name and description. After you do that, you see a red box at the top of the page that says: "Akismet is not active. You must enter your WordPress.com API key for it to work." Sort of a contradiction there — WordPress tells you that Akismet isn't active after you've activated it. That's because the plugin file is active, but the Akismet service isn't yet active (Figure 10-9 shows you the warning that Akismet gives you when Akismet is not active, telling you that you still need to enter your WordPress.com API key).

Go ahead and click the link in the red box to obtain your WordPress.com API key. You need to create a WordPress.com account in order to get an API key (See Chapter 3 for information on creating a WordPress.com account.) Although you do have to create a WordPress.com account, you don't need to use it; you just need to get the API key, as shown in Figure 10-10. When you have it, return to the Akismet Configuration page by clicking the Plugins tab in your WordPress Administration panel and then clicking the Akismet Configuration subtab. Enter the API key into the WordPress.com Akismet Key box and click the Update Options button to fully activate the Akismet plugin.

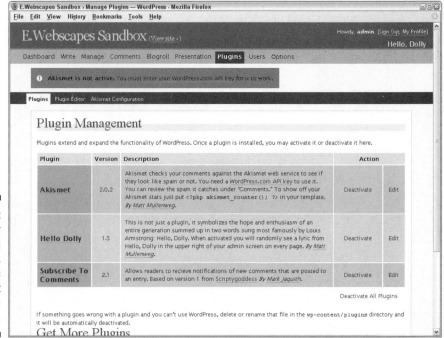

Figure 10-9:
After activating Akismet, WordPress tells you it isn't active yet.

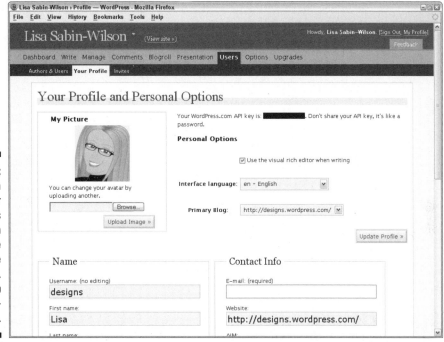

Akismet catches spam and throws it into a queue, where it holds it for 15 days and then completely deletes it from your database. It's probably worth your while to check the Akismet Spam panel once a week to make sure it hasn't captured any legitimate comments or trackbacks.

You can rescue those nonspam captured comments and trackbacks by doing the following, after you've logged into your WordPress Administration panel:

1. **Click the Comments tab on the Administration panel.**

   The Comments page appears and displays a list of the most recent comments on your blog.

2. **Click the Akismet Spam subtab on the Administration subpanel.**

   The Akismet Spam page displays any comments that were caught by the Akismet spam plugin.

3. **Scroll through the list of spam comments, looking for any comments or trackbacks that are legitimate.**

4. **If you locate one that's legitimate, select the Not Spam Box check box directly beneath the entry.**

   This marks that comment as legitimate. In other words, this is a comment you do not consider to be spam.

 5. Click the De-Spam Marked Comments button at the bottom of the page.

 This reloads the page and the comment you've "de-spammed" is no longer listed in the Akismet Spam section.

You know, I have to say, I'm really glad I just wrote this section. As I write, I'm testing all this stuff on my own blog. I just found four legitimate comments caught in my Akismet spam filter and was able to "de-spam" them, releasing them from the binds of Akismet and unleashing them upon the world.

I've been blogging since 2002. I started blogging with the Movable Type blogging platform and moved to WordPress in 2003. As blogging became more and more popular, comment and trackback spam became more and more of a nuisance to bloggers everywhere. I remember one morning in 2004 when I woke up and found that a total of 2,300 pieces of disgusting comment spam had been published to my blog. Something had to be done! The folks at Automattic did a fine thing with Akismet. Since the emergence of Akismet, I barely have to think about comment or trackback spam, except for the few times a month I check my Akismet spam queue.

Hello Dolly

Matt Mullenweg, co-founder of WordPress, developed the Hello Dolly plugin. Anyone who follows the development of WordPress at all knows that Matt is a huge fan of jazz. How do we know this? Every single release of WordPress is named after some jazz great. For example, one of the most recent releases of the WordPress software is named Ella, after jazz great Ella Fitzgerald.

So, knowing this, it isn't surprising that Matt Mullenweg developed a plugin named Hello Dolly. Here's the description of it that you see in the Plugin Management page in your WordPress Administration panel:

 "This is not just a plugin, it symbolizes the hope and enthusiasm of an entire generation summed up in two words sung most famously by Louis Armstrong: Hello, Dolly. When activated you will randomly see a lyric from Hello, Dolly in the upper right of your admin screen on every page."

Is it necessary? No. Is it fun? Sure!

Activate the Hello Dolly plugin in the Plugin Management page in your WordPress Administration panel. When you've activated it, your WordPress blog greets you with a different lyric from the song "Hello, Dolly!" each time.

If you want to change the lyrics in this plugin, you can edit them by clicking the Edit link to the right of the Hello Dolly plugin on the Plugin Management page. This opens the Plugin Editor and allows you to edit the file in a text editor. Make sure that each line of the lyrics has its own line in the plugin file.

Widgets

Widgets are wonderful — and you can quote me on that! If you ever used WordPress prior to version 2.2, you will know that Widgets used to be a plugin that you had to install. With version 2.2, widgets are now included within the software files and are available to you as long as you have a widget-ready WordPress theme (more about that later).

Widgets are plugins developed by the folks at Automattic that allow you to add WordPress functionality to your blog (such as to list recent posts and recent comments, and to category lists in your sidebar) without having to muck around in the code of the template. You can drag widget boxes and drop them into your sidebar, arranging the order in which you want them to appear on your site without having to know HTML or even opening the template files at all!

Note: This section assumes you're using the default Kubrick theme.

To use Sidebar Widgets, follow these steps:

1. **Click the Presentations tab on the Administration panel.**

   This displays the Themes page, with a list of WordPress themes installed on your blog. (Usually, you see the title of each theme and a preview; sometimes, you see only the title of the theme.)

2. **Click the Widgets subtab on the Administration subpanel.**

   This displays the widgets options page shown in Figure 10-11.

3. **Select a widget you want to use by clicking and dragging a widget box from the Available Widgets palette to the sidebar.**

   Here's where widget magic happens. Click one of those widget boxes in the Available Widgets palette with your mouse and, while holding down your mouse button, drag it into the Sidebar 1 box that you see in Figure 10-11. See what happens? This is called drag-and-drop because you drag a box, or widget, into the sidebar and drop it there.

4. Repeat these Steps 1–3 for every widget you want to use.

When you have all the widgets you want in the sidebar, you can rearrange them using the same drag-and-drop method to put them in the order that you would like them to appear on your blog.

5. Click the Save Changes button at the bottom of the page when you're done.

This saves the changes you've just made to the widget options. View your blog, and you will now see that the widgets you chose to use are displayed on your blog, in the order you chose to display them.

Figure 10-12 shows you the widgets I chose to drag into my sidebar (Pages, Recent Posts, Categories, and Archives), and Figure 10-13 shows you the sidebar on my live blog. You can see that the widgets on my blog are the same as the ones I chose in the Sidebar Widgets options, and they're in the same order, as well.

Almost all of the widgets have options that you can set for them. The Pages widget, for example, displays a list of your static pages on your blog. After you drag and drop the Pages widget to your sidebar, you can edit the title that appears above the list of static pages shown on your blog.

Figure 10-11: Sidebar Widgets plugin options page in the WordPress Administration panel.

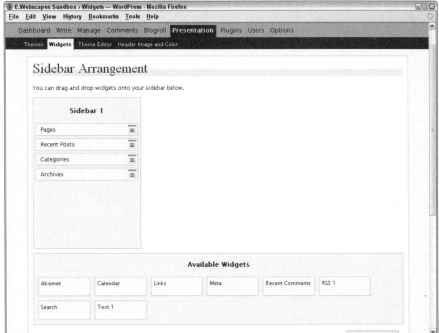

Figure 10-12:
My Sidebar Widgets options show the widgets I chose for my blog.

Figure 10-13:
The sidebar widgets as they appear on my live blog.

Click the Presentations tab in your WordPress Administration menu and then click the Widgets subtab. Doing so opens the Sidebar Arrangement page. Drag the Pages widget to the sidebar. To edit the settings of the Pages widget, follow these steps:

1. **Click the icon in the right corner of the widget.**

   This opens the Pages widget options window with settings such as Title, Sort By, and Exclude (as shown in Figure 10-14).

2. **Type a title in the Title field.**

   This title is the heading that you want to appear on your blog, above the list of static pages that appear on your blog. The default heading is Pages, but you can change it to whatever you want (for example, My Pages).

3. **Select a sorting option from the Sort By drop-down menu.**

   With this menu, you can sort by Title (alphabetical), Page Order (creation date) or Page ID (ID assigned to the page).

4. **Click the X at the top-right corner of the box to save your options.**

   This closes the small window and returns you to the widgets options page that you see in Figure 10-12.

5. **Click the Save Changes on the Sidebar Arrangement page.**

   This saves the changes you just made and returns you to the widgets options page again. (Actually, this page has two buttons labeled Save Changes; you can click either one to save your changers here.)

Widgetized themes

For blogs not using the default Kubrick theme, it isn't enough to have widget functionality; the theme you're using needs to be widget ready (already configured to use sidebar widgets). Most of the free WordPress themes available for download include widgets — or at least they should. Because WordPress includes the widget functionality as part of the core software now, the use of widgets has become a standard expectation of most users of free WordPress themes. There really is no excuse anymore for theme designers to build WordPress templates that don't have widget functionality built into them.

How do you know whether your theme is widget ready? Don't worry — WordPress will let you know! In the Administration panel, when you click the Presentations tab and the Widget subtab, if the theme you currently have active isn't widget ready, you won't see the widget options as shown in Figure 10-11. Rather, you'll see a friendly message telling you that your current WordPress theme isn't widget ready.

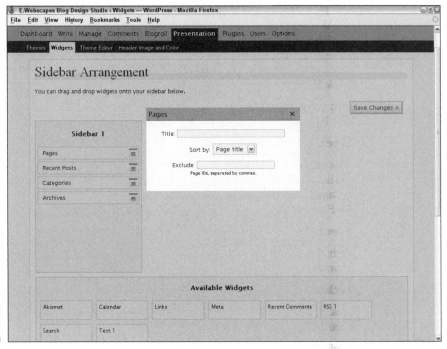

Figure 10-14:
Configuring
the options
for the Page
Widget
plugin.

If your current theme is not widget ready, you need to make some adjustments to it to make it so. Automattic, the creator of the WordPress widgets, gives you very detailed and useful instructions on adjusting your theme files for widgets. You can find the instructions at `http://automattic.com/code/widgets/themes`.

See It and Say It with WordPress Plugins

Sometimes, just writing your thoughts, ideas, and opinions isn't enough for visitors to be completely satisfied with their overall blogging experience. For some, it isn't enough to read blog content — they want to see it and hear it as well. Really, about the only technology that blogging hasn't produced yet is the scratch-and-sniff blog. I should invent that. However, it could be a scary thing, depending on the blog. I think I'll stick with the visual and auditory senses and leave it at that!

I'm talking about the emerging popularity of blogging technologies such as podcasting, vblogging, and photoblogging. These three aspects of blogging allow you to provide even more interaction with your visitors by presenting your content as audio files (podcasting), videos (vblogging), and photos (photoblogging).

Podcasting: The talking blog

Imagine talk radio on the Internet. Okay, maybe you don't have to stretch that far to imagine it. Podcasting has become more and more popular on the Internet and in the blogosphere. It doesn't quite hold the mystery that it used to.

In a nutshell, *podcasts* are recorded audio files available for download. You can listen to them on your computer or download them onto an MP3 player and listen to them while you drive to work.

The name *podcast* is a mashup of Apple's *iPod* and *broadcasting* as a method to broadcast audio files on the Internet. You don't need an Apple iPod in order to listen to a podcast, though — any MP3 player will do.

There are some great advantages to providing a podcast on your blog:

✔ Podcasting lets the average Joe (or Jill) publish a radio show on a blog.

✔ You can provide short, recorded snippets of just you talking — or expand it and do audio interviews with people of interest. It's a great way to distribute knowledge on topics that interest you and your site visitors.

✔ Podcasts are distributed via RSS feeds, and this is what really connects podcasts to blogging. The ability to enclose a podcast in an RSS feed also allows you to organize your podcasts by category, making them very easy for browsing.

Podcasting with WordPress

You can create podcasts and include them on your blog without any enhancements, add-ons, or plugins at all in WordPress. However, listed a bit later in this chapter are some great plugins that WordPress users have developed to help you along a bit with sharing your podcasts with the world!

Here are five easy steps you can take to create podcasts in WordPress:

1. **Create your audio file using your microphone and the software of your choosing.**

   Literally hundreds of programs are available for creating audio files. Audacity is a good, free program that you can find at http://audacity. sourceforge.net.

   If you'd like more information about podcasting, pick up a copy of *Podcasting For Dummies,* by Tee Morris and Evo Terra (Wiley Publishing).

2. **Upload your new MP3 audio file to your Web server using FTP.**

3. **Create a new post in your WordPress Administration panel and include the link to the new MP3 file you just uploaded.**

   The link you create needs to be the full Internet address, for example:

   ```
   http://yourdomain.com/yourfile.mp3
   ```

4. **Click the Publish button.**

   This saves and publishes your post, including the link to the audio file.

5. **Tell all your friends, family, and any strangers you run into on the street about your great podcast!**

Photoblogging

The very simple definition of a *photoblog* is this: It's a blog with photos. That's pretty much it, and it's all you really need to know about how to explain what a photoblog is to your friends and family.

Oh, but wait! The photoblog purists out there are ready to kick me in the butt because there is so much more to it than that . . . sort of. Photobloggers range from professional photographers who share their portfolio of work on the Web to amateur photographers who do it for fun and use photoblogging to document their lives in pictures, kind of like a photo diary.

Usually, you can spot a blog that's dedicated to photography because almost all the posts are done with photographs and you'll usually find thumbnails in the sidebar that, when clicked, are linked to the bigger photographs. Most regular blogs rely on words to get their message across to their readership. Photoblogs use photographs — or a mixture of both photos and words — to communicate.

Three great WordPress podcasting plugins

Some super plugins have been developed for WordPress podcasting. Here's a list of three truly great ones:

- ✔ **WP-iPodCatter:** Helps WordPress users create an iTunes podcast directory. You can download it at `http://garrick vanburen.com/wordpress-plugins/wpipodcatter`.

- ✔ **PodPress:** Displays a nice MP3 player in any post you include an MP3 file in. It also adds the RSS feed automatically. You can download it at `www.mightyseek.com/podpress`.

- ✔ **Podcast Quicktag:** Adds a convenient button to the WordPress post page that makes adding audio file links to your posts easy. You can download it at `www.tamba2.org.uk/wordpress/podcast`.

Three super photoblog plugins for WordPress

Here are some of the best photoblog plugins available:

YAPB (Yet Another Photoblog plugin): Turns your WordPress installation into functional photo gallery software, allowing you to take full advantage of the functionality that WordPress offers, including plugins and themes. It's an excellent choice for photobloggers. You can download it at `http://johannes.jarolim.com/blog/wordpress/yet-another-photoblog`.

Pictorialis: Helps you create a photoblog/photo gallery using your WordPress software installation and is pretty easy to install, configure, and style. You can download it at `http://pictorialis.wltc.net`.

ANIga Gallery: Allows you to use your WordPress blog as a photo gallery by giving you options for photo uploads and display that gives your readers the chance to comment on your photos. You can download it at `www.animalbeach.net/aniga`.

Vblogging

The final bit of extra blogging technology I'm addressing in this chapter is video blogging, also known as *vblogging*. Vblogging got a slow start in the world of blogging, and users didn't really latch on to the practice of publishing videos on the Internet until the YouTube rage took the Internet world by storm. By then, all bets were off, and everybody was publishing videos on the Web.

It has become popular for bloggers to embed YouTube videos in their blog posts as a way of sharing favorite music, videos, and clips of interesting items they find in the video archives at `http://youtube.com`.

Another way to add videos to your blog is to create them yourself, but the technologies, equipment, and software available are far too abundant for coverage in this book. Check out *Digital Video For Dummies,* by Keith Underdahl, which is a great resource for creating digital video; also see *Videoblogging For Dummies,* by Stephanie Cottrell Bryan, for a great videoblogging resource.

Embedding YouTube videos in your posts

Follow these steps to embed a video from YouTube in your blog posts:

1. **Visit YouTube and find a video to share in your blog post.**

2. **Look for the Embed box that contains the code for the video.**

3. **Copy the code and then paste it into your blog post.**

4. **Click Publish.**

   You're done!

In Table 10-3, I share with you some great plugins that have been developed by WordPress users to make adding videos to your blog much easier.

Table 10-3	Some Great Plugins to Help You Vblog	
Plugin Name	**Location**	**Description**
Anarchy Media Player	`http://an-archos.com/anarchy-media-player`	Allows you to play videos, of any format, on your blog. This plugin also gives you a convenient button (quicktag) in the WordPress posts page that allows you to easily insert video files in your posts.
WPvideo	`www.skarcha.com/wp-plugins/wpvideo`	Gives you the ability to insert any Flash-based video in your WordPress post. It also lets you insert the video author's name, title, and description.
Viper's Video Quicktags	`http://wordpress.org/extend/plugins/vipers-video-quicktags`	Gives you a nice video options page, where you can configure the settings and display options for videos on your blog.

Keep in mind that providing your own audio and video files on your blog can be a costly exercise, just because of the hard drive space and bandwidth required to run them. You can resolve disk space and bandwidth issues by hosting your video files on a free service, such as YouTube, if you don't mind the whole world having access and the ability to publish your videos elsewhere on the Net.

Open Source Development

The WordPress software was built upon an existing platform called b2. Matt Mullenweg, co-founder of WordPress, was using b2 as a blogging platform at the time, and the developer of that program abandoned the project. What did this mean for its users? It meant no more development unless someone somewhere picked up the ball and continued with the platform. Enter Matt Mullenweg and welcome WordPress.

Apply this same concept to plugin development and you'll understand how, sometimes, plugins can and do fall by the wayside and drop off the face of the earth. Unless someone's there to pick up the ball when the original developer loses interest, future development of that plugin ceases. It's important to understand that most plugins are developed in an open source environment, and this means a few things for you, the end user:

✔ The developers who created your favorite plugin aren't obligated to continue development on the project. If they find a new hobby, or simply tire of the work, they can give it up completely. If no one picks up where they left off, you can kiss that plugin goodbye if it doesn't work with the latest WordPress release.

✔ Developers of popular plugins are generally extremely good about updating them when new versions of WordPress are released, or when a security bug or flaw is discovered. However, keep in mind that no timetable exists for these developers to hold to. Many of these folks have day jobs, school, or families that can keep them from devoting as much time to the project as *you* would like them to.

✔ Beware of the pitfalls of completely falling in love with any particular WordPress plugin because in the world of plugin development, it's easy come, easy go. Try not to allow your Web site to become dependent on a plugin, and don't be surprised if the plugin you love doesn't exist tomorrow. You can use the plugin for as long as it continues to work for you, but when it stops working, such as with a new WordPress release or a security exploit that makes it unusable, you have a rough decision to make. You can:

   • Stop using the plugin and try and find a suitable solution.

   • Wait and hope that some other developer picks up the ball and continues where the original developer left off.

   • Try to find someone to provide a fix for you — in which case, you'll more than likely have to pay someone for her time.

I don't want to make it all sound so gloom and doom in the world of WordPress plugins, but I do think it's very important to understand the dynamics in play here. It's all food for thought.

Finding Plugin Resources

Chapter 18 of this book highlights ten of the most popular plugins available for WordPress and tells you where to find them. Be sure to check out that chapter to find some of the most used and most useful WordPress plugins.

The WordPress Codex has a wealth of information on plugins, as well, including information on how to write and develop your own plugin, if you want to.

You can find the WordPress Codex resource on plugins at `http://codex.wordpress.org/plugins`.

Lorelle VanFossen keeps a popular blog at `http://lorelle.wordpress.com`. On this blog, Lorelle writes about WordPress tips, tricks, and how-to's. Lorelle dedicated an entire month to WordPress plugins. The entire series is a great plugin resource, and you can find it at `http://lorelle.wordpress.com/tag/wordpress-plugins`.

Weblog Tools Collection keeps track of new WordPress plugin releases and updates. You can always find great information on new and updated, WordPress plugins at `http://weblogtoolscollection.com/archives/category/wordpress-plugins`.

Chapter 11

Designing Your Blog

In This Chapter

▶ Doing it yourself with free WordPress themes

▶ Exploring professional services

▶ Finding a professional who can accommodate your needs

▶ Keeping the communication lines open

My grandma was fond of saying, "Don't judge a book by its cover," but I wonder whether she would apply the same concept to blogs. The design of your blog gives your visitors an immediate first impression, and in this chapter, you explore a few different methods for designing your blog. I help you figure out whether you want to go it alone by taking advantage of the free WordPress themes available to help you design your own blog, or whether you should take the leap and hire a professional to do the dirty work for you.

This chapter also covers how to find WordPress design professionals and consultants who can provide design solutions for you, as well as some tips on communicating your design needs to the pros.

Deciding Whether You Need a Professional

For some people, hiring a professional is a solution — and sometimes, the only viable solution — for creating a blog that's different from all the rest. Let's face it, some folks would rather chew on nails than try to figure out all the template tags, CSS, and graphic design techniques it takes to create a custom-made WordPress template. I hear it from WordPress users (and other blogging platform users) all the time: "I want a unique look, but I don't know how to do it. I just want to blog."

The question for you to answer is whether you'll be completely satisfied by using a free theme available for all WordPress users, or if you prefer to hire a professional to provide you with a custom theme that will be unique to your blog only. This chapter explores both options to help you make a decision for your own blog.

Getting Started Quickly and Easily with Free Themes

WordPress comes packaged with two free themes for you to use. Most bloggers who use WordPress usually don't waste any time at all in finding a theme that they like better than the Default or Classic WordPress themes. Those packaged themes, which you can find under the Presentation tab on your WordPress Administration panel, are meant to get you started. But you are by no means limited to using just those two themes. Although the themes are functional, they're visually kind of plain.

Free WordPress themes, such as those I discuss in Chapter 17, are popular because of their appealing designs and ease of installation and use. They're great tools to use when you launch your new blog, and if you dabble a bit in the area of graphic design and CSS (Cascading Style Sheets), it's totally possible to take one of the available free WordPress themes and customize it to fit your own needs. (See Chapter 9 for some resources and tools for using templates and template tags, as well as to find some great CSS references that can help you explore the world of Cascading Style Sheets.)

By using free themes, you can have your blog up and running with a new design — without the help of a professional — pretty fast. And with thousands of themes available, you can change your theme as often as you want. (If you've already decided that you'd prefer to hire a professional, you can skip ahead to the section "Checking Out the Types of Blog Professionals," later in this chapter.)

Finding and installing free themes

It may take you some time to find the theme that fits you best; but with thousands available, it won't be that difficult to find one that suits you. The WordPress Themes site currently has more than 1,600 free themes available for download. Using and trying out several different free themes lets you try on different "outfits" for your blog, allowing you to change outfits, as needed, until you find just the right theme.

Installing and using free themes couldn't be easier. The first thing you want to do is visit a site that has free WordPress themes available for download, such as the WordPress Themes site at `http://themes.wordpress.net`.

Spend some time on that site, browse through the hundreds of offerings, and find one — or two or ten — that you like. On the WordPress Themes site, you can preview and then download a theme by following these steps:

1. **Click the image of the theme you'd like to preview.**

   This displays a page with a larger picture of the theme, along with author information and some descriptive information, such as the number of columns, the primary color scheme, and so on.

2. **Click the Test Run link that appears at the bottom of the picture, as shown in Figure 11-1.**

   This opens a new browser window that shows you a working version of the theme you're previewing and allows you to see how the different elements of the blog look and work together. Go ahead and click around on that theme to check out some of the key features of the theme, such as how the comments are displayed and how the search function works.

Figure 11-1: Click the Test Run link to preview a theme on the WordPress Themes site.

3. **Return to the theme page at the WordPress Theme site. If you like the theme, click the Download link.**

   Underneath the theme image, you see some information about the theme, including the number of times the theme has been downloaded by other people. If it's a really good theme, the download number will be high. This number also tells you how many other people are potentially using the same theme (if you're worried about individuality in design, this may be a concern for you).

The theme files are compressed in a `.zip` file. Use your favorite decompression program (Chapter 6 gives you some information on these programs) to unpack the files to your own computer.

From there, connect to your Web server via FTP and upload the entire theme folder into the `/wp-content/themes/` directory of your Web server.

Activating your new theme

At this point, you can activate the theme by following these simple steps after logging in to your WordPress Administration panel:

1. **Click the Presentation tab on the WordPress Administration panel.**

   This displays the Presentation page, which lists all the themes currently installed on your WordPress blog. The name of each theme appears next to a small screenshot of the theme.

2. **Select the theme you'd like to use and click the theme name.**

   This reloads the page, and the theme you just selected now appears underneath the Current Theme heading.

3. **View your blog to see the change.**

   The theme you just activated appears on your live blog.

Chapter 9 provides a far more detailed look into WordPress themes and how to manage and edit them within your WordPress Administration panel.

Each theme has its own folder in the `/wp-content/themes/` directory on your Web server. For every functional theme in that directory, you see the themes listed in your WordPress Administration panel under the Presentation tab.

Checking Out the Types of Blog Professionals

You have big plans for your blog, and your time is valuable. Hiring a professional to handle the backend design and maintenance of your blog enables you to spend your time creating the content and building your readership on the front end.

Many bloggers who've made the decision to go the custom route by hiring a design professional do it for another reason: They want the design/theme on their blog to be completely unique and individual to them — a design that no one else has. Free themes are nice; however, you do run the risk of your blog looking just like hundreds of other blogs out there.

Branding is a term often used in advertising and marketing. It refers to the recognizable identity of a product — or in this case, of a blog. Having a unique brand or design for your site sets yours apart from all the rest. If you have a custom look to your blog, people will begin to associate that look with you. You can accomplish this by using just a single logo — or an entire layout and color scheme of your choosing.

Many consultants and design professionals on the Web put themselves up for hire to help you realize the custom, unique look you seek for your blog and Web site. Who are these people? I get to that in just a second. First, you want to understand what services they offer, which can help you decide if hiring a professional is the solution for you.

Take a quick look at some of the many services offered:

- ✔ Custom graphic design and CSS styling for your blog
- ✔ Custom template creation
- ✔ WordPress plugin installation and integration
- ✔ Custom WordPress plugin creation, based on your individual needs
- ✔ WordPress software installation on your Web server
- ✔ Upgrades of the WordPress software
- ✔ Upgrades of WordPress plugins
- ✔ Web site hosting and domain registration services
- ✔ Search engine optimization and Web site marketing

Some bloggers take advantage of the full array of services provided, whereas others use only a handful. The important thing to remember is that you aren't alone out there. Help is available for you and your blog.

In Table 11-1, I pair the three types of blog experts — designers, developers, and consultants — with the different services they typically offer.

Many of these folks are freelancers with self-imposed titles, so it can be a semantics thing. However, by and large, I've matched titles to duties as best I could. Keep in mind that some of these professionals wear all of these hats and are considered a Jack (or Jill)-of-all-trades, whereas others specialize in one area of expertise.

Table 11-1	Types of WordPress Professionals
Title	*Services*
Blog designer	These folks excel in graphic design, CSS, and the development of custom-designed blog templates.
Blog developer	These guys and gals are code monkeys. Some of them don't know a stitch about design; however, they can provide you with custom code to make your blog do things you never thought possible. Usually, you'll find these people releasing WordPress plugins in their spare time for the WordPress community to use for free.
Blog consultant	If you're blogging for a business, these folks can provide you with a marketing plan for your blog or a plan for using your blog to reach clients and colleagues in your niche field. Many of these consultants also provide search engine optimization consulting and services to help your domain reach high ranks in search engines.

I wish I could tell you what kind of price to expect from any one type of consultant. Truth is, there's no real way for me to make an "On average, you can expect to pay. . . . " statement because the level of expertise can vary so wildly. I have seen these types of services on the Web range anywhere from $5 per hour all the way up to $300 per hour — and all points in between. As with any purchase, do your research and make an informed decision before you buy. That's the absolute best advice I can give.

Blog designers

Blog designers can take a simple blog and turn it into something dynamic and exciting. These people are experts at the graphic design, CSS styling, and template tagging needed to create your working templates. Most often, you'll also find that blog designers are skilled in the installation and upgrade of WordPress software and plugins and sometimes even skilled in the area of custom PHP or custom plugin creation. These are the folks you want to contact when you are looking for someone to create a nice, custom design for your blog (see Figure 11-2).

Some blog designers post their rates directly to their Web site through the use of design *packages,* whereas other designers choose to quote projects on a case-by-case basis because every project is unique. When you are searching around for a blog designer, if the prices are not displayed on the site, feel free to drop the blog designer an e-mail and ask for an estimate. Armed with this information, you can do a little comparison shopping while you search for just the right designer.

The designers and design studios listed in Table 11-2 represent a range of style, pricing, services, and experience. All of them excel at creating custom WordPress blogs and Web sites. This list is by no means exhaustive, nor is it a complete reflection of what's available. It is, however, a nice starting point for you to begin the process of hiring a professional for your project.

Figure 11-2: Moxie Design Studios is a company that provides custom designs for blogs.

It's impossible for me to list all the different professionals who provide WordPress consulting services, but I do list some of the popular ones (in Tables 11-2 through 11-4). My goal here is to cover a diverse level of services so that you have the knowledge to make an informed decision on which professional to choose.

Table 11-2	Established WordPress Blog Designers
Who They Are	*Where You Can Find Them*
E.Webscapes Design Studio	`http://ewebscapes.com`
Moxie Design Studios	`http://moxiedesignstudios.com`
The Blog Studio	`http://theblogstudio.com`
Hop Studios	`http://hopstudios.com`

Blog developers

The WordPress motto sits at the bottom of its home page:

"Code is poetry."

And no one knows this better than the extremely talented blog developers out there today, including the developers on the core WordPress development team. A developer can take some of the underlying code, make a little magic happen between PHP and the MySQL database that stores the data and content for your blog, and create a dynamic display of the content on your blog — all for you. Most likely, you will contact a developer when you want to do something with your blog that is a little out of the ordinary, and you can't find a plugin that does the trick.

If you've gone through all the available WordPress plugins and still can't find the exact function that you want your WordPress blog to perform, get a hold of one of these folks. Explain what you need — the developer can tell whether it can be done, if he or she is available to do it, and how much it will cost — don't forget that part! You might recognize some of the names in Table 11-3 as the developers/authors of some of the more popular WordPress plugins you find on the Web.

Table 11-3	Established WordPress Developers for Hire
Who They Are	*Where You Can Find Them*
Mark Jaquith	`http://txfx.net`
Alex King	`http://crowdfavorite.net`
Aaron Brazell	`http://technosailor.com`

Blog consultants

Blog consultants may not be able to do any design work or coding work for your blog, but they're probably connected to the people who can. Consultants can help you achieve your goals for your blog in terms of online visibility, marketing plans, and search engine optimization. Most of these folks can help you find out how to make money with your blog and connect you with various advertising programs. Quite honestly, you can do what blog consultants do by investing just a little time and research into these different areas. However, as with design and coding, it takes time to figure it all out and then implement it. Sometimes, it's easier — and more cost effective — to hire a professional rather than do it yourself.

Who hires blog consultants? Typically, a business that wants to incorporate a blog with its existing Web site, or a business that has already started a blog but wants a little extra help in taking it to the next level to increase its exposure online. Table 11-4 gives you the names and Internet locations of some people and organizations that offer this kind of consulting.

Table 11-4	Established Blog Consultants for Hire
Who They Are	*Where You Can Find Them*
La Shawn Barber	`http://thelanguageartist.com`
Toby Bloomberg	`www.divamarketingblog.com`
Debbie Weil	`www.blogwriteforceos.com`
Blog Business Summit	`http://blogbusinesssummit.com/consulting`

Hiring a Professional

With the growing popularity of WordPress, you and I are treated to an ever-expanding market of WordPress consultants, developers, and designers. This is an extremely good thing because the competition keeps them sharp and gives us a wide variety of choices at the same time. This section provides information on how to find, hire, and communicate with the professionals who make the WordPress magic happen.

Finding professionals

Search engines are the most obvious tools to use to look for blog designers, developers, and consultants. By entering the applicable keywords into the search engines, you can find professionals who provide the services you seek. I suggest keywords like these, just to name a few:

- *blog consultant*
- *blog designer*
- *WordPress designer*
- *WordPress developer*
- *custom WordPress themes*

Aside from search engines, here are some ideas on other places you can find blog professionals:

- **Other blogs:** Word of mouth is probably the best testimonial when it comes to the services and skills of a group or individual. If you visit blogs on a regular basis, you might notice that bloggers who have paid for custom design, development, or marketing services usually display a link to the Web site of the professional they used and are more than happy to talk about their project details. So when you see a custom blog that you really like, drop the blogger an e-mail and ask about it, or visit the Web site of the professional the blogger used.

- **WordPress Support Forum** (http://wordpress.org/support): You can find many WordPress experts hanging out here, and some of them are available for hire. Or at the very least, people in the forum can provide you with great recommendations.

  This is a community forum of people from all walks of life — from the novice to the very experienced. You will, of course, want to check the credentials of anyone you find in the forum to make sure that he or she has the experience and knowledge to do what you're asking for.

- ✔ **WordPress Themes site (**`http://themes.wordpress.org`**):** The designers who provide free themes for the WordPress community often hire themselves out for custom projects, as well. If you see some work from a particular designer that you like on this site, consider dropping that designer an e-mail to find out if he or she is available for hire.

- ✔ **Automattic Web site (**`http://automattic.com/services/` `wordpress-consultants`**):** The folks at Automattic have brought us Akismet and Sidebar Widgets, and they're some of the original developers of the WordPress software. They provide a list of qualified WordPress design and development consultants, with each listing hyperlinked to that professional or company's site.

Auditioning your prospects

There are hundreds of designers, consultants, and developers on the Web today, each with his or her own style and skill. There is, literally, something for everyone.

Here are some questions to keep in mind when deciding on the professional you want to work with:

- ✔ Does he/she have any experience working with WordPress?

- ✔ How much experience does he/she have?

- ✔ Does his/her skill encompass just one aspect of what you're looking for? Will you have to hire more than one professional to get the entire job done (for instance, design, development, and marketing).

This section helps you evaluate the credentials and skills of the various professionals out there so that you can make a decision about which one to hire for your project.

Blog design practices: What to look for

There are certain expectations you, as a consumer, should have when hiring a professional to design and develop your project. Before paying out any amount of money for a professional, make sure the person is as skilled as you need him or her to be. Keep one very important point in mind: As with anything else in life, you get what you pay for. You wouldn't pay for a Ford and expect a Mercedes, right?

As with any industry, blog designing has a few standards in place that you should expect from any professional that you hire. If the designer you're considering can't meet these basic standards, I recommend moving on until you find one who can. I'm not trying to criticize anyone here; I've just been on the receiving end of some projects that didn't meet these basic standards. And in keeping with my previous car-buying analogy, if you don't get it right the first time, this lemon will nickel and dime you to death — either in money or time investment — for months, and sometimes years, to come. So make sure that the person you hire is skilled in the following areas:

✔ **XHTML validation:** You understand that sites on the Web are built with a certain programming language, typically using HTML. XHTML validation is kind of like spell checking or grammar checking the HTML code against a set of standards put in place by the World Wide Web Consortium (W3C). When your site validates, it's easier for all types of browsers to read and display the underlying code that is the foundation of the design.

The easiest way to see if a Web site or blog validates is by visiting the W3C Web site and using its validation service at `http://validator.w3.org`.

✔ **CSS-based designs:** The expected standard for Web site and blog designing today is to make sure that the design is *CSS based,* which means that the format and layout of the site is completely powered by a Cascading Style Sheet. (Other methods include *inline styles,* which are styles written directly inside the code rather than pulled in from a Cascading Style Sheet, and table-based designs that don't render or display as well as CSS-based designs.) CSS-based sites also have less *code bloat,* meaning that the code contained within the pages is light and the markup lean, which is something that search engines will love you for!

The easiest way to tell whether a designer has used table-based design techniques, with inline styling, is to look at some of the other sites he's designed (you can usually find these in the portfolio or gallery section of the designer's site). View a few sites this person has designed and then view the HTML source of the site (right-click in the browser window and choose View Source). Designs created with tables and inline styles usually have code that looks something like this:

```
<table width="100%" border="0" cellspacing="0" cellpadding="0"
       background="#ffffff">
```

Instead of using tables and inline styling, the same results can be achieved by using CSS. And CSS provides a better browsing experience for your visitors.

✔ **Cross-browser rendering:** Multiple browsers are available today — including Internet Explorer, Firefox, Opera, Netscape, and Safari, just to name a few. Each browser has its own way of rendering code and CSS; in particular, Internet Explorer is especially unique in the way it renders CSS, which creates a bit of a challenge from a design standpoint. The site needs to look the same in Internet Explorer as it does in all other browsers. As a blog owner, you want your site to display correctly for all visitors. That means that the site must be optimized for the various browsers that visitors use. This cross-browser rendering is something every professional designer should be able to accomplish; however, it is always best to ask and not make any assumptions.

A word about XHTML validation: You can't always gauge a designer's expertise in this area simply by visiting the sites she has designed. It's very easy
for anyone who has administrator access to break validation by just a few
simple keystrokes. When a designer hands a project to a client, it's possible
for the client to do something, either within the code or within the content of
the site, to break XHTML validation.

You can find a great deal more information about XHTML validation on the
W3C Web site at `www.w3.org/QA/Tools`.

Looking at the pro's virtual resume

Before you contact a blogging professional who you're considering hiring to
help with your blog, you can find out some pertinent information about who
he is, what he does, and what his style is. A little planning and research can
go a long way in helping to ensure that you're finding a good fit for your project.

Usually, you can find a portfolio for the professional you're considering on
his or her Web site. This lets you browse through some samples of projects
the person has worked on. When you get to the professional's site, look for
links labeled something like *Portfolio, Gallery,* or *Clients.*

You can get a good feel for the blogging professional's style and design abilities by browsing through his or her portfolio of projects. If looking at the
portfolio causes you to run screaming from the computer monitor, it's a good
bet that this particular professional isn't the one for you. Keep browsing until
you find one who's done some design work that you really admire.

Browsing through a blogging professional's portfolio should give you an idea
about whether that person has experience working with the WordPress software. If that seems to be the case, keep reading; you'll likely find a wealth of
information about the services offered by looking a bit deeper on the site.

When you're looking at a blogging professional's Web site, determine what
standards are most important to that person by trying to find out if he or she
does the following:

✔ Develops XTHML-valid code, as well as provides nice graphic design
work.

✔ Ensures that the product provided renders properly in all browser systems. (If you see excuses for why the product renders in only one
browser, move on.)

✔ Provides the services you need. (Can all of your project needs —
domain registration, Web hosting, design work, and software setup and
upgrades — be met under one roof?)

While you're on the blogging professional's Web site, make a note of some client URLs and then visit those sites. Get in contact with these clients and find out what kind of experience they had with the professional you're considering. You may want to contact multiple clients to get a good sampling of client satisfaction. Don't have a lot of time for this? Professional blogging designers, developers, and consultants often post client testimonials right on their Web sites for you to read.

Another way to find out more information is to do a Google search on the individual or company name. Type the name directly into Google's search engine to find out what people are saying on their sites about the professional you're looking to do business with. Usually, bloggers write about their experiences, good or bad, with vendors they've worked with.

Making contact

When you've narrowed your list of candidates, drop them all an e-mail with your questions. Be as specific as possible about your particular needs. Designers and developers can do a lot of things, but I have yet to meet one who can read minds.

Sending an e-mail that says, for example, "I need my blog designed. How much would you charge?" is less effective than something like this:

> *"I'm looking for a professional who can create a custom design for my blog.*
>
> *You can find my blog at* www.yourdomain.com *[enter your URL].*
>
> *I'm looking for a new template with a three-column layout done in shades of dark and light blue.*
>
> *The new design must accommodate all my current content and advertising.*
>
> *In addition to my current content, I have an image that I'd like to include on my blog (which I can send to you when needed). I also need recommendations for plugins."*

An e-mail structured like this gives a much better idea of what you're seeking and arms the professional with a better idea of what direction to head in and what questions to ask before beginning your project.

In return, e-mails from the person you're thinking about hiring should tell you what to expect in terms of price and when you can expect the project to be completed, and should answer any questions you've posed.

These professionals all have their own ways of getting from point A to point B in terms of communication. Some communicate via e-mail, some via phone, and some via an online help desk. Whichever method they use, open communication is the key. You fully expect your professional to communicate with you; do her the return favor of giving her your ideas and identifying the aspects of your blog that you think are vital and important. A relationship with a good professional can be one that lasts a lifetime — or at the very least, for the lifetime of your blog.

Agreeing on the contract

When you have made your final decision on the blogging professional you want to work with, the next step is a contract — the agreement between you and the professional — that states what you can expect from each other.

A professional may fax a paper contract to you to sign. Some professionals, however, use virtual agreements in which all the details of the project are agreed upon either through e-mail or through an online form that you fill out. The decision is yours as to which format you are most comfortable with.

At the very least, the contract (or agreement) should contain the following information:

- ✔ **Pricing and Payment Schedules:** This is the project price quote that you and the professional have agreed on. This quote should contain information on how and when payments will be made.

- ✔ **Completion date:** This is the date that you and the professional expect the project to be finished.

- ✔ **Project Delivery:** This is the method the professional will use to deliver the completed project to you. Delivery may be in the form of electronic transfer via e-mail, project materials published to your Web site, or project materials provided on CD-ROM or DVD.

- ✔ **Project Details:** These are the specifics of the services you can expect the professional to provide. If this is a design project, the details usually include specifications of the design work. If you're hiring someone to handle marketing services, the professional should detail the services to be performed, such as developing a marketing plan, advertising, and search engine submission.

I'm not a lawyer. The information I've provided here is very general and focuses on the key elements that any contract or agreement should include. Be sure to consult with an attorney for specific legal advice concerning contracts.

It's Your Blog: You Can Cry If You Want To

Whether you decide to take advantage of some of the hundreds of free WordPress themes available or choose to have a custom design done by a professional, keep one thing in mind: It's *your* blog. You're the one who has to live with it, so don't be afraid to speak up and ask questions about how things work and what you can expect.

If you have questions about one of the free themes you're using, the theme author is usually willing to answer them. Generally, you can find the theme author's Web site address in the theme itself (often in the style sheet, as shown in Figure 11-3). Drop by the Web site and see whether the site provides an FAQ (Frequently Asked Questions) section about the theme you are using, or any other type of documentation regarding the theme. Many theme authors don't have a lot of time to devote to e-mail, so be sure to check the theme designer's site first for any information you can find about the theme before you consider sending him an e-mail.

Figure 11-3: An example of the style sheet of a WordPress theme that shows the theme author's name and Web site URL.

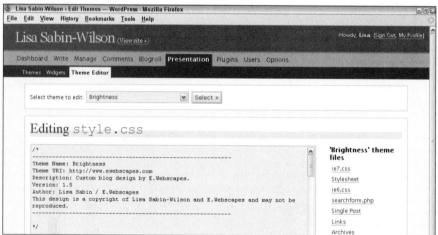

Ditto goes for custom design solutions. When you've chosen a designer you want to work with, ask the questions that are burning inside your mind. The professional you hire may be the expert at what he does, but don't let that intimidate you at all. Don't forget that you're paying for the service. Your designer should be able to answer the questions you have about the process of creating your design. Remember, it's all about open communication.

That goes for consultants, developers, and hosts, as well. You'll never know unless you ask. That's what my grandma used to tell me.

Part IV

Going Multiuser with WordPress MU

The 5th Wave   By Rich Tennant

NO BLOG HOST

PLEASE

In this part . . .

*H*ave you ever considered running a community with hundreds of users who operate their own blogs? And accomplishing all that using just one domain name? You *can* do that — with WordPress MU. In this part, I introduce you to the sometimes complicated but always exciting WordPress MU, and I tell you how you can create and maintain a multi-user blogging community.

Chapter 12

Implementing WordPress MU

. . . .

In This Chapter

▶ Introducing WordPress MU

▶ Arranging Web hosting for WordPress MU

▶ Setting server configurations

▶ Installing WordPress MU

▶ Downloading WordPress MU

▶ Brushing up on FTP

▶ Initial setup of WordPress MU

. . . .

*I*n this chapter, I introduce you to the WordPress MU software and the technical requirements — such as downloading and installing the software, understanding Web hosting requirements, and completing the initial setup and configuration of WordPress MU — needed to manage and maintain a multi-user environment.

With the self-hosted WordPress.org software (as discussed in Part III of this book), you can create a blog that has multiple authors, and each author contributes to the content and conversation of the same blog. With the WordPress MU software, each author/user has his own individual blog instead of being a contributor to one blog.

Meeting WordPress MU

I've heard people pronounce the name WordPress MU various ways, including the following:

✔ *WORDpress moo*

✔ *WORDpress my*

✔ WORDpress *em you*

The third one is correct. Say it with me now: *WORDpress em you*. But no matter how you say it or what you call it, you're talking about a powerful piece of software that lets you run hundreds of thousands of blogs with one installation, on a single domain. It's the WordPress software on steroids. More important, WordPress MU is free — as are all the versions in the WordPress software family.

MU stands for *multi-user*, which means that you can set up multiple user blogs within one installation of WordPress MU.

Each blogger on one WordPress MU system can choose from a variety of themes and blog settings without affecting any of the other bloggers on the system. As the administrator of a WordPress MU site, you can have unlimited users with an unlimited number of blogs, and you control the central system. Users can't install their own plugins on their blogs. The WordPress MU system administrator handles all plugins, and users can use the plugins selected and installed by that person.

The best example of a multi-user blog is the hosted version at WordPress.com. WordPress.com has the bragging rights of almost 1 million users. And it's managed and operated with WordPress MU. At WordPress.com, an unlimited number of people can sign up for free blogs, and each gets a personalized domain name in this format: *yourusername*.`wordpress.com`. Likewise, when you install WordPress MU on your domain, you can offer personalized domains to an unlimited number of bloggers, with you as the administrator of the entire community.

You can find some really super examples of WordPress MU in action at Weblogs at Harvard Law School (`http://blogs.law.harvard.edu`), Edublogs (`http://edublogs.org`), and, of course, WordPress.com (`http://wordpress.com`).

You can find information and support for WordPress MU in the support forums located at `http://mu.wordpress.org`. It's important to make the distinction between the regular WordPress support forums and the WordPress MU support forums because they deal with two very different pieces of software. If you head into the regular WordPress support forums at `http://wordpress.org/support` with a question about WordPress MU, you'll be gently redirected to the WordPress MU support forums. Save yourself some time and make sure you're in the right place to begin with.

I think it's important for anyone, no matter what type of software she's running on her Web server account, to be able to communicate with her Web host provider. With WordPress MU, it's more important than ever to have a Web host that you're comfortable with, can get in touch with, and trust. I say this based on the warning that the WordPress MU folks give you, right off the bat in the Read Me (`readme.txt`) file contained within the installation files:

Something to consider before deciding on WordPress MU for your blogging solution

If you're not comfortable editing PHP code, taking care of a complex Web server and database system, and being proactive about following developments of this project, run — don't walk — to http://wordpress. com *and sign yourself and your friends up for free blogs. It's easier in the long run, and you'll save yourself a lot of pain and angst.*

Hosting WordPress MU

This chapter assumes that you already have a domain name and a Web hosting provider. However, you do need to make sure that your Web host meets the basic hosting requirements for a WordPress MU blog community. This section provides you with an overview of those requirements.

If you need information on registering a domain name or finding a Web host, flip back to Chapter 6, where I discuss both of those topics.

Hosting services generally provide (at least) these services with your account:

- ✔ Hard drive space
- ✔ Bandwidth
- ✔ Domain e-mail with Web mail access
- ✔ File Transfer Protocol (FTP) access
- ✔ Comprehensive Web site statistics
- ✔ MySQL database(s)
- ✔ PHP

Because you intend on running WordPress MU on your Web server, you need to look for a host that provides the minimum requirements needed to run the software on your hosting account, which are:

- ✔ PHP version 4.2 (or greater)
- ✔ MySQL version 4.0 (or greater)

In addition to the requirements above, the Web server needs to have the Apache mod_rewrite module installed. It's this module that creates the custom permalinks for WordPress (which I discuss in Chapter 8). If you don't know if your Web server has this installed, ask your hosting provider. If it isn't installed, your hosting provider should be able to install it for you at your request. If, for some reason, the host can't do this for you, finding a hosting provider who can isn't that hard and just takes a little research on your part.

You can install and use WordPress MU even if you aren't a Web server administrator or database systems guru. You can accomplish the installation and setup of it in one of three ways:

- ✔ Handle it all yourself if you have the capability and knowledge.
- ✔ Hire a consultant to handle the dirty details for you.
- ✔ Ask your Web hosting provider to handle the details for you; however, be prepared to pay for those additional services.

Here are a few Web hosting providers who have proven track records with WordPress MU users:

- ✔ **A Small Orange:** `http://asmallorange.com`
- ✔ **Blogs About Hosting:** `http://blogs-about.com`
- ✔ **Laughing Squid:** `http://laughingsquid.net`
- ✔ **WPMUDEV Premium:** `http://premium.wpmudev.org`

Here are a few consultants who have extensive experience with WordPress MU design and development:

- ✔ **Automattic:** `http://automattic.com/services/support-network`
- ✔ **E.Webscapes:** `http://ewebscapes.com`
- ✔ **Incsub:** `http://incsub.com`

Before installing and using WordPress MU, you need to make your best guess as to how big your blogging community will be. WordPress MU can easily handle thousands of individual blogs with one installation, and if you plan on having a very large blogging community, you need to make your hosting decisions accordingly. It's much easier for you to make the right decisions in the beginning than it is to make those decisions long after you have an active community up and running.

Many WordPress MU communities start out with grand dreams of being large and active. Be realistic about how your community will operate in order to make the right hosting choice for yourself and your community.

Small blogging communities can be easily handled on a shared server solution, whereas larger, more active communities should really consider a dedicated server solution for operation. The difference between the two lies in their names:

- ✔ **Shared server solution:** You have one account on one server that has several other accounts on it. Think of this as apartment living. One apartment building has several apartments for multiple people to live, all under one roof.

✔ **Dedicated server:** You have one account on one server that's dedicated
only to your account. Think of this as owning a home, where you don't
share your living space with anyone else.

A dedicated server solution is a more expensive investment for your blog
community, whereas a shared server solution is the most economical.
Your decision on which solution to go with for your WordPress MU blogging
community should be based on your realistic estimates of how big and how
active your community will be. You can move from a shared server solution
to a dedicated server solution if your community gets larger than you
expected. However, it's easier to start with the right solution for your
community from day one.

As I stated previously in this chapter, managing a WordPress MU community
is a large undertaking that requires some knowledge of managing Web servers
and complex database systems. If you don't have this knowledge to begin
with, be prepared to do some research or bring an experienced consultant
on board to help you manage the system, once you have it up and running.

Installing WordPress MU

WordPress MU has its own dedicated space on the WordPress.org Web site.
You can find all of the information about WordPress MU you need — such as
the history of the project, the installation files, and user documentation and
support forums — on its Web site at `http://mu.wordpress.org`. (See
Figure 12-1.)

This section takes you through the steps of installing WordPress MU on your
own Web server.

Downloading and decompressing the installation files

The first step you need to take in getting WordPress MU up and running on
your Web server is to download it from the WordPress MU Web site. Click the
Download link at the top of the Web site. WordPress MU gives you two compression formats for the software: `.zip` and `tar.gz`. (I recommend getting
the `.zip` file, as it's the most common format for compressed files.) Then,
unpack it with the decompression program of your choice and save the files
to your own local hard drive. (I provide information about recommended
decompression programs in Chapter 6.)

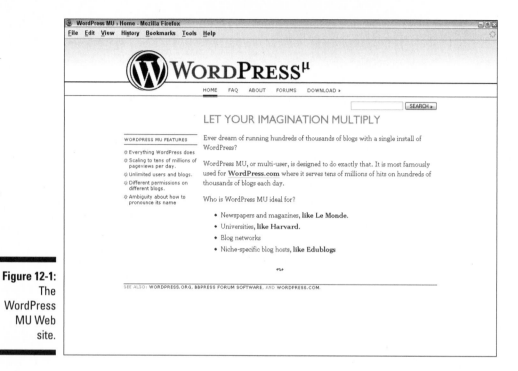

Figure 12-1:
The WordPress MU Web site.

When you unpack the WordPress MU files, you might notice that the unpacked files are now located in a folder named wordpress-mu-X.x *(X.x* is the version number; for example, wordpress-mu-1.2.4). Double-click that folder and you see all the files needed to run WordPress MU on your Web server.

Setting up the MySQL database

MySQL is a database structure that stores all of your WordPress options, posts, comments, and other pertinent data. Every Web host is different in how it gives you access to set up and manage your MySQL database(s) for your account. Contact your Web host if you aren't sure what interface to use or how to access it.

cPanel is a popular account administration interface for managing MySQL databases, and the following steps tell you how to use cPanel to create a new MySQL database for your WordPress MU installation. If your host provides a different interface, the same basic steps apply.

1. Log in to cPanel using your Web browser.

Most often, the URL to access it is something like this:

```
http://yourdomain.com/cpanel
```

If you're unsure of the URL for your cPanel login page, please check with your hosting provider.

2. **Locate the MySQL Database Administration section and click the MySQL Databases icon.**

   The MySQL Account Maintenance page appears; from here, you can set up a new MySQL database.

3. **Choose a name for your database and type it in the Name field.**

   Usually, I give my database a name that I will easily recognize later. This is especially helpful if you're running more than one MySQL database on your account. For example, if I name this database *WordPress* or *WPBlog,* I can be reasonably certain that a year from now, when I want to access my database to make some configuration changes, I know exactly which one I need to deal with.

   Make absolutely sure that you take note of the database name you select in this step. Jot it down on a piece of paper or copy and paste it into a text editor window. Just keep the database name close at hand — you *will* need it later.

4. **Click Create Database.**

   A new page loads with a message confirming that the database has been created.

5. **Click the Go Back link.**

   This returns you to the MySQL Account Maintenance page. (You can also click the Back button in your browser menu.)

6. **Under the Current Users section, type your desired username in the Username field and your desired password in the Password field.**

   For security reasons, make sure your password isn't something that's easily guessed by sneaky hackers.

   Again, make absolutely sure that you take note of the username and password you set up in this step. Jot them down on a piece of paper or copy and paste them into a text editor window. Just keep your username and password close at hand — you *will* need them later.

7. **Click the Create User button.**

   A new page loads with a message confirming that the database user was created. It also confirms the username and password.

8. **Click the Go Back link.**

   This returns you to the MySQL Account Maintenance page. (You can also click the Back button in your browser menu.)

9. **Under the Add Users to Your Database section, select the user you just set up (you) from the User drop-down menu.**

10. **From the Database drop-down menu, select the new database you just set up.**

11. **In the Privileges section, select the All check box.**

    This assigns all privileges to the user (you), which gives you full access to the database in the future.

12. **Click Add User to Database.**

    A new page loads with a confirmation message that the user has been added to the database.

Uploading the WordPress MU files

Now is the time to revisit the WordPress MU files that you have on your local computer. But having them on your computer isn't enough; you need to upload them to your Web server so that you can run the installation.

You can accomplish this by transferring the files to your Web server via FTP. Using FTP to upload files to your Web server involves connecting an FTP client to your Web server account and uploading (or moving) the files from your computer to your Web server. (If you need more information on FTP programs and practices, page back a few chapters to Chapter 6.)

The ReadMe text file (`readme.txt`) gives you two different options on where you can install the WordPress MU files on your server; your choice here is a matter of personal preference. Here are instructions for both options:

- ✔ **Integrate WordPress MU into the root of your domain (with a URL in this format:** `http://yourdomain.com/`**).** Upload all contents of the unzipped WordPress MU folder (excluding the folder itself) into the root directory of your Web server. (In many cases, the root directory of your Web server will be something like the `public_html` or `httpdocs` folder. Check with your hosting provider if you're unsure what the root directory of your Web server is.)

- ✔ **Install WordPress MU in its own subdirectory on your Web site (with a URL in this format:** `http://yourdomain.com/blogs/`**).** Rename the WordPress MU folder to the name you'd like the subdirectory to have and upload it to your Web server. (For example, if you want the WordPress MU installation in a subdirectory called `blog`, you should rename the `WordPress MU` folder to `blogs` and upload it to the root directory of your Web server.)

Make your choice about where you want to place WordPress MU on your server and upload all of the files via FTP.

Web server configurations for WordPress MU

This section gives you important information about the configurations of your Web server. These configurations need to be in place in order to run WordPress MU successfully. If you can perform the configurations in this section yourself (and if you have access to the Apache configuration files), this section is for you. If you don't know how, are uncomfortable with adjusting these settings, or don't have access to change the configurations in your Web server software, you'll need to ask your hosting provider or hire a consultant to perform the configurations for you.

This step is essential, so one way or another, make sure that you get it done before trying to run WordPress MU.

Apache

Apache (http://httpd.apache.org) is Web server software that's loaded and running on your Web server. Not everyone has access to Apache files, however. Usually, the only person who has access to those files is the Web server administrator. (This is usually your Web host.) Depending on your own Web server account and configuration, you may or may not have access to the Apache software files.

mod re_write

The Apache module that's necessary in order for WordPress MU to create nice permalink URLs is called mod_rewrite. This must be configured so that it's active and installed on your server.

You or your Web host can make sure that the Apache mod_rewrite is activated on your server; open the httpd.conf file and verify that the following line is included within:

```
LoadModule rewrite_module /libexec/mod_rewrite.so
```

If it isn't, type that line on its own line and save the file. You will probably need to restart Apache before the change takes effect.

Virtual host (or vhost)

In the same httpd.conf file that I discuss two paragraphs ago, you need to make some adjustments to the <VirtualHost> section of that file. Follow these steps:

1. **Find the** <VirtualHost> **section in the** httpd.conf **file.**

   This line of the httpd.conf file provides directives, or configurations, that apply to your Web site.

2. **Find a line in the** `<VirtualHost>` **section of the** `httpd.conf` **that looks like this:**

   ```
   AllowOverride None
   ```

3. **Replace that line with this line:**

   ```
   AllowOverride FileInfo Options
   ```

4. **On a new line, type** ServerAlias *.*yourdomain.com.*

   Replace *yourdomain.com* with whatever your domain is. This line defines the host name for your MU site and is essential for the virtual host to work correctly.

5. **Save the** `httpd.conf` **file and close it.**

DNS (domain name server)

WordPress MU gives you two different ways to run a network of blogs on your domain. You can use the subdomain option or the subdirectory option. The most popular option (and recommended structure) sets up subdomains for the blogs created by your WordPress MU community. With this subdomain option, the URL of each blog looks cleaner, and the username of the blog appears first. Also, if you intend to take advantage of plugins that are available for WordPress MU, you'll find that most of the plugin structures are written with a subdomain setup in mind.

You can see the difference in the URLs of these two options by comparing the following examples:

 ✔ A **subdomain** looks like this: `http://username.yourdomain.com`.

 ✔ A **subdirectory** looks like this: `http://yourdomain.com/username`.

In the subdomain example, see how the username appears first? That's the most desired method of setting up a WordPress MU network of blogs.

If you want to use a subdomain for each blog in your WordPress MU community, you must add a wildcard record to your DNS records. You need to add a hostname record pointing at your Web server in the DNS configuration tool available in your Web server administration software (like WebHost Manager, a popular Web host administration tool). The hostname record looks like this: `*.yourdomain.com` (where `yourdomain.com` is replaced with your actual domain name).

PHP (PHP Hypertext Processor)

In this section, you edit the PHP configuration on your Web server. PHP needs to have the following configurations in place in the `php.ini` file on your Web server in order to run WordPress MU on your server:

✔ Set your PHP to *not* display any error messages in the visitor's browser window. (This is usually already turned off by default; just double-check that to be sure.)

✔ Find out if your PHP is compiled with memory limit checks. You can find this out by looking for the text `memory_limit` in the `php.ini` file. Usually, the default limit is 8MB. Increase the memory limit to at least 32MB, or even 64MB, to avoid PHP memory errors when running WordPress MU.

✔ Global variables should be set to Off. Usually, the default setting does have global variables turned off; double-check to be sure. An easy way to configure this is to open the `.htaccess` file (found on your Web server in the same directory you installed the WordPress MU files) and add the following two lines to the very top of the `.htaccess` file:

```
php_flag register_globals 0
php_flag display_errors 0
```

Running the Install Script

For such a complex piece of software, the installation really couldn't be easier. Assuming that you've correctly uploaded the WordPress MU files, set up the MySQL database, and set your Web server configurations correctly, these next few steps should be a breeze. WordPress MU guides you along, every step of the way.

Open a new browser window and follow these steps to run the installation of WordPress MU:

1. **Type the URL for your domain in the address bar.**

   For example, type *yourdomain.com* (where *yourdomain.com* is your actual domain name). This displays the Installing WordPress MU page that you see in Figure 12-2.

2. **In the Blog Addresses section, select either the Sub-domains or the Sub-directories radio button.**

   You need to choose how you would like to set up your network of blogs here. If you aren't sure which option to choose, review the "DNS (domain name server)" section earlier in this chapter.

   You can't go back and change the options from Step 2 later — so be sure you check the right option for your setup in this step.

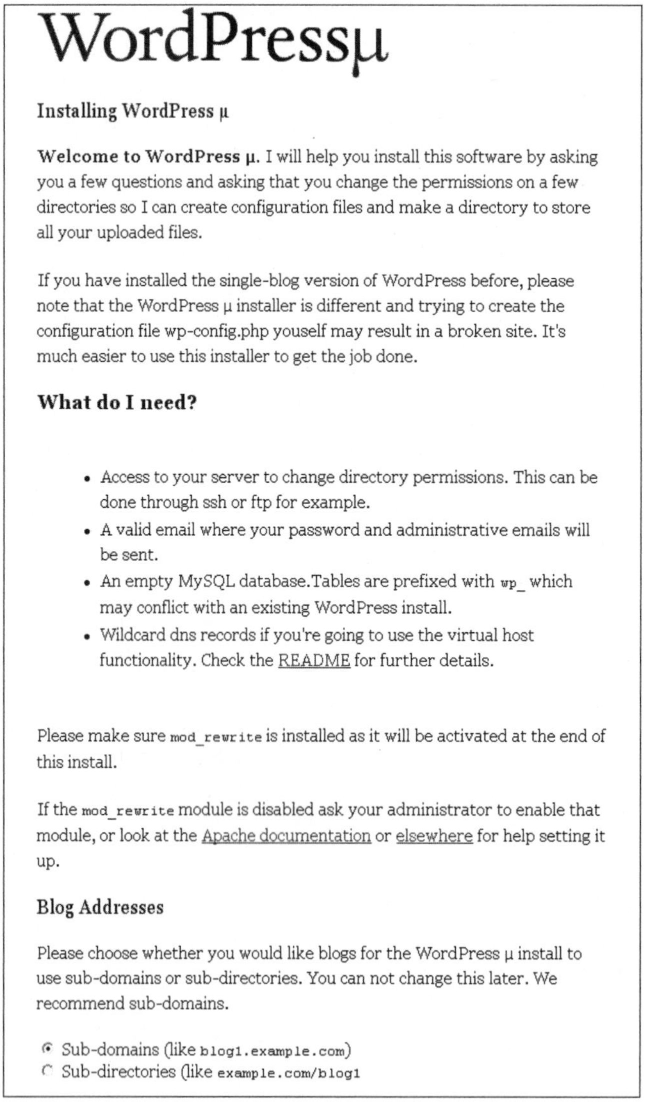

WordPressμ

Installing WordPress μ

Welcome to WordPress μ. I will help you install this software by asking you a few questions and asking that you change the permissions on a few directories so I can create configuration files and make a directory to store all your uploaded files.

If you have installed the single-blog version of WordPress before, please note that the WordPress μ installer is different and trying to create the configuration file wp-config.php youself may result in a broken site. It's much easier to use this installer to get the job done.

What do I need?

- Access to your server to change directory permissions. This can be done through ssh or ftp for example.
- A valid email where your password and administrative emails will be sent.
- An empty MySQL database.Tables are prefixed with `wp_` which may conflict with an existing WordPress install.
- Wildcard dns records if you're going to use the virtual host functionality. Check the README for further details.

Please make sure `mod_rewrite` is installed as it will be activated at the end of this install.

If the `mod_rewrite` module is disabled ask your administrator to enable that module, or look at the Apache documentation or elsewhere for help setting it up.

Blog Addresses

Please choose whether you would like blogs for the WordPress μ install to use sub-domains or sub-directories. You can not change this later. We recommend sub-domains.

- ⦿ Sub-domains (like `blog1.example.com`)
- ○ Sub-directories (like `example.com/blog1`)

Figure 12-2:
The first step in running the WordPress MU installation script.

3. Type the name of your database, the username, the password, and the host in their respective text boxes, as shown in Figure 12-3.

You set up the database name, username, and password in the "Setting up the MySQL database" section, earlier in this chapter. This area is case-sensitive, so be sure you have your upper- and lowercase letters correctly typed in these text boxes.

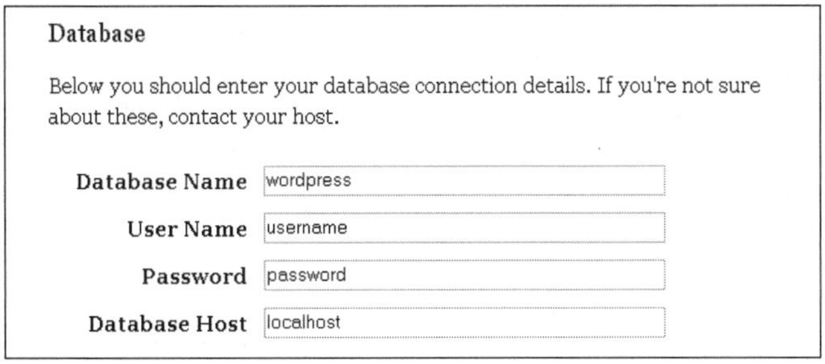

Figure 12-3:
Enter the
connection
details for
your MySQL
database.

4. **Type the database host in the Database Host text box.**

   Ninety-nine percent of the time, you'll leave *localhost* in this field.

   However, some hosting providers set a different host for the MySQL database server. If *localhost* doesn't work, contact your hosting provider to find out the name of the MySQL database host.

5. **Type your domain name in the Server Address text box, as shown in Figure 12-4.**

   This should be the shortest version of your domain name. For example, type **yourdomain.com**, not **www.yourdomain.com** (where *your domain.com* is your actual domain name). Don't include the http:// portion of the domain name here either.

6. **Type the title of your WordPress MU site in the Site Title text box.**

   The title is what you would like your WordPress MU site to be called. You can edit this later, if you change your mind.

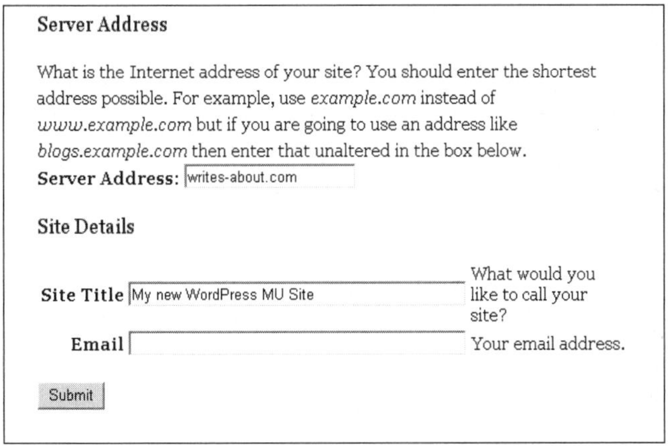

Figure 12-4:
Enter the
server
address
and other
identifying
information
for your site.

7. **Type your e-mail address in the Email text box.**

   This is the e-mail address where you want to receive all site-related information (such as contact information, notifications, and so on). Consider it the site administrator's contact e-mail address.

8. **Click the Submit button.**

   This puts the WordPress MU installation script to work, and you see a page with the message: Installation Finished! This page also has the login information you need for your new WordPress MU site (the username and password) — make note of that and save it someplace safe.

The login details for your new WordPress MU site are also e-mailed to you at the e-mail address that you provided in the previous steps. This e-mail contains your username and password so that you're able to log in to your new WordPress MU site.

Visit your new site by typing your domain name in your browser's address bar. You'll recognize the theme as the default Kubrick theme used by the regular WordPress software, as shown in Figure 12-5.

Figure 12-5:
The front page of your WordPress MU site after successful installation.

Using the login information given to you after installation (and in the e-mail), you can log in to your WordPress MU administration panel and start having a look around. Chapter 13 takes you through some of the important sections of the WordPress MU administration panel.

Giving Your New Blog Community a Test Run

You can do a quick test to make sure all your server and DNS configurations are working correctly. Just set up a test blog in your community and make sure it works correctly.

To set up a test blog, follow these steps:

1. **Type the URL of your new WordPress MU site in your browser's address bar.**

   This displays the front page of your new WordPress MU site (see Figure 12-6).

Figure 12-6:
Set up a test blog on your WordPress MU Site.

2. Click the Create a New Blog link.

This takes you to a new page (`http://yourdomain.com/wp-signup.php`, where *yourdomain.com* is your actual domain name). It should look something like mine in Figure 12-6.

3. Type the username of your choice in Username text box.

This is the name that will appear in the URL of the first blog in your WordPress MU community. The username appears in the URL in one of the following formats, depending on your settings: `http://username.yourdomain.com` if you've set up your WordPress MU to use subdomains or `http://yourdomain.com/username/` if you're using subdirectories.

4. Type your e-mail address in the Email Address text box.

This is the e-mail address that you would like to use for contact notifications on this blog. Also, your new blog password is sent to this e-mail address, so double-, triple-, and quadruple-check that you've typed it correctly (no typos!).

5. Click the Gimme a Blog! radio button.

There are actually two options here: Gimme a Blog! and Just a Username, Please. The second option reserves a username within the WordPress MU network of blogs on your site, but will not create a new blog.

6. Click the Next button.

This displays a new page with a confirmation of the new blog creation, along with a message that asks you to confirm your intentions to set up this new blog. Follow the directions in that e-mail and you'll receive another e-mail with the username and password for the blog you just created.

Check that the new blog displays correctly by typing its Internet address in your browser address bar. If all goes well, you should see your new blog displaying in your browser window. Kudos!

If all doesn't go well, see Table 12-1 for some common problems — along with their solutions — that users run into when installing and setting up WordPress MU on their Web servers. If you don't find a solution to your issue here, pay a visit to the WordPress MU support forum at `http://mu.wordpress.org` and ask the friendly people there if they can assist you with your particular problem.

Table 12-1	Common WordPress MU Installation Problems	
Error	*Common Cause*	*Possible Solution*
500 Internal Server Error	The `mod_rewrite` module isn't installed.	Go to the "Web server configurations for WordPress MU" section in this chapter to view the requirements for the `mod_rewrite` module. Double-check your `httpd.conf` file to make sure it contains the correct information; or ask your Web host to check that file for you, if you don't know how or don't have access to the `httpd.conf` file.
		If the correct information is in the `httpd.conf` file, contact your Web hosting provider to make sure the Apache `mod_rewrite` module is installed properly.
	`AllowOverride` is set incorrectly in the `<Directory>` section.	Go to the "Web server configurations for WordPress MU" section in this chapter and follow the instructions to set the `AllowOverride` option. The `<Directory>` section of your `httpd.conf` file should say: `AllowOverride FileInfo Options` — or even `AllowOverride All`.
		If you don't know how to edit, or don't have access to the `httpd.conf` file, contact your hosting provider to make sure it's set correctly.

(continued)

Table 12-1 *(continued)*

Error	Common Cause	Possible Solution
404 Page Cannot Be Found	The DNS wildcard isn't set up correctly.	Go to the "Web server configurations for WordPress MU" section in this chapter and follow the instructions for setting up DNS wildcards in your DNS configuration settings for subdomain use. If you do not know how to edit, or don't have access to, your DNS, contact your hosting provider to make sure it is set correctly.
	vhost is set up incorrectly.	In the `<VirtualHosts>` section of your configuration file, you should have the following: `SeverAlias *.your domain.com` where *yourdomain.com* is your actual domain name. If you don't know how to edit, or don't have access to the `httpd.conf` file, contact your hosting provider to make sure it's set correctly.
Error Establishing Connection to the Database	The MySQL database information is incorrect.	During the process of running the installation script, you provided the details of the MySQL database for this WordPress MU installation. If that information is incorrect, the connection to the database will fail. Double-check your MySQL database information in the `wp-config.php` file in your installation directory.

Error	Common Cause	Possible Solution
You didn't receive the confirmation e-mail after installation.	The e-mail might be filtered as spam or junk mail in your e-mail program.	Check your mail logs to see whether the e-mail is caught in spam or junk folders.
	You might have mistyped your e-mail address.	Log in to the WordPress MU Administration panel, click Options, and check the E-Mail Address field to edit the administrator e-mail address, if needed.

Troubleshooting and Bug Reporting

When troubleshooting installation problems, keep these things in mind:

- ✔ Read the `ReadMe.txt` file included in the installation files and make sure you've followed each step correctly.

- ✔ Check your `wp-config.php` file to make sure the database information is correct.

- ✔ Check the closed tickets at the WordPress MU Bug Tracking site at `http://trac.mu.wordpress.org/report/6`. You might find that someone else experienced the same issue you're having — along with a solution to the problem.

- ✔ Visit the WordPress MU Support Forum at `http://mu.wordpress.org` and search through the messages there to see if anyone else has experienced an issue similar to the one you're experiencing.

- ✔ If you're unable to solve your problem with the preceding methods, you can submit a bug report to the WordPress MU Bug Tracking site. Make sure you include the following information in your bug report:

  - Is your virtual host (vhost) true or false?

  - What is the path to your WordPress MU installation? (Did you install it in the root directory of your Web server or in its own folder?)

  - Is there anything in your error logs? Make a copy of the complete text of any message(s) that shows in your error logs. Include this text when requesting support.

  - Is the database information in your `wp-config.php` file correct?

  - Please make sure you mention the version number you're using.

If you don't include the basic information in your bug report, don't be surprised if you're redirected to this page: `http://trac.mu.wordpress.org/wiki/DebuggingWpmu`. This isn't meant to be unhelpful. The moderators of the list do want to help you; however, they need some specific information on your setup so that they can help you help yourself.

Chapter 13

Managing Your WordPress MU Community

*E*xcept for certain areas that I discuss in this chapter, the Administration panel for WordPress MU has several similar options and settings to the original WordPress software it was built on.

In this chapter, you discover the WordPress MU Administration panel in depth. This includes the configurations to set as the administrator of your WordPress blog, managing your network of bloggers, and installing, managing and using WordPress MU themes and plugins.

You can also use WordPress MU to manage and maintain your WordPress-powered Web site by taking advantage of all the WordPress features available in the WordPress.org software. You can use Part III of this book to review how you can manage your site using these features.

It's important to note that you should be familiar with the regular WordPress software available for download from Wordpress.org. Many aspects and concepts of WordPress MU are similar to the original software. WordPress MU is based on the original software, after all, and it isn't a good idea to jump into WordPress MU without first fully familiarizing yourself with the original WordPress software. Please don't say I didn't warn you.

Logging In to WordPress MU

When you log in to WordPress MU, you see the Administration panel, which is similar to the WordPress.org Administration panel that I discuss in Chapters 7 and 8. Along the top of the Administration panel, you see a row of menu tabs, as shown Figure 13-1. I discuss the following tabs in this chapter:

- ✔ Site Admin
- ✔ Plugins
- ✔ Presentation (Themes subtab only)

The rest of the Administration panel menu tabs have the same basic settings and options as the WordPress.org software. Although I do so love to quote and requote myself, I don't have the space to repeat it here, so you can find information on those options in Chapters 7 and 8 of this book.

Administration panel   Site Admin tab   Presentation tab   Plugins tab

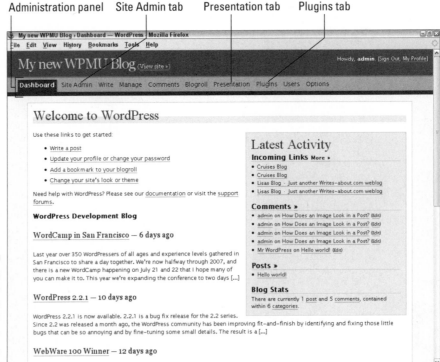

Figure 13-1:
The
WordPress
MU
Administra-
tion panel.

Exploring Your Site Admin Options in WordPress MU

One of the first things you want to do, after you install WordPress MU and log in, is to click the Site Admin tab on the Administration panel to display the Admin, Blogs, Users, Themes, Options, and Upgrade subtabs. This is where you set the user and administrative options for your WordPress MU blog. You won't need to use some of these options until you start to take new bloggers into your community; however, I cover them now so that you will be prepared for the onslaught of new blogger signups when it happens.

 Speaking of your new users, you don't want to miss the information provided in Chapter 14, where I talk about staying on top of WordPress MU news so that you can take care of your blogging community by providing the most current updates to it. A big part of keeping your community thriving is keeping your community happy and informed so that members can't find a reason to leave!

Performing searches on the Site Admin page

Click the Site Admin tab in the main menu and then click the Admin subtab to display the Admin page, shown in Figure 13-2. On this page, you can perform searches for users and blogs within your community by simply typing the name or keyword into one of the two text fields and clicking the associated button. Obviously, you won't perform this search if you don't have any users yet. However, this function is extremely useful when you do have a community of users who are keeping active blogs.

The Search Users function searches usernames and user e-mail addresses and provides you with return results accordingly. This means that if you search for the user *Lisa,* for instance, it will give you returns with any user that has the name *Lisa* in either the username or e-mail address for the blog — so you can get multiple returns when using one search term.

The Search Blogs feature allows you to input any keyword, and it will return any blog content within your community that contains your chosen keyword.

Admin subtab

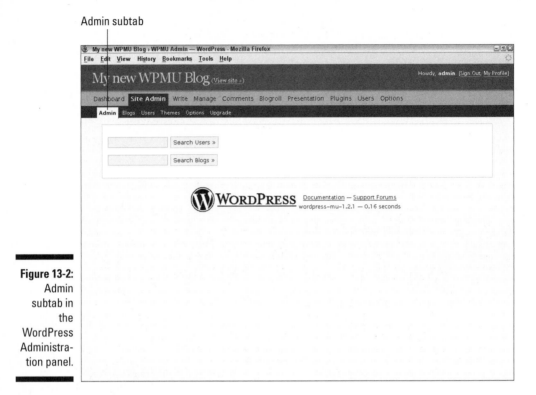

Figure 13-2:
Admin subtab in the WordPress Administration panel.

Managing all the blogs in your community

Click the Blogs subtab to display the Site Admin Blogs page, as shown in Figure 13-3. This page includes search tools that find blogs and bloggers, and a table with the names of all your blogs, blog IDs, and tons of other handy features that I cover in this section.

Searching for specific bloggers and blogs

At the top of the Site Admin Blogs page, you have the Search Blogs feature. Here, you can search for blogs by name, Blog ID, or IP Address. This is especially helpful if you have a large community and a user e-mails you with a problem or question he has on his blog. You can visit the Blogs page and pull up that particular blog pretty quickly by using the search feature available at the top.

To the right of the Search Blogs feature you see a heading called Blog Navigation with links underneath labeled Previous Blogs | | Next Blogs. The Site Admin Blogs page will display only 20 blogs, so if you have more than 20 blogs in your community, you can use the Blog Navigation links to navigate to the next page (by clicking Next Blogs) that lists out the next 20 blogs, and then use the Previous Blogs link to navigate back.

Managing individual blogs

Next, you see each blog listed by ID with various displays and options to the right of it. The display shows you the following information about each blog within your community:

- ✔ **ID:** Blog ID number
- ✔ **Blog Name:** The username associated with the blog
- ✔ **Last Updated:** The date the blog was last updated (or posted to)
- ✔ **Registered:** The date the blog was registered
- ✔ **Users:** The e-mail address associated with the user(s) of that blog
- ✔ **Actions:** Tools for managing individual blogs

The final column in the Blogs display is labeled Actions, and Table 13-1 describes those actions and how they can help you manage your blogging community users.

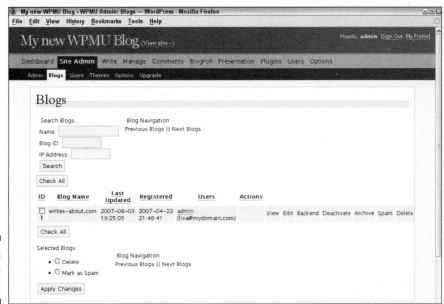

Figure 13-3:
The Blogs
page.

Table 13-1	Working with the Blog Administration Tools
Action	**What Happens when You Click It**
View	The user's blog opens in a new browser window, allowing you to view it.
Edit	Opens the Edit Blog page, which allows you to view and edit settings within the blogger's Administration panel. You use this more for diagnostic and troubleshooting purposes than for altering user settings for the user.
Backend	Opens the user's blog Administration panel, allowing you (the community administrator) to view the Administration panel as if you were the user. It's excellent for troubleshooting purposes.
Deactivate	Deactivates the user's blog but doesn't delete it. When you click the Deactivate link, you're given a chance to confirm that you're absolutely sure you wish to deactivate the blog. After you confirm it, the Deactivate link on the Blog page changes to Activate, allowing you (the community administrator) to reactivate the user and that user's blog at any time in the future. Visiting the user's blog after deactivation gives you a message that says, "This user has elected to delete their account and the content is no longer available."
Archive	Suspends the user's blog and deactivates it. When you click the Archive link, you're given a chance to confirm that you're absolutely sure you wish to archive the blog. After you confirm it, the Archive link on the Blog pages changes to Unarchive, allowing you (the community administrator) to unarchive the user and his blog at any time. Visiting the user's blog after archiving it gives you a message that says, "This blog has been archived or suspended."
Spam	Marks the user and that user's blog as spam and archives/suspends it. When you click the Spam link, you're given a chance to confirm that you're absolutely sure you wish to mark the blog as spam. After you confirm it, the Spam link on the Blog page changes to Not Spam, allowing you (the community administrator) to mark it as Not Spam at any time.
Delete	Deletes the user's blog. When you click the Delete link, you're given two chances to confirm that you're absolutely sure you really want to delete the blog. After you've confirmed it, *you can't undo this action.* This does not delete the user's account, however; the user can create new blogs with his or her existing account.

When you (or a user) delete a blog within the system, that action can't be undone. It's a permanent action, so be absolutely, 100-percent positive that you really, really want to delete the blog before you confirm the action. This is why the WordPress MU software provides not one, but two, confirmation messages, forcing you to think twice before you act.

Getting rid of multiple blogs at one time

Notice, in Figure 13-3, the check box to the left of each blog listing. You use these check boxes in conjunction with the Selected Blogs tool (shown in Figure 13-4) that you see beneath the table of blogs and bloggers. Use this tool to delete or mark as spam multiple blogs at one time.

To use the Selected Blogs tool, select the check box to the left of each of the blogs you wish to edit. Then select either the Delete or Mark as Spam radio button and click the Apply Changes button to, well . . . apply the changes.

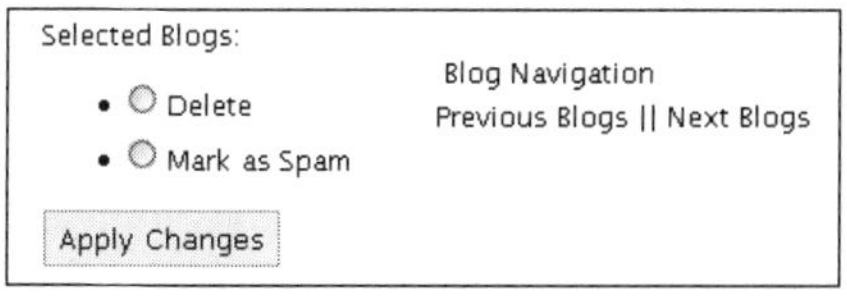

Figure 13-4:
You can delete multiple blogs or mark multiple blogs as spam with just a couple of clicks.

Selected Blogs:

Blog Navigation
Previous Blogs || Next Blogs

- ○ Delete
- ○ Mark as Spam

Apply Changes

Adding a blog to the community

Finally, at the bottom of the Blogs page (as shown in Figure 13-5), you find that you can manually add blogs to the system. This feature is especially helpful if you want to create your own blogs within the community, or if you want to set up a blog for a friend and save him the trouble of going through the necessary motions of creating a blog on his own. (We all have friends like that, don't we?)

In the Add Blog area of the Blogs page, take the following steps to create a blog in this section:

1. **Type a username in the Blog Address text box.**

2. **Type the title of the blog in the Blog Title text box.**

3. **Type the user's e-mail address in the Admin Email text box.**

4. Click Add Blog.

This reloads the Blogs page, and you now see the blog you just set up in the list of blogs.

If the e-mail address you give for the administrator of the new blog doesn't already exist in the database, WordPress MU creates a new user for this account. An e-mail confirmation with the link to activate the blog is sent to that e-mail address, followed by a second e-mail with the login information (username and password).

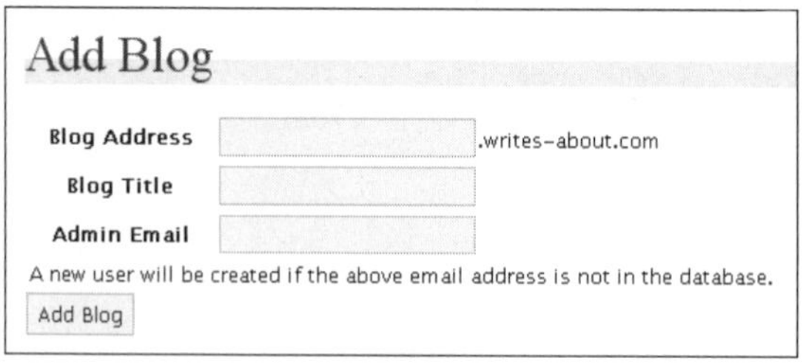

Figure 13-5:
WordPress
MU allows
you to
create blogs
within the
Administra-
tion panel.

Add Blog

Blog Address	[ ] .writes–about.com
Blog Title	[ ]
Admin Email	[ ]

A new user will be created if the above email address is not in the database.

[Add Blog]

Editing the settings of one blog at a time

As I mention in Table 13-1, you can edit some very specific details and settings on a per-blog basis by using the Edit link on the Blogs page. Some of the options that are available don't really require editing, and other settings are already set by the user in her own Administration panel. This Edit link gives you a glance at what a user's blog settings are and allows you to make some modifications to the user's blog configurations.

Figure 13-6 shows you the Edit Blog page. Refer to Table A-1, in the appendix of this book, for many more details on the multiple settings you can look at or configure.

On the right side of the Edit Blog page, you see two additional headers:

✔ **Blog Themes:** This is a list of available themes for this blog. Each theme has a check box to the right that you can select to enable the theme for that blog, or leave the box unchecked to indicate that the theme is not available for that blog's use.

✔ **Blog Users:** This is a list of current users on this blog. Each user has an Edit link to the right. Clicking that Edit link takes you to the user's profile page, where you can edit the different options for the user's profile, such as e-mail address and password. (See Chapter 7 for more information about user profiles.)

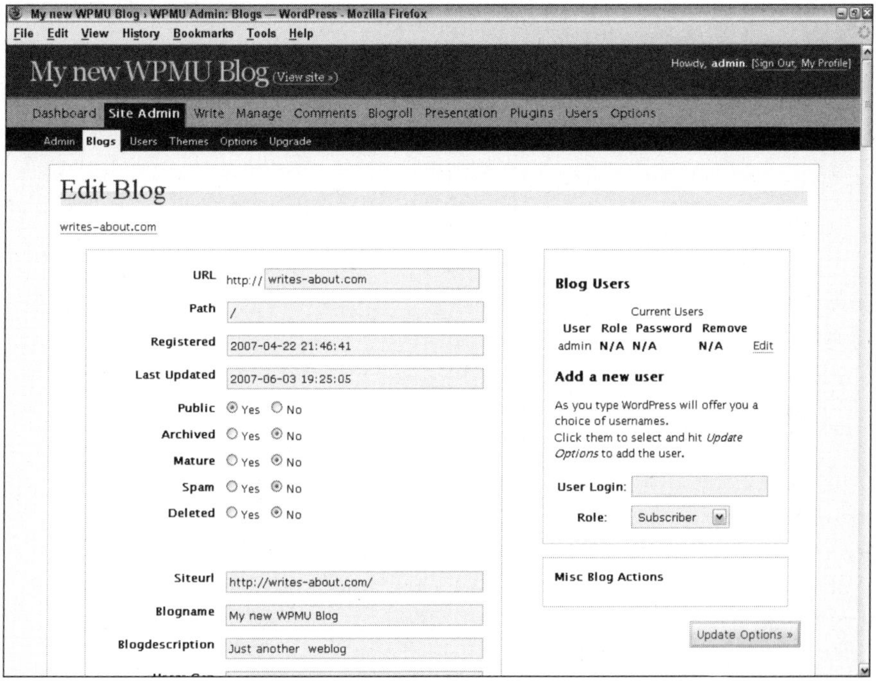

Figure 13-6:
Edit
individual
blog
settings by
clicking the
Edit link on
the Blogs
page.

Managing community users

Click the Users subtab to display the Users page, shown in Figure 13-7. Here, you can view the list of user accounts within your WordPress MU community and manage their accounts. The Blogs page, discussed in the previous section, deals with editing and managing specific blogs; however, the Users section deals with managing specific users (who can have multiple blogs listed for their account).

Searching users

At the top of the Users page, you can search for specific users in your community by using the search box that appears at the top under the Search Users heading. You can find the steps for using this search feature in the "Searching for specific bloggers and blogs" section, earlier in this chapter. The Users page lists 20 users; if your community has more than 20, you can use the User Navigation links to the right of the search box to navigate to the next page of users.

Figure 13-7:
Manage
users in the
WordPress
Administra-
tion panel.

List of users

Beneath the Search function, all of the users within your WordPress MU blog community are listed, in order of ID. This user list provides you with the following information about your users:

- ✔ **ID:** When new users sign up for an account in your WordPress MU community, they are automatically assigned a unique ID number that you see in the ID column at registration.

- ✔ **Login:** This column includes the username (login name) of each member of your blog community.

- ✔ **Email:** This is the e-mail address they used when they signed up for a blog within your community.

- ✔ **Name:** This is the user's name.

- ✔ **Registered:** This is the date the user registered.

- ✔ **Blogs:** This is the list of current blogs this user has in your blog community. Users can have multiple blogs under the same account (same username and e-mail address).

Two additional tools appear to the right of the user list, and you can use them to perform these functions:

- ✔ **Edit:** Click this link, and you can edit the user's account details and profile — including the password for this user.

- ✔ **Delete:** Click this link and you delete this user from your blog community. Be careful — this action also deletes all of the blogs that this user has.

Notice the check box to the left of each user ID. Use these check boxes in conjunction with the Selected Users tool below them to apply the following edits to multiple user accounts:

- ✔ **Delete:** This deletes the selected users from your blog community. Be careful with this action; it deletes the users' blogs from your community, as well.

- ✔ **Mark as Spammers:** This marks the selected users as spammers. Not only does this delete the user accounts and any blogs associated with those users, it also disallows a user with the same e-mail address from registering a new blog within your community.

To apply these changes to the selected users, you must first select the check box for each user you'd like to apply the action to. Then select the function (the Delete or Mark as Spammers radio button) and click the Apply Changes button when you're done.

Add a user

At the bottom of the Users page, you see the Add User section (as shown in Figure 13-8), where you can add new users to your WordPress MU community.

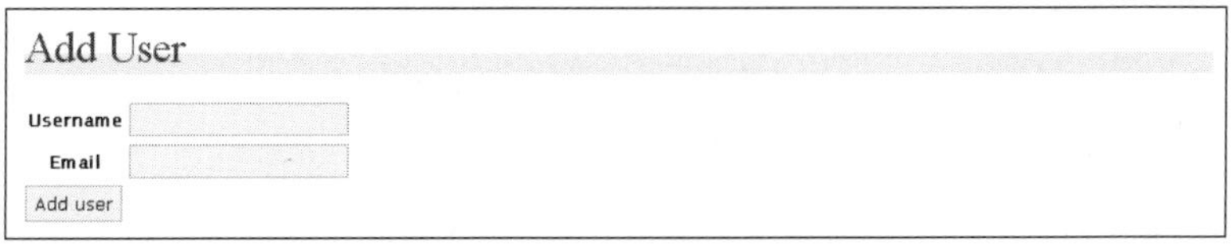

Figure 13-8:
Add a user
to your
WordPress
MU blog
community
manually.

Maybe you have a reluctant friend who you've been begging and pleading with to join your new community. She keeps promising you that she will — yet days go by, and you're not seeing her user registration come through your administration e-mail. (Mom, are you listening?) Well, fix her up with a registration right this very minute! To register for a user, do the following:

1. **Type the desired username in the Username text box.**

2. **Type the user's e-mail address in the Email text box.**

3. **Click the Add User button.**

   The page reloads with an Options Saved message at the top. You now see the new user in the list of users on this page.

Okay, so the new user will receive a confirmation e-mail, and you do have to rely on the fact that your friend will actually confirm the registration you so graciously performed for her. But at least you're one step closer to having your best friend on board!

Installing Themes for Your Users

This section of this chapter answers the burning question of how you can provide a variety of different themes within your WordPress MU blogging community so that your bloggers have choices as to which themes they'd like to use. As I mention in several chapters of this book, literally thousands of free WordPress themes are available for use on both personal blogs and WordPress MU setups. Finding the ones that best suit you and your community takes a bit of time and research.

Not all WordPress themes are created equal. You will find some free WordPress themes that weren't created with WordPress MU in mind and therefore don't work with WordPress MU. So don't make assumptions. It's good practice to test every theme you include in your WordPress MU setup.

While several great themes are available for WordPress MU, here are four that are guaranteed to work for you and are already very popular with many WordPress bloggers:

- **Cutline:** `http://cutline.tubetorial.com`
- **Tarski:** `http://tarskitheme.com`
- **Farms Really Big Theme Pack:** `http://wpmudev.org/project/Farms-Really-Big-Theme-Pack/`
- **MegaPress:** `http://wpmudev.org/project/WPMU-Theme:-MegaPress/`

Figure 13-9 shows the Site Themes page within the Site Admin section of the Administration panel, without additional themes installed, aside from the default themes provided and packaged with the WordPress MU installation:

- WordPress Classic
- WordPress MU Default
- WordPress Default

After you install a few new themes, you'll see those themes show up on the Site Themes page. You must activate each theme to make it available for use by your community of bloggers. To activate a theme, take these steps:

1. **Select Yes in the Active column to the left of the theme name on the Site Themes page.**

Figure 13-9:
Displaying
available
themes in
your
WordPress
MU
Administra-
tion panel.

2. **Click the Update Themes button.**

   This reloads the page with an Options Saved message at the top.

Uploading and installing themes

The process of uploading and installing themes for a WordPress MU community blog is really no different than doing it for a regular, self-hosted WordPress
blog using the software available for download at WordPress.org (And I give
instructions for doing that in Part III of this book.) Here's a quick overview of
the process:

1. **Download the desired theme from the theme Web site.**

2. **Unpack (unzip) the theme files onto your computer.**

   See Chapter 6 for more specific instructions on unpacking zip files,
   including information on the software you use to accomplish this.

3. **Connect to your Web server via FTP.**

   See Chapter 6 for information if you need more information about using
   FTP.

4. **Upload the theme folder to** `/wp-content/themes/`.

5. **Log in to your WordPress MU Administration panel.**

6. **Click Site Admin and then click Themes.**

   This displays the Site Themes page, with a list of available themes currently installed on your WordPress MU site.

7. **Select Yes or No in the Active column to the left of the theme name. (Refer to Figure 13-9.)**

8. **Click the Update Themes button at the bottom of the page.**

   This reloads the page with an Options Saved message at the top.

From here, you (and your users) can see the theme by clicking the Presentations tab on the Administration panel (see Figure 13-10). You can then activate that theme by clicking the theme's name, or the screenshot of the theme if it has one.

Figure 13-10: I installed the Tarski theme and activated it in my MU Administration panel.

Testing themes for your WordPress MU community

It's probably — no, scratch that — it *is* a great idea to test themes on your own blog before you activate the theme for anyone in your blog community to use. To accomplish this, follow the steps that follow in the "Enabling themes on a per-blog basis" section and activate it for your own blog first. Test the functions and the different way it behaves. For example, test the comments display, links display, how the formatting looks for the different widgets you have available, and so on. Fully test the theme on your own site, and then when you've given it your stamp of approval, go ahead and activate it for your user community.

Enabling themes on a per-blog basis

Say you have one theme that you want to enable for only one blog in the system. In other words, you don't want all of the blogs in your community to be able to use it — just one blog only. To accomplish this, follow these steps:

1. **Select No in the Active column next to the theme on the Site Themes page. (Refer to Figure 13-9.)**

   This ensures that no other user within the community (except the community [WordPress MU] administrator) can see or use this theme.

2. **Click the Site Admin tab on the Administration panel.**

   This loads the Admin page, and you see the available subtabs in the navigation menu.

3. **Click the Blogs subtab. (Refer to Figure 13-5.)**

   This loads the Blogs page, where you see a list of all the blogs within your WordPress MU network.

4. **Click the Edit link to the right of the desired blog.**

   This loads the Edit Blog page. (Refer to Figure 13-6.) You now see the Blog Themes section at the top right.

5. **Select the check box next to the theme name.**

   This enables that theme for this user.

6. **Click the Update Options button at the bottom of the page.**

   This reloads the page with an Options Saved message at the top.

Configuring site options

The very next tab over in the Site Admin subpanel is Options. Click the Options subtab, and you see the Site Options page, which gives you options such as operational settings (for example, the site name, administrator e-mail address, the text of the welcome e-mail that gets sent to new users, and others) that you can set for your WordPress MU blog setup, as shown in Figure 13-11. The options are many, and the following steps take you through each setting and what it does:

1. **Type the name of your site in the Site Name text box.**

2. **Type your e-mail address in the Site Admin Email text box.**

   You use this e-mail address to send site registration notices, password reminders, and support e-mails to the users within your WordPress MU network. Just a suggestion — make it an easy, generic one like `support@ yourdomain.com`. You want to keep in mind that this e-mail address is used to send out notices to your users, so some of those users may e-mail you back at that e-mail address seeking support or assistance.

Figure 13-11:
The Site
Options
page.

3. **In the Welcome Email text box, type the text of the e-mail you'd like WordPress MU to automatically send to new users.**

   Alternatively, you can leave this area alone and use the default text provided for you.

   There are a few variables you can use in this e-mail that aren't explained on the Options page:

   - *SITE_NAME:* Inserts the name of your WordPress MU site.
   - *BLOG_URL:* Inserts the URL of the new member's blog.
   - *USERNAME:* Inserts the new member's username.
   - *PASSWORD:* Inserts the new member's password.
   - *BLOG_URLwplogin.php:* Inserts the hyperlinked login URL for the new member's blog.
   - *SITE_URL:* Inserts the hyperlinked URL for your WordPress MU site.

4. **In the First Post text box, type the text that you want to appear in the first post on every blog that's created in your blogging community.**

   You can use this area to provide useful information about your site and services. This also serves as a nice guide for new users, as they can view that post in their Administration panels and see how it was entered. You can also use the variables mentioned in Step 3 to have WordPress MU automatically add some information for you.

5. **In the Banned Names text box, type the usernames that you would like banned from your network.**

   If you enter more than one name, make sure to separate the names with spaces.

   By default, WordPress MU bans a few names — such as www, web, root, admin, main, invite, and administrator — from registration. For good reason, you don't want a random user to register a username such as admin because the URL to that user's blog would look like this: `http://admin.yourdomain.com`. A URL like that would give people the false impression that this individual holds some position of authority in your network.

6. **In the Limited Email Registrations text box, type the domain names of the e-mail addresses you want to limit registration to.**

   This option allows you to limit new user registration to only certain domains. People who try to register with e-mail domains that aren't on this list can't register. To keep registration open to everyone, regardless of their domain, leave this field blank.

7. **Type the domain names you would like to ban (restrict) from registering.**

   Any domains you enter here will not be allowed to register.

Enter one domain per line. If you don't wish to restrict any domains, leave this field blank.

Some MU administrators ban free e-mail services, such as Hotmail.com, because doing so cuts down on the amount of *spam* (illegitimate) registrations.

8. In the Blog Upload Space text box, type the hard drive space allotment you want to give each blog.

This space allotment is given in megabytes (MB). The default number is 10. This is the amount of hard drive space you want to give each user to store her files.

9. In the Upload File Types text box, type the file types you will allow users to upload.

Any file types that don't appear in this list aren't allowed.

By default, WordPress MU gives you the following file types: JPG, `.jpeg`, PNG, GIF, MP3, MOV, AVI, WMV, MIDI, `.mid`, PDF.

10. In the Max Upload File Size text box, type the number for the maximum file size allowed.

This number is given in kilobytes (K). The default file size is 1500K. This means that a user cannot upload a file that's larger than 1500K. Adjust this number as you see fit.

11. In the Site Admins text box, type the usernames allowed for site administrators.

The usernames in this text box are allowed to log in to the main blog and administer the site.

The default is admin. Separate names with spaces.

12. Choose Default from the Default Language drop-down menu in the Site Wide Settings section.

This sets the default language for the entire site. Individual blog owners may override this setting in their Administration panels.

WordPress MU doesn't currently support any language other than English for your WordPress MU and your users' Administration panels. You can, however, visit the WordPress MU Forums and perform a search for language packs that have been developed by community users. With luck, you'll find just the language pack that you need here: `http://mu.wordpress.org/forums/tags.php?tag=language`.

13. In the Menus section, select the Plugins text box.

This makes the Plugins page visible. If leave this deselected, you won't see the Plugins tab on the WordPress MU Administration panel.

14. Click the Update Settings button at the bottom of the Site Options page.

This reloads the page with an Options Saved confirmation message at the top.

Upgrading WordPress MU

The final tab on the Site Admin subpanel is Upgrade, as shown in Figure 13-12, and you can use this page when you upgrade the WordPress MU software. Chapter 14 discusses the importance of staying informed of news and updates of the WordPress MU software project so that you can stay on top of new version releases when they happen. When you upgrade the WordPress MU software, you also need to upgrade the user blogs, and that's what the Upgrade subtab is for. It allows you to run the upgrade script for every user blog in your community with just one click. Depending on the size of your community, this could take a very long time. Check out Chapter 14 for step-by-step instructions for upgrading your WordPress MU site.

Figure 13-12:
Upgrading individual user blogs is as easy as a single click on the Upgrade Site link.

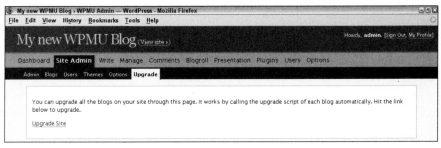

Using Plugins with WordPress MU

When thinking of using plugins with your WordPress MU site, you need to think in two directions:

✔ **Which plugins will you install for all blogs in your community?**

You install these plugins for *all* blogs in your community.

✔ **Which plugins will you install for your bloggers to use only if they want to?**

These plugins will be installed. Users can activate them within their own Administration panels, if they choose to, or leave them inactive.

Read Chapter 10 if you need someone to walk you through the basic mechanics of finding, downloading, unpacking, uploading, installing, and activating plugins for WordPress. Chapter 10 focuses on plugins for the self-hosted version of WordPress, but the same basic concepts apply to WordPress MU plugins; the only difference is the location you place your plugin files on your Web server. The location of the files determines whether it's a plugin for the overall community to use or a plugin for individual blog users to activate if they want.

Five great plugins for WordPress MU (mu-plugins)

I've tried and tested each of these great plugins for WordPress MU:

✔ **WPMU Anti Splog:** This plugin blocks a user from registering a new blog in your WordPress MU network if her IP is black-listed as a spammer on Spamhaus.org. (You can download it at `http://wpmudev.org/project/WPMU-Anti-Splog`.)

✔ **Theme Stats:** This is a helpful plugin that allows you, the site administrator, to see the statistics on which WordPress themes are in use throughout your WordPress MU network. (You can download it at `http://wpmudev.org/project/Theme-Stats`.)

✔ **Z-Space Upload Quotas:** This handy plugin allows you, the site administrator, to set the upload quota on a per-user basis. This also allows the users to see their space usage in the Dashboard page of their Administration panels. (You can download it at `http://wpmudev.org/project/Z-Space-Upload-Quotas`.)

✔ **MU Admin Bar:** When logged in, users see all the important WordPress Administration panel tabs across the tops of their blogs, making it easy to access the Administration section of their accounts. (You can download it at `http://wpmudev.org/project/MU-Admin-Bar`.)

✔ **Widgets MU:** This plugin allows you to use WordPress widgets in a WordPress MU environment. (You can download it at `http://wpmudev.org/project/Widgets-MU`.)

The next section assumes that you understand the concepts of plugin installation and activation from Chapter 10. If you need to brush up on that knowledge, now would be a good time to do it.

Plugins for the overall MU site

In the self-hosted WordPress software setup, administrators upload plugins into the `/wp-content/plugins` folder. The difference with WordPress MU is this: When you want to install and activate plugins that you'll activate for your entire community, you upload the plugins into the `/wp-content/mu-plugins/` folder. These plugins won't show up in your WordPress Administration panel under the Plugins tab, and *you don't need to activate them.*

The mere act of uploading plugins to the `/wp-content/mu-plugins/` folder activates them automatically, so you probably want to be selective about what plugins you decide to install into this folder. Every plugin you place in this folder is loaded and executes on every blog within your community. So be *very* picky about what you place here.

Plugins for your users to choose from

The second type of plugin installation you can perform on your WordPress MU site is one that installs plugins but doesn't activate them. Instead, each user within your community has the choice as to whether she wishes to activate and use that plugin. Members are given this choice on their Administration panels under the Plugins tab, where they can activate only those plugins they choose. (Figure 13-13 shows the Plugins Management page with a list of the plugins I installed on my WordPress MU site.)

Instead of uploading these plugins into the `/wp-content/mu-plugins/` folder, as in the previous section, you install these plugins into the `/wp-content/plugins/` folder.

In order to give your users access to activate and use these plugins, you do need to make sure you complete the following steps in your WordPress Administration panel:

1. **Click the Site Admin tab on the Administration panel.**

   This loads the Site Admin page.

2. **Click the Options subtab.**

   This loads the Site Options page.

Figure 13-13: Plugins installed in the wp-content/plugins folder allow users to activate them, if they want.

3. **Scroll to the bottom of the page to the Menus section.**

4. **Select the Plugins check box.**

   This enables the Plugins menu on the Administration panel.

5. **Click the Update Options button.**

   This reloads the page with an Options Saved confirmation message at the top. You now see the Plugins tab on the Administration panel.

Completing those steps makes the Plugins tab visible in each of your user's Administration panel menus — including yours as the site administrator — allowing your users to click the Plugins tab to view and activate the plugins that you've made available to them.

Chapter 14

Maintaining WordPress MU

● ●

In This Chapter

▶ Real-world perspectives

▶ Staying current with MU news and updates

▶ Upgrading your WordPress MU site

▶ Managing spam and splogs

● ●

Your decision to run and maintain a WordPress MU blogging community comes with the responsibility of keeping your users happy with your service. When you are the manager of an online community, your online life, as you know it, changes because you're responsible for the correct functioning and display of other user blogs. WordPress MU is *not* a "set it and forget it" application that runs itself. It requires your tender loving care and attention to keep it running.

Scared yet?

Good! You're still with me! This chapter covers some important aspects of managing a WordPress MU community, going beyond just the necessary knowledge needed to install and use the software. These aspects include keeping up-to-date on the latest news that comes from the WordPress MU developers, new plugins, old plugins that have been updated, and any ideas, tips, and tricks that will benefit your users. It's a lot to keep up with. However, it's worth it if you're planning on running a successful community that gives your users a satisfying experience with your services.

Getting a Real-World MU Perspective

I had the fortunate opportunity to catch up with Andrew Billits while writing this book. Andrew runs the WPMUDEV Web site (shown in Figure 14-1) at `http://wpmudev.org`, which is a directory of plugins, themes, and just about anything related to WordPress MU. Here, MU users can share tips, tricks, and hacks they've come across.

Along with his business partner, James Farmer, Andrew also runs the Edublogs WordPress MU development and hosting company. Edublogs, which you can find online at `http://edublogs.org`, is a large WordPress MU community that caters to the educators. Andrew's WPMUDEV site is a directory of plugins, themes, and just about anything related to WordPress MU.

Regarding the overall size of the WordPress MU community, Andrew gave me some statistics for WPMUDEV that he started recording in April 2005. He reported total downloads of 76,348, noting that the data for individual files had been logged for only the last 6 months, which means if you add every download for each file, you have 12,000 average monthly hits to the site. Andrew cautions that he certainly wouldn't take those numbers to the bank, but it does give an idea as to the size of the WordPress MU community. At this time, the official WordPress MU site hasn't given out the actual statistics on the number of WordPress MU downloads.

Obviously, WordPress MU is an emerging star in the multi-user blogging community. I spoke with Andrew on some of the challenges faced with running a large MU community, the advantages of having a multi-user blogging community, and some of his favorite themes and plugins that he uses to help make his community top notch. Considering that he was in the middle of moving (he was literally sitting on a box while answering my questions), you can tell that this is a guy who is passionate about what he does!

Figure 14-1: WPMUDEV is directory information related to WordPress MU.

Here are some of the highlights from my talk with Andrew regarding what he feels are the pros and cons of using WordPress MU:

- ✔ **Lack of expertise:** Whereas small communities are fairly easy to maintain, the large ones pose difficulties. Having 35,000 accounts requires dedicated equipment, and if you're not a Linux expert who is thoroughly familiar with Apache, MySQL, and PHP, you'll have problems. Andrew estimates that he spends 50 percent of his time helping people manage large WordPress MU communities.

- ✔ **Lack of proper support:** What most people don't realize is that you're going to have glitches when managing a large WordPress MU site. Each site owner is responsible for handling support for his users, as well as managing feedback and troubleshooting problems. With WordPress MU, there is no built-in method for handling support, so you have to make up your own methods — whether it's through use of e-mail, an online help desk, forums, and so on.

- ✔ **Money, money, money:** Be prepared to financially support your WordPress MU community because bandwidth and server costs can get pretty steep if your community grows large.

- ✔ **Advantages over WordPress.com:** The advantage is that you can tailor WordPress MU to fit a specific group, or niche. A good example of this is the Digital Photography Blogs site (which you can find at `http://dpblogs.com`) — or even the site that Andrew runs with his partner, James, at Edublogs (which you can find at `http://edublogs.org`). WordPress.com is nice, but it's a generic blog provider. WordPress MU lets you custom fit the community to you and your users' needs.

- ✔ **Time investment:** Andrew manages the servers for his large WordPress MU site, fixes bugs, and programs code for new features. His partner James handles all the user interaction. Andrew states that he easily spends 50 percent of his time maintaining the entire Edublogs community. What most people don't realize is that a blog community is a 24/7 operation. If a user needs help trying to figure something out, she doesn't necessarily want to wait for you to wake up in the morning and send a reply.

- ✔ **User support versus maintenance:** Andrew states that he learned pretty quickly that blog users are a pretty savvy bunch, and if you provide them with how-to articles and keep them informed of current issues, they can pretty much handle themselves. Andrew and James currently spend about an hour a day taking care of support issues. The rest of the time is spent maintaining the backend of the WordPress MU environment.

- ✔ **Plugins and themes:** While Andrew does a fair amount of development for his WordPress MU community — creating custom plugins of his own, rather than using already existing ones — he does use plugins that are available to the general public. He uses the Anarchy Media Player plugin and SpamKarma 2, both of which are currently available for download at the WPMUDEV.org Web site. Andrew prefers WordPress themes — such as Cutline, by Chris Pearson — that are clean and clutter free. (See Chapter 17 for information on the Cutline theme.)

I want to send big thanks to Andrew for his time and the responses he provided. I think it's important for anyone considering starting a WordPress MU blog community to approach it in a pragmatic way. You need to be realistic about your expectations of the product, the amount of time you have to dedicate to your project, and any financial concerns that you may face for your MU project.

Being in the Know

One of the most important things you can do as a WordPress MU site administrator is to keep up-to-date on recent news that comes out of the WordPress MU development community. Your users are counting on you to keep the software running and current, as well as provide them with the latest and greatest tools for their blogging experience. This is a challenge, and I'm going to say something now that you need to reread a few times to make sure it sticks in your grey matter:

> **When you find a good WordPress MU resource site, bookmark it and check it often!**

Did you read that twice? Really good WordPress MU resource sites are somewhat hard to come by, as there are precious few sites on the Web dedicated to the software. I provide a few resource sites in this chapter; however, bookmarking them in your browser isn't enough. You need to take whatever steps necessary to make sure you get new information as it comes out. The vital pieces of information you're looking for are:

- New releases of the WordPress MU software so you know when to upgrade.

- Information about any security bugs or new vulnerabilities found — and what security patches, if any, are released.

- Updates to the WordPress MU plugins or themes you're currently using in your community.

I offer you the following recommendations on how you can get updates on the latest news:

- Subscribe to its RSS feed, if the WordPress MU resource site has one.

- Subscribe to its newsletter, if the WordPress MU resource site has one.

- Subscribe to any mailing lists the WordPress MU resource site has available.

- Get to know the guru behind the WordPress MU site of your choice and rent a room at her home and offer to do housekeeping chores in exchange for MU tips.

- I'm really just joking on that last point.

Table 14-1 gives you a start with some good WordPress MU resources on the Web.

Table 14-1	WordPress MU Resources on the Web		
Name of Resource	*Type of Resource*	*Where to Find It*	*How to Get Updates*
WordPress MU Support Forum	Support forums for users. Support is provided by volunteer members.	`http://mu.wordpress.org/forums`	Register as a user. Visit the site regularly. Subscribe to the RSS feeds for the tags (categories) that interest you.
WordPress MU Site	You'll find the latest version of MU available for download and some FAQs on the software.	`http://mu.wordpress.org`	Visit the site regularly.
Donncha O. Caoimh	Donncha is the lead developer for WordPress MU.	`http://ocaoimh.ie`	Subscribe to his WordPress category RSS feed. Visit his site regularly.
WPMUDEV.org	You'll find plugins, themes, tips, tricks, and hacks here.	`http://wpmudev.org`	Visit the site regularly.
WordPress Multi-User Trac	A collection of assistance files and FAQs for your MU installation.	`http://trac.mu.wordpress.org/wiki`	Visit the site regularly.
WordPress Multi-User Trac Tickets	Tickets and problems submitted to the Trac and ongoing discussions by users and developers	`http://trac.mu.wordpress.org/report/1`	Subscribe to the RSS feed. Visit the site regularly.
Technorati - WordPress MU Tag	Technorati collects blog feeds from all over the Web and sorts them into tags (or categories).	`http://technorati.com/tag/wordpress+mu`	Subscribe to the RSS feed for the WordPress MU tag to find out what other users are saying about it.

When using the WordPress MU Support Forums at `http://mu.wordpress.org/forums`, keep in mind that all of the users you find there are volunteers who give their time to the support forums as a way of giving back to a project that they are passionate about. Do yourself and the volunteers on the forum a huge favor: Use the search function before you submit your question. More often than not, your question has already been asked and discussed previously in the forums, and you'll most likely find the answer you seek by searching the forums first. Also remember that the support forum for the WordPress.org software is *not* the place to be asking questions about the WordPress MU software. Likewise, the support forums for WordPress.com are not the place to submit your requests for support for WordPress MU. I know it's confusing. However, make sure you're in the right forum before you start asking questions. Oh — and *please* and *thank you* go a very, very long way with the forum crowd.

Upgrading WordPress MU

Occasionally, Donncha O. Caoimh, the lead developer for WordPress MU, releases an upgrade for the software. Typically, he makes those announcements on his personal blog, so that's definitely an RSS feed that you'll want to subscribe to. The WordPress MU developers don't release new versions as frequently as the WordPress.org software (which is *very* frequent). However, when they do, it's important for you to schedule a time to upgrade your system and give your users some warning as to when you'll be performing the upgrade so that they can expect to experience a bit of system down time.

The upgrade process is similar to the installation process, except you don't have to set up the DNS or vhost because that part is already completed. The process of upgrading involves replacing the program files on your Web server with the new, upgraded program files from WordPress MU.

It is extremely important to back up your database before proceeding with an upgrade — using phpMyAdmin, or whichever tool your Web hosting provider gives you, to make a full backup of your WordPress MU database.

As long as you've backed up, you can proceed with the upgrade.

The steps to upgrade are as follows:

1. **Download the WordPress MU software.**

    a. Visit the WordPress MU Web site at `http://mu.wordpress.org`.

    b. Click the Download link on the menu at the top of the page.

    c. Click either the Download.zip or Download.tar.gz link to download the files to your computer.

2. **Unpack (unzip) the files into a folder on your computer.**

   See Chapter 6 for information on unpacking files using decompression programs such as WinZip, WinRar, and so on.

3. **Upload the files to your Web server — making absolutely sure you don't overwrite or delete the original** `wp-config.php` **file!**

   Connect your FTP client to your Web server and open the folder where you originally installed WordPress MU. (This is the same directory that contains the `wp-config.php` file.)

4. **Open the** `htaccess.dist` **file.**

       a. Compare this file to the old `.htaccess` file saved on your server.

       b. If there are any new lines in the `htaccess.dist` file that aren't in the old `.htaccess` file, copy them from the htaccess.dist file to the `.htaccess` file.

       c. The text `BASE/` should be replaced with the path to your own Web site.

5. **Upgrade the MySQL database of each blog.**

       a. Log in to your WordPress MU Administration panel.

       b. Click the Site Admin tab on the Administration panel.

       c. Click the Upgrade subtab.

       d. Click the Upgrade Site link.

       e. Wait for the script to finish loading.

       You know it's finished when you see the All Done! message at the top of the page.

Leave a note for your users

Before and during an upgrade, let your users know what's going on behind the scenes by using a special WordPress MU plugin developed by Thunder Lounge. (The plugin is available for download at `http://thunder lounge.com/word-press/plugins/ mu-dashboard-notes.html`.) With this plugin, you can leave notes for your users that they'll see whenever they log in to their own WordPress blogs in your community. The notes appear in the Administration panel on the Dashboard page, and you can update your users on things such as planned system maintenance and upgrades, new themes and plugins you've added to the system, and new services you've provided for your users.

Fighting Spam and Splogs

Along with providing your users with great customer service, you need to control spam within your community. In a WordPress MU community, spam comes in two forms:

- Comment spam on user blogs.
- Splog spam with new user signups. (See the "What on earth is a splog?" sidebar for a definition.)

Fighting spam in your WordPress MU community does require the use of a plugin . . . or two, or three. It depends, really, on how bad the spam problem is. Trust me when I say that spam will, eventually, become a very large problem for your community because no WordPress blogging system is immune to spam problems. Your community does not even need to be very large, or very active. The whole goal for spammers is to get their links and advertisements published, live on the Internet, and your free blogging community that provides free sign-ups that can be done within mere minutes are like a Petri dish for spammers. You may as well cover all your anti-spam bases from day one to make sure your community is as protected as it can get.

Preventing splog signups

The dark side of the blogosphere is filled with users trying to *game the system* (trick it) by publishing fake blogs in hopes of earning money through advertising and/or page rank from Google. Upon first glance, these blogs look like the real thing. They are set up to look like blogs, are designed like blogs, and have all the features of blogs (including RSS feeds, categories, archives, and so on). However, some of these blogs have no content at all. Or, if they do have content, it's usually content that is stolen from other blogs through a method called *scraping*.

Scraping is the practice of stealing content from Web sites and blogs in order to fill a blog with what looks like original content. Some of the scraping techniques actually grab the content right from the Web sites; other techniques grab the content from the RSS feeds published by the targeted blogs. Both techniques are fully automated processes resulting in the creation of full-fledged blogs with posts that the splog owner barely had to lift a finger to create.

Aside from the obvious copyright violations going on with these splog sites, the sploggers are gaming the search engines, tricking them into believing that the sites contain original content. The splogs put up gobs of advertising in hopes that visitors who land on their splog click away from the splog sites through one of its Google AdSense or affiliate links — putting money directly into their pockets.

What on earth is a splog?

Splog. It's such an odd word, isn't it? Yet, it's a word that has, unfortunately, become known in the blogosphere as a very negative thing. The term *splog* is the combination of two words:

spam + blog = splog

While spam is typically identified as unwanted, junk e-mail, the concept here is the same.

People put blogs up on the Internet, fill them with keywords and phrases, and then load them with Google Ads in hopes that you, the Internet surfer, will find your way onto their site, find a bunch of useless garbage for content, decide you didn't find what you're looking for, and click one of their Google ads — putting money in their pockets for, essentially, doing nothing.

Often, you find these same splog sites in the comment and trackback spam that ends up on your own blog. Sploggers stop at nothing to promote their sites and get you to click their links.

Regarding splogs, the Web site Plagiarism Today (at `http://www.plagiarismtoday.com/2005/11/08/behind-splogging-why-sploggers-splog`) has this to say:

> *"Sploggers are almost certainly the most prolific plagiarists on the Web. A handful of determined and capable sploggers can swipe content from literally thousands of different sites, scraping their RSS feeds and taking their content as their own."*

At `http://www.sifry.com/alerts/archives/000335.html`, Dave Sifry, from Technorati, calls them fake blogs that look like real ones, and states

> *"They [splogs] are created in order to perpetuate click fraud or sometimes as a part of a "make money fast" scam on the Internet by again taking advantage of traffic brought to them by search engines and Web rings."*

Lorelle VanFossen, from Lorelle on WordPress at `http://lorelle.wordpress.com/2006/09/23/how-to-spot-a-splog`, says that she just reports splogs as spam when she comes upon one, saying, " . . . as I believe that if we all fight against splogs, splogs will die."

It all sounds rather nefarious, doesn't it? What can you do about it? A few plugins available for WordPress MU can really help prevent splog signups in your blog community; see Table 14-2.

Table 14-2	**Plugins to Help Prevent Splog Signups**	
Name of Resource	*Where to Find It*	*How It Works*
WPMU Anti Splog	`http://wpmudev.org/ project/WPMU-Anti- Splog`	Blocks the user from signup if his IP address is blacklisted as a spammer on Spamhaus.org.
WP Captcha Registration	`http://mu.bloggles. info/2007/02/10/ updated-wpmu- captcha- registration`	A Captcha (completely automated public turing test to tell computers and humans apart) validates users to avoid autoscript signups for blog accounts.

You should install the plugins in Table 14-2 into the `/wp-content/mu-plugins/` folder and activate them for your community. (See Chapter 13 for plugin installation procedures for WordPress MU.)

Preventing comment spam

Comment and trackback spam is a topic I've covered a few times in this book already. You get a sense of how much of a problem this is for bloggers everywhere based on the amount of times I have mentioned it already. It's not different for WordPress MU communities, and your users are going to expect that you have the problem under control, as much as possible. Table 14-3 has a few plugins that work well for WordPress MU to help you stamp out spam in your community.

Table 14-3	**Plugins to Help Combat Comment Spam in WordPress MU Communities**	
Name of Resource	*Where to Find It*	*How It Works*
Spam Karma 2	`http://unknowngenius. com/blog/wordpress/ spam-karma`	An antispam plugin for WordPress that can be used with WordPress.org or WordPress MU.

Name of Resource	Where to Find It	How It Works
Bad Behavior	`www.homelandstupidity.us/software/bad-behavior`	Bad Behavior is an antispam plugin for WordPress MU. It can also be used with the WordPress.org software.
Akismet	`http://akismet.com`	Akismet makes comment and trackback spam a thing of the past. *Note:* Akismet has different licensing terms for personal versus commercial sites, so be sure to check its terms, which are posted at `http://akismet.com/commercial/`.

You can install the plugins in Table 14-3 into the `/wp-content/mu-plugins/` folder if you want these plugins automatically activated for all blogs in your system (I recommend this approach!), or you can install them into the `/wp-content/plugins/` folder if you want your users to be able to choose whether they want to use the plugin. (See Chapter 13 for plugin installation procedures for WordPress MU.)

Although no spam protection is 100-percent foolproof, using the tools provided in Tables 14-2 and 14-3 can put you several steps ahead of sploggers and spammers. The users in your community will thank you a thousand times!

Part V
Flexing and Extending WordPress

The 5th Wave — By Rich Tennant

FREELANCER NED WILLIS CONSULTS WITH A MEMBER OF HIS TECHNICAL STAFF

"...and that's pretty much all there is to migrating your blog to WordPress."

In this part . . .

This part of the book is about moving a blog that you created with another blogging platform (such as Blogspot) to WordPress, and using WordPress as a full-fledged content management system (CMS). Want to find out how you can use the WordPress software for an entire Web site that might include a blog? I tell you how in this part.

Chapter 15

Migrating Your Blog to WordPress

$\mathcal{S}$o, you have a blog on a different blogging system and want to move your blog to WordPress? This chapter helps you accomplish just that. WordPress makes it relatively easy to pack up your data and archives from one blog platform and move into a new WordPress blog.

WordPress lets you move your blog from platforms such as Blogspot, Typepad, Movable Type, and others. It also gives you a nifty way to migrate from any blogging platform through the use of RSS Feeds. In this chapter, you discover how to prepare your blog for migration and how to move from the specific platforms that WordPress provides the migration scripts for.

Movin' On Up

Bloggers have a variety of reasons to migrate away from one system to WordPress, such as the following:

✔ **Simple curiosity:** There is a *lot* of buzz around the use of WordPress and the whole community of WordPress users. People are naturally curious to check out something that all the cool kids are doing.

✔ **More control over your stuff:** This is true particularly for those who have a blog on Blogspot, Typepad, or any other hosted blog. Hosted programs have limits to what you can do, create, and mess with. When it comes to plugins, addons, and theme creation, hosting a WordPress blog on your own Web server wins hands down. In addition, you have complete control over your data, archives, and backup capability by hosting it on your own server.

 ✔ **It's easier to use:** Many people find the WordPress interface easier to use, more understandable, and a great deal more user friendly than many of the other blogging platforms available today.

WordPress.org and WordPress MU currently accept imports from the following platforms:

 ✔ Blogspot: `http://blogspot.com`

 ✔ Blogware: `http://home.blogware.com`

 ✔ DotClear: `http://www.dotclear.net`

 ✔ GreyMatter: `http://noahgrey.com/greysoft`

 ✔ LiveJournal: `http://www.livejournal.com`

 ✔ Movable Type: `http://movabletype.org`

 ✔ TypePad: `http://typepad.com`

 ✔ Textpattern: `http://textpattern.com`

 ✔ WordPress: `http://wordpress.com` and `http://wordpress.org`

 ✔ RSS: Import using any RSS feed

WordPress.com currently accepts imports from Blogspot, LiveJournal, Movable Type, TypePad, and WordPress. You can find the URLs for these platforms in the preceding list.

Preparing for the Big Move

Depending on the size of your blog (that is, how many posts and comments you have), the migration process can take anywhere from 5 to 30 minutes. Obviously, if you have a lot of data to move, it will take a bit longer than if you have only a little. As with any major change or update you make to your blog, no matter where it is hosted, the very first thing you need to do is create a backup of your blog before you attempt to move it anywhere. This means a back up of

 ✔ **Your archives:** Posts, comments, trackbacks

 ✔ **Your template:** Template files, image files

✔ **Your links:** Any links, banners, badges, and elements you have on your current blog

✔ **Your images:** Back those images up by making sure you have them on your own computer hard drive

Table 15-1 gives you a few tips on how to create the export data for your blog on a few of the major blogging systems.

Table 15-1   Backing Up Your Blog Data on Major Blog Systems*

Blogging System	Backup Information
Movable Type	Click the Import/Export button in the menu on your Movable Type Administration panel. Click the Export Entries From. . . link. Wait until the page stops loading and then save the page as a `.txt` file on your computer.
TypePad	Click the name of the blog you'd like to export and then click the Import/Export link in the Overview menu. Click the Export: link at the bottom of the Import/Export page. Wait until the page stops loading and then save the page as a `.txt` file on your computer.
Blogspot	Back up your template by copying the text of your template to a text editor such as Notepad. Save it as a `.txt` file on your computer.
LiveJournal	Browse to `www.livejournal.com/export.bml` and enter your information; choose XML for the format. Save this file to your computer.
WordPress.com	Click the Manage tab in the Administration panel. Click the Export tab in the Administration subpanel. Choose your options. Click the Download Export File button and save this file to your computer.
RSS	Point your browser to the RSS URL you want to import. Wait until it loads fully (you may need to set your feed to display ALL posts). View the source code of the page, and copy and paste that source code into a text file. Save the page as a `.txt` file on your computer.

*This table assumes that you are logged in to your blog software.

Converting Templates

Every blogging program has a unique way of delivering content and data to your blog. Template tags vary from program to program; no two are the same, and each template file requires conversion if you want to use *your* template with your new WordPress blog. If this is the case, you have two options available to you:

✔ **Convert the template yourself.** Knowledge of WordPress template tags and HTML is required in order to accomplish this. If you have a template you're using on another blogging platform and you would like to convert it for use with WordPress, you need to swap out the original platforms tags for WordPress tags. Chapter 9 gives you the rundown on basic WordPress template tags, and you may find that information useful if you are planning to attempt a template conversion yourself.

✔ **Hire an experienced WordPress consultant to do the conversion for you. (See Chapter 11 for a listing of WordPress consultants.)**

To use your own template, make sure you have saved *all* the template files, images, and the stylesheet from your previous blog set up. You will need them to convert the template(s) for use in WordPress.

Remember, hundreds of free templates are available for use with WordPress, so it may be a lot easier if you abandon the template you're currently working with and find a free WordPress template that you like. Some bloggers, however, have paid to have custom designs done for their blog. In this case, you can usually contact the original designer of your theme and hire that designer to perform the template conversion for you. There also are several WordPress consultants whom you can hire to perform the conversion for you — including yours truly.

Moving Your Blog

You've packed up all your stuff and have your new place all prepared and ready. Moving day has arrived!

This section takes you through the steps to move your blog from one blog platform to WordPress. This section assumes that you already have the WordPress software installed and configured on your own Web server (see Chapter 6 for information about installing WordPress.org). You can also apply these steps to moving your blog to a WordPress.com hosted blog (Part II is all about WordPress.com).

Find the import function that you need by following these steps in your WordPress Administration panel:

1. **In the Administration panel, click the Manage tab.**

   This displays a page with a listing of all your blog posts.

2. **Click the Import subtab.**

   This displays the Import page, listing available blogging platforms that you can import content from (for example, Blogger and Blogware). Figure 15-1 shows the Import page for WordPress.org and WordPress MU; Figure 15-2 shows this page for WordPress.com.

3. **Click the link for the blogging platform you are working with.**

   This displays a page that lists directions and information you need to fill in before you begin the import. The following sections contain directions for each platform.

Figure 15-1:
The Import feature in your WordPress. org and MU Administration panel.

Figure 15-2:
The Import
feature
in your
(hosted)
WordPress.
com
Administra-
tion panel.

Importing from Blogspot/Blogger

I call it Blogspot, you call it Blogger — a rose by any other name still smells as sweet. The blogging application owned by Google is referenced either way: Blogspot or Blogger. In the end, we're talking about the same application.

To begin the import process, follow the steps at the start of "Moving Your Blog" to find the Import feature in your WordPress Administration panel. Click the Blogger link, and you receive a message that says, Howdy! This importer allows you to import posts and comments from your Blogger account into your WordPress blog. The message goes on to explain that you need a Google account, and you need to tell Google that you are authorizing your WordPress blog to access your Blogger blog.

Next, click the Authorize button to tell WordPress to access your account. Be ready to enter your username and password for Google, as shown in Figure 15-3.

When you have successfully logged in, you receive a message from Google stating that your blog at WordPress is requesting access to your Blogger account so that it can post entries on your behalf. Give your permission by clicking the Grant Permission button on that page. If you have many posts and comments, on your Blogger blog, this can take 30 minutes or more.

Figure 15-3:
Enter your
Google login
information
to authorize
WordPress
to access
your
account.

After the import script has performed its magic, you are redirected to your WordPress Administration panel. The name of your Blogger blog is now listed here. To complete the import of the data from your Blogger blog, click the Import button (underneath The Magic Button header) that appears to the right.

The text on the button changes to "Importing" while the import takes place. When it is done, the text on the button changes to "Set Authors" (no wonder it's called the Magic Button!). Click the button when it appears as Set Authors; this allows you to assign the authors to the posts.

Assigning authors to posts is an easy process — after you've clicked the Set Authors button, the Blogger username appears to the left with a drop-down menu to the right with the WordPress author name. If you have just one author on each blog, the process is especially easy. If you have multiple authors on both blogs, go through and match the Blogger username with the correct WordPress.com author name and then click Save Changes — and you're done!

Importing from Blogware

Compared with some of the major players out there today, Blogware is not a hugely popular blogging platform, and as of this writing, the Blogware import script imports posts only — it does not import comments or trackbacks. Also, the Blogware importer is available only for the self-hosted software at WordPress.org. WordPress.com does not currently provide an import script for Blogware.

If you do use Blogware, follow these steps to migrate your blog to WordPress:

1. **Create an XML file within your Blogware administration interface.**

   To do so, follow the directions that Blogware provides on its site.

2. **Save the XML file as a text file onto your computer.**

   Save the file with the .txt extension (for example, import.txt).

3. **Go to the Import page in your WordPress Administration panel.**

   To get to the Import page, follow the steps at the very start of this section ("Moving Your Blog").

4. **Click the Blogware link.**

   This opens the Import Blogware page, where you can extract the XML file into your WordPress blog.

5. **Click the Browse button.**

   This opens a window from your computer with a listing of files. Double-click the `.txt` file that you saved earlier from the XML file you created in Blogware.

6. **Click the Upload and Import button.**

   Sit back and let the import script do its magic. When it's done, it reloads the page with a confirmation message that the process is completed.

Importing from DotClear

Follow the steps at very start of this section ("Moving Your Blog") to go to the Import page. Click the DotClear link, and a page appears that asks for several items of information about your DotClear blog, as shown in Figure 15-4.

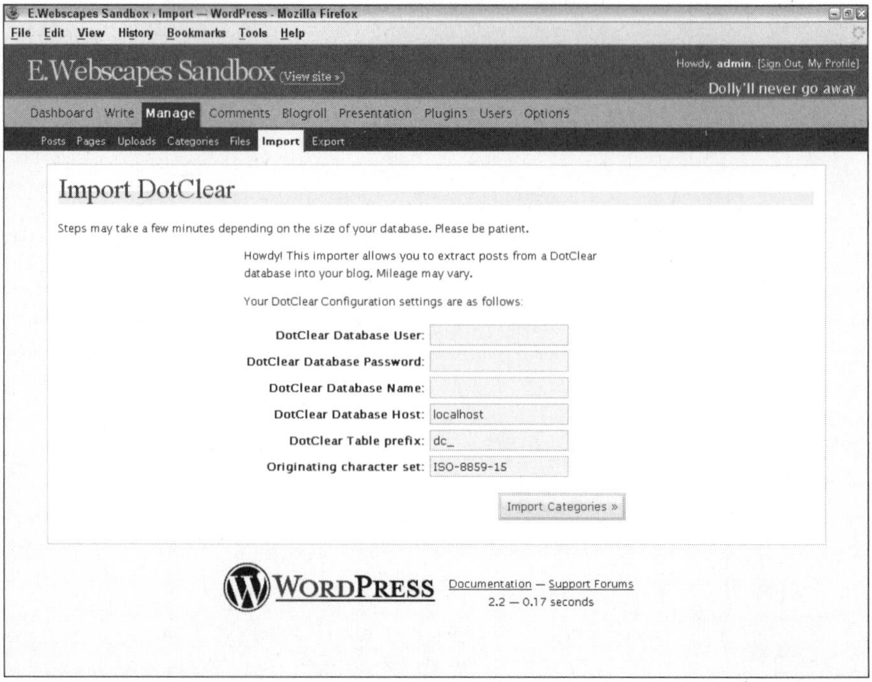

Figure 15-4: Import from a DotClear blog to WordPress.

Enter the information asked for on this page, including the database user, password, database name, host, table prefix, and originating character set. (If you're not sure where to find the information you need, contact your hosting service provider or DotClear to find help.) Then click the Import Categories button.

As of this writing, WordPress.com does not provide an import option for DotClear-powered blogs.

Importing from GreyMatter

GreyMatter is an old blogging platform that was popular in the early 2000s. Not many bloggers are using GreyMatter anymore, but for the one or two of you reading this book who may still be using it, WordPress does provide an import script to migrate your blog posts, comments, and users from your GreyMatter blog.

Go to the Import page of the WordPress Administration panel by clicking the Manage tab and then Import subtab. Then click the GreyMatter link and enter the details that the import script asks for, such as the path to your GreyMatter files and entries and the last entry number, which you can obtain from your GreyMatter control panel. Fill in that information and then click the OK button to start the import process, as shown in Figure 15-5.

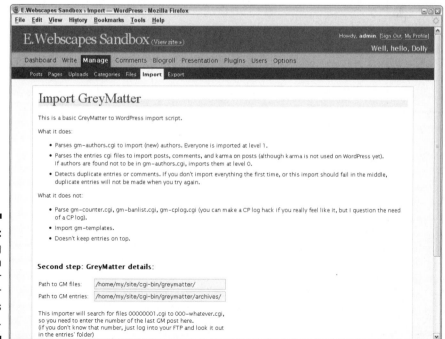

Figure 15-5:
Import blog data from GreyMatter into your WordPress blog.

If you are unsure where to find the information about your GreyMatter files and entries, consult your Web hosting provider or contact the developers of GreyMatter.

WordPress.com does not offer an import script from a GreyMatter blog.

Importing from LiveJournal

Both WordPress.com and WordPress.org offer an import script for LiveJournal users, and the process of importing from LiveJournal to WordPress is the same for each.

Go to the Import page in your WordPress Administration panel (using the steps at the very start of this section ("Moving Your Blog"). Then click the LiveJournal link.

To export your blog content from LiveJournal, log in to your LiveJournal blog and then type this URL into your browser's address bar: `www.livejournal. com/export.bml`.

LiveJournal lets you export the XML files one month at a time, so if you have a blog with several months of posts, be prepared to be at this for a while, because you have to export the entries one month at a time, and then you have to import them into WordPress — yep, you guessed it — one month at a time.

To speed the process a little, you can save all the exported XML LiveJournal files into one text document by copying and pasting each month's XML file into one plain-text file (created in a text editor such as NotePad), thereby creating one, long XML file with every month of posts from your LiveJournal blog. You can then save the file as an XML file to prepare it for import into your WordPress blog.

After you have exported the XML file from LiveJournal, return to the Import page in your WordPress Administration panel and follow these steps:

1. **Click the LiveJournal link.**

    This displays the Import LiveJournal page, where you can extract the XML file into your WordPress blog.

2. **Click the Browse button.**

    This opens a window from your computer with a listing of files. Double-click the filename of the file you saved earlier from the XML file that you created in LiveJournal.

3. **Click the Upload and Import button.**

    When the import script finishes, it reloads the page with a confirmation message that the process is complete.

WordPress then runs the import script and brings over all your posts from your LiveJournal blog.

Importing from Movable Type and TypePad

Movable Type and TypePad were created by the same company, Six Apart. These two blogging platforms run on essentially the same code base, so the import/export procedure is basically the same for both. Refer to Table 15-1, shown previously, for details on how to run the export process in both Movable Type and TypePad.

Go to the Import page in your WordPress Administration panel by following the steps at the very start of this section ("Moving Your Blog"). Click the Movable Type and TypePad link to display the instructions for importing the data you exported from your Movable Type or TypePad blog.

This import script will move all your blog posts, comments, and trackbacks into your WordPress blog.

In Table 15-1, I describe how to create an export file from either Movable Type or TypePad. You should have saved that export file to your own computer. To import this file into your WordPress blog, follow these steps:

1. **Click the Browse button.**

   This opens a window from your computer with a listing of files. Double-click the filename of the export file you saved earlier from your Movable Type or Typepad blog.

2. **Click the Upload File and Import button.**

   Sit back and let the import script do its magic. When it's done, it reloads the page with a confirmation message that the process is completed.

This import script allows for a maximum file size of 2MB. If you get an "out of memory" error, try dividing the import file into pieces and uploading them separately. The import script is smart enough to ignore duplicate entries, so if you need to run the script a few times to get it to take everything, you can do that without worrying that it will duplicate your content.

After the import script is done, it asks you to assign users to the posts by giving you the Movable Type or TypePad username and asking you to match it with the WordPress usernames. If you have just one author on each blog, this is an easy process. If you have multiple authors on both blogs, go through and match the Movable Type or TypePad usernames with the correct WordPress author name and then click Save Changes — and you're done!

Importing from Textpattern

Go to the Import page in your WordPress Administration panel by following the steps at the very start of this section ("Moving Your Blog"). Click the Textpattern link to display a page that asks you for specific information about your Textpattern blog.

In addition to warning you that the import process "may take a few minutes depending on the size of your database," WordPress also warns that it imports from Textpattern 4.0.2+ only. So if you have an earlier version, you need to upgrade your Textpattern version before importing. WordPress even warns you that this import script has not been tested on earlier versions of Textpattern, so it's probably a grand idea to upgrade your Textpattern blog before attempting to run this import.

Enter the requested information — the TextPattern database user, password, name, host, and table prefix — and then click the Import Categories button to begin the import process.

WordPress.com does not currently offer an import option from Textpattern.

Importing from WordPress

With this WordPress import script, you can import one WordPress blog into another, and this is true for both the hosted and self-hosted versions of WordPress. Refer to Table 15-1, earlier in this chapter, to find out how obtain your blog data using the export feature. After you've completed the export-ing, to import the data into your WordPress blog, click the WordPress link on the Import page. (To get to the Import page, see the steps at the start of the "Moving Your Blog" section, earlier in this chapter.)

On the Import page, WordPress informs you that using the WordPress extended RSS (WXR) file will import all your posts, comments, custom fields, and categories into your blog.

Follow these steps to perform the import:

1. **Click the Browse button.**

   This opens a window from your computer with a listing of files. Double-click the export file you saved earlier from your WordPress blog.

2. **Click the Upload File and Import button.**

The import script gets to work, and when it's done, it reloads the page with a confirmation message that the process is completed.

WordPress gives you the friendly warning that the file cannot be over 2MB in size in order for it to be uploaded via the Import page in the WordPress.com Administration panel.

Importing from an RSS feed

If all else fails, or WordPress does not provide an import script that you need for your current blog platform, you can import your blog data via the RSS feed for the blog you want to import. With the RSS import method, you can import posts only; you can't use this method to import comments, track-backs, categories, or users.

Refer to Table 15-1, earlier in this chapter, for the steps required to create the file you need to import via RSS. On the Import page in the WordPress Administration panel, click the RSS link. There, you find the instructions to import your RSS file, as shown in Figure 15-6.

Figure 15-6: Import your blog into WordPress via RSS.

Follow these steps to import the data from the RSS file:

1. **Click the Browse button on the RSS Import page.**

   This opens a window from your computer with a listing of files. Double-click the export file you saved earlier from your RSS feed.

2. **Click the Upload File and Import button.**

   The import script does its magic and then reloads the page with a confirmation message that the process is completed.

WordPress.com does not currently allow you to import blog data via an RSS feed. This is a function that you can perform only with the self-hosted WordPress and WordPress MU blogs.

Finding Other Resources to Import

The WordPress Codex has a long list of other available scripts, plugins, workarounds, and outright hacks for importing from other blog platforms. You can find that information at `http://codex.wordpress.org/Importing_Content`.

Note, however, that the WordPress Codex is run by a group of volunteers who donate their time and efforts to keeping the WordPress documentation up-to-date. Be aware that not all the information listed in the Codex is necessarily up-to-date or accurate. Please keep that in mind when referring to the WordPress Codex for import information (or any other information as it relates to help with running your WordPress blog).

Chapter 16

Beyond Blogging: WordPress as a Content Management System

*I*f you've avoided using WordPress as a solution for building your own Web site because you think it's only a blogging platform and you don't want to have a blog (not every Web site owner does, after all), it's time to rethink your position. The self-hosted version of WordPress, WordPress.org, is a powerful content management system (CMS) that is flexible and extensible enough to run an entire Web site — with no blog at all, if you prefer.

This chapter shows you a few ways that you can use the self-hosted WordPress.org software to power your entire Web site, with or without a blog.

This chapter covers different template configurations that you can use to create separate sections of your site using static page templates, category templates, and various sidebar templates. Here, you find out how to include these elements in various areas of your site. You also discover how to use the front page of your site as a *landing page* (the display of a static page) or *portal* (the display of a page that contains small snippets from other sections within your site with links to those sections), which can include a link to an internal blog page if you want one.

Understanding What a Content Management System Can Do for You

A *content management system* (CMS) is a system used to create and maintain your entire site. It usually includes tools for publishing and editing, as well as for searching and retrieving information and content. A CMS enables users who have little or no knowledge of HTML to maintain their Web sites, with easy methods to create, modify, retrieve, and update their content without ever having to touch the code required to perform those tasks.

CMS programs such as WordPress give you, the site owner, all the tools and advantages of blog software for managing and maintaining your site. These programs make setting up a Web site much easier than it ever used to be. In the past, if you didn't know HTML, you had to hire a Webmaster to manage, update, and maintain your Web site. With WordPress, you can do all that yourself, with or without HTML knowledge. That capability translates into a *huge* cost savings and opens the door to anyone who wants to run a Web site but doesn't have the resources or knowledge to do it. Now you can!

Creating the Front Page of Your Web Site

For the most part, when you visit a blog powered by WordPress, you see the blog on the main page. For example, my personal blog at http://justa girlintheworld.com, powered by WordPress (of course), shows my latest blog posts on the front page, along with links that take you to the blog post archives (by month or by category) on my site. This setup is typical of a site run by WordPress.

However, the front page of my business site at http://ewebscapes.com, also powered by WordPress, contains no blog at all. Instead, it is a *static* page, which means that it does not display any blog posts, but rather displays the contents of a static page I created within the WordPress Administration panel. This static page on my site serves as a portal to my design blog, my portfolio, and other sections of my site that contain information about my service. The site includes a blog but also serves as a full-blown business Web site, with all the sections I need to provide my clients with the information they want.

Both of my sites are powered by the self-hosted version of WordPress.org, so how can they differ so much in what they display on the front page? The answer lies in the templates you use and the options you set within the WordPress Administration panel.

In the steps that follow, I start by using a new WordPress installation with the default Kubrick theme to show how you can easily change the front page of your blog to display a static page instead of the full blog listing.

You use the static page feature in WordPress to create content that you do not want to be displayed as a part of your blog posts but do want displayed as part of your overall site (such as a bio page, a page of services, and so on). To have a static page display on the front page of your site, first you need to create that page, which you do by following these steps:

1. **Click the Write tab on the Administration panel.**

   This brings up the page where you can write a new post to your WordPress blog.

2. **Click the Write Page subtab.**

   This displays the Write Page page, where you write and save a new page to your WordPress site. (Check out Chapter 7 for the difference between a page and a post in WordPress.)

3. **Type the title of your choice in the Page Title text box.**

   This is the title for the page you're creating.

4. **Type the content of your page in the Page Content text box.**

5. **Set the options for this page.**

   I explain all these options in Chapter 6.

6. **Click the Publish button.**

   This saves the page to your database and publishes it to your WordPress site.

Figure 16-1 shows you the page I created as an example front page for a site. Note that the Page Template option is set to Default Template. This tells WordPress that you want to use the default page template to format the page you're creating.

Next, you need to tell WordPress that you want the page you just created to serve as the front page of your site. Say, for instance, that the title of your page is Welcome to My Front Page. When you complete the following steps, WordPress makes that page available for you to use as your static front page:

1. **Click the Options tab on the Administration panel to display the General Options page.**

2. **Click the Reading subtab to display the Reading Options page.**

3. **In the Front Page area, select the A Static Page radio button.**

4. **From the Front Page drop-down menu, select the page you just created.**

   In Figure 16-2, I'm choosing to display a static page, and Welcome to My Front Page is the page I want to display.

Page Template

Figure 16-1:
Create the
static page
you want to
use to
display on
your front
page.

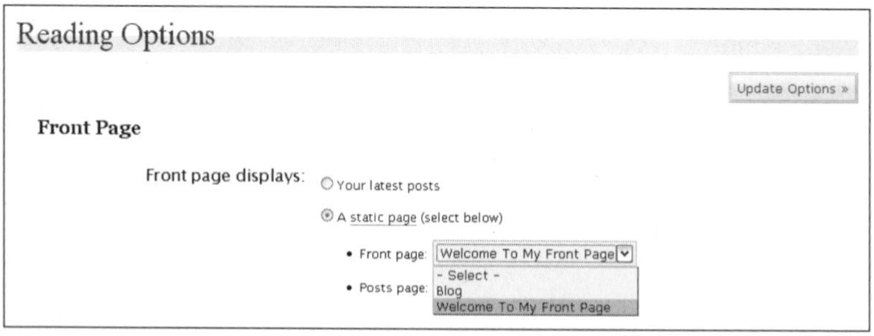

Figure 16-2:
Choosing
which page
to display as
the front
page.

5. Click the Update Options button.

This tells WordPress to display the page you selected in Step 4 as the front page of your site. Figure 16-3 shows my site displaying the page I created as my front page.

Figure 16-3:
WordPress
displays the
page you
select as
your front
page.

With a little adjustment of the code in the page.php (Page) template in the default Kubrick theme, you can create a front page that doesn't look like a blog at all. In Figure 16-4, you see my front page without the usual "bloggy" sidebar that contains archive links, blogrolls, meta information, and so on.

Chapter 9 covers template tags and templates that you can use in WordPress, including setting up static page templates. However, you can use the quick-'n'-dirty way, as I did, to change your front page from a bloggy-looking page to a nonbloggy-looking page with the default Kubrick theme. Just follow these simple steps:

1. **Click the Presentation tab on the Administration panel.**

   This displays the Current Theme page, which lists your current theme and all available WordPress themes on your blog.

2. **Click the Theme Editor subtab.**

   This displays the Editing page, with all the templates included in the current theme listed on the right side of the page.

3. **Click Page Template on the right side of the page.**

   This reloads the Editing page with the contents of the page.php template displayed in the text box on the left side of the page.

4. Locate this code:

```
<div id="content" class="narrowcolumn">
```

5. Replace the code in Step 4 with this code:

```
<div id="content" class="widecolumn">
```

6. Remove the following code found near the bottom of the page.php **template:**

```
<?php get_sidebar(); ?>
```

7. Click the Update File button.

This saves the file and updates your site with the changes you just made.

Now visit your front page, and you should have something that looks similar to Figure 16-4.

Using this method, you can create unlimited amounts of static pages to build an entire Web site. You don't even need to have a blog on this site, unless you want the functionality of a blog included as a part of the site.

The next section tells you how to create a blog on your site.

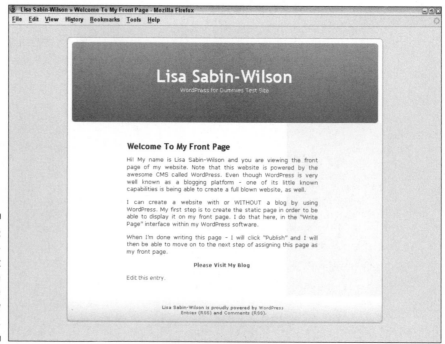

Figure 16-4:
A WordPress front page without the bloggy sidebar.

Adding a Blog to Your Web Site

This is a test of just how much of an eye for detail you have. Did you notice anything in Figure 16-4 that wasn't in Figure 16-3? Take a moment to have a look while I enjoy the last drops of my espresso. Done?

If you spotted the Please Visit My Blog link at the bottom of Figure 16-4, you would be correct. I added that link to my front page so that when a visitor clicks it, he or she will be taken to my blog page once I create it.

If you want a blog on your site but don't want to display the blog on the front page, you can find the solution to that to that issue on the WordPress Administration panel. Right now, that Please Visit My Blog link doesn't work because I haven't created the blog yet. To create the blog for your site, follow these steps:

1. **Click the Write tab on the Administration panel.**

   This brings up the page where you can write a new post to your WordPress blog.

2. **Click the Write Page subtab.**

   This displays the Write Page page, where you can write and save a new page to your WordPress site.

3. **Type** Blog **in the Page Title text box.**

   Doing this automatically sets the page slug to /blog. (Read more about slugs in Chapter 8.)

4. **Leave the Page Content box blank.**

5. **Click the Publish button.**

   This saves the page to your database and publishes it to your WordPress site.

You now have a blank page that redirects to http://yourdomain.com/blog. Next, you need to assign the page you just created as your blog page. To do so, follow these steps:

1. **Click the Options tab on the Administration panel.**

   This displays the General Options page.

2. **Click the Reading subtab.**

   This displays the Reading Options page.

3. **Select the page you just created in the Posts Page drop-down menu.**

   This sets the page as your blog page. (Figure 16-5 shows the Posts Page drop-down menu, where you select your blog page.)

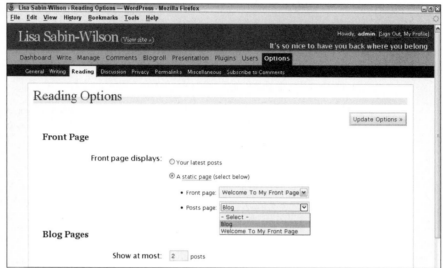

Figure 16-5:
Set these
options
to tell
WordPress
where
you want
your blog
displayed.

4. **Find the Blog Pages section of the page and type the number of posts you want displayed in the Show at Most text box.**

   This number sets the number of posts you want displayed on that page all at one time. If you enter **5**, the blog page shows the last five posts you've made to your blog.

5. **Click the Update Options button.**

   This saves the options you just set, and you now see your blog loaded at `http://yourdomain.com/blog` (where *yourdomain.com* is your actual domain name).

Now when you navigate to `http://yourdomain.com/blog`, you see your blog displayed. In Figure 16-6, you can see my blog page, which shows how a page looks when the administrator chooses to display two posts.

On the blog page, the sidebar displays any page you create under the Pages heading. However, earlier in Figure 16-4 where I adjusted the Kubrick theme to remove the sidebar, I had to add the link to my blog page. You can accomplish this trick by using the following bit of code in the content of the static page you created for your front page display:

```
<a href="/blog">Please Visit My Blog</a>
```

Figure 16-6:
My blog
display at
/blog with
two posts
showing.

This method of using the /blog page slug works only if you're using custom permalinks with your WordPress installation. (See Chapter 8 if you'd like more information about permalinks.) If you're using the default permalinks, the URL for your blog page is different. You can easily find the URL for a page by clicking the Manage tab on the Administration panel and then clicking the Pages subtab. Find the page you created for your blog display and click the View link that appears on the right side of the page. Clicking the View link opens the blog page in your browser, and you can copy the URL from the address bar in your browser and paste it in the code provided in the previous section.

Defining Specific Templates for Static Pages

As I explain in the "Creating the Front Page of Your Site" section, earlier in this chapter, a *static page* contains content that is not displayed on the blog page, but rather as a separate page of content within your site. You create a static page in your WordPress Administration panel by clicking the Write tab on the Administration panel and then clicking the Write Page subtab on the subpanel. (See Chapter 8 for more about creating a static page.) You can have numerous static pages on your site, and each page can have a different design, which is governed by the template you create. (See Chapter 9 to find out all about choosing and using templates.) You can create several static page templates and assign them to specific pages within your site by adding the following bit of code to the very top of the static page templates:

```
<?php
/*
Template Name: About Page
*/
?>
```

The `Template Name` is a name that you choose for each template.

For example, this is the code that appears at the top of the static page template I use for my About Us and Our Blog Designers page on my site (`http://ewebscapes.com/about`). You can create the same type of page template by following these steps:

1. **Create a template with the filename** `about.php`.

   You can create this file in a text editor program, such as Notepad. (To refresh your memory about how to create a template, flip back to Chapter 9.)

2. **Upload the new** `about.php` **template file to your WordPress theme folder.**

   You can find your WordPress theme folder on your Web server in the `/wp-conent/themes/` folder. Upload `about.php` via FTP. (See Chapter 6 for more information about FTP.)

3. **Log in to your WordPress Administration panel, click the Presentation tab, and then click the Theme Editor subtab.**

   This loads the Theme Editor page, where you can edit the template files in your current WordPress Theme.

4. **Click the** `about.php` **template located on the right side of the page.**

5. **Type the Template Name tag directly above the header template tag.**

   The header tag looks like this: `<?php get_header(); ?>`.

6. **Type the Template Name tag like this:**

   ```
   <?php /* Template Name: About Page /* ?>
   ```

7. **Click the Update File button.**

   This saves the file and reloads the page. Notice that the `about.php` template is now called About Page in the template listing on the right side of the page.

See Figure 16-7, which shows some of the code to enter for the template.

Editing `about-page.php`

```php
<?php
/*
Template Name: About
*/
?>
```

Figure 16-7:
Naming a
static page
template.

Figure 16-7 doesn't show all the code required for the template, but I include the figure to show you where the code for naming the template belongs.

To create a new kind of layout for each static page on your site, you use the naming convention described previously in the "Defining Specific Templates for Static Pages" section of this chapter and shown in Figure 16-7; however, you change the template name (in this example, About Page) to a different name, of your choosing, for each page template you create.

When you have the template created and named the way you want it, you assign that template to a page by following these steps:

1. **Click the Write tab on the Administration panel.**

   This brings up the page where you can write a new post to your WordPress blog.

2. **Click the Write Page subtab.**

   This displays the Write Page page, where you write and save a new page to your WordPress site.

3. **Type the title in the Page Title text box and the page content in the Page Content text box.**

   You're entering the title of the page you're creating and the text you want the page to contain.

4. **Select the page template from the Page Template drop-down menu.**

   This menu appears at the right side of the page under the Page Template heading. If you've named your page template correctly using the template naming convention I describe earlier in the "Defining Specific Templates for Static Pages" section of this chapter, you see that page template name in the drop-down menu.

5. **Click the Publish button to save and publish the page to your site.**

Figure 16-8 shows you the layout of my home page (using a template named `home.php`) and the information it contains, whereas Figure 16-9 shows you the layout and information provided on my Blog Design and Web Site Services page (using a template named `services.php`). Both pages are on the same site, in the same WordPress installation, with different static page templates to provide a different look, layout, and set of information.

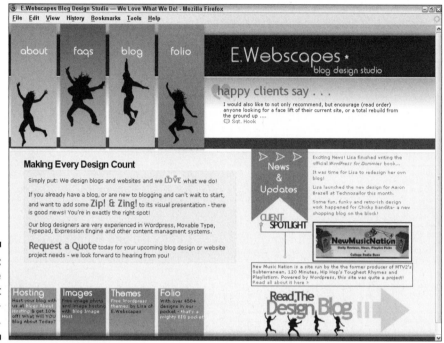

Figure 16-8:
My home
page at
E.Web-
scapes.

Figure 16-9:
The
Services
Page at
E.Web-
scapes.

Creating a Template for Each Post Category

You don't have to limit yourself to creating a static page template for your site. No, you can completely gorge yourself at the table of possible WordPress templates that you can use to create unique sections of your site, as I did (with an espresso chaser, of course).

For example, Figure 16-10 shows you my design portfolio. Design Portfolio is the name of a category that I created in my WordPress administration panel. Instead of using a static page for the display of my portfolio, I've used a category template to handle the display of all posts made to the Design Portfolio category.

Figure 16-10: My Design Portfolio page, using a category template file.

You can create category templates for all categories on your blog by simply creating template files with names that correspond with the Category ID numbers and then uploading those templates to your WordPress themes directory (see Chapter 9). The logic to this is as follows:

- ✔ A template with the filename `category.php` is a catch-all for the display of categories.

- ✔ Add a dash and the Category ID number to the end of the filename (as shown in Table 16-1) to specify a template for an individual category.

- ✔ If you don't have a `category.php` or `category-#.php` file, the category display pulls from the Main Index Template (`index.php`).

Table 16-1 shows you three examples of the category template naming requirements.

Table 16-1	WordPress Category Template Naming Convention
If the Category ID Is . . .	*The Category Template Filename Is . . .*
1	category-1.php
2	category-2.php
3	category-3.php

Using Sidebar Templates

Notice in Figure 16-8 that some of the information in the right sidebar is different from the right sidebar in Figure 16-9. It is possible to create separate sidebar templates to use in different pages of your site by using a simple include statement. When you write an include statement, you're simply telling WordPress that you want it to include a specific file on a specific page.

The code used to pull the usual Sidebar Template (sidebar.php) into all the other templates, such as the Main Index Template (index.php), looks like this:

```
<?php get_sidebar(); ?>
```

That pulls the Sidebar Template onto your page. What if you create a page and want to use a sidebar that has different information than what you have in the Sidebar Template (sidebar.php)? Follow these steps:

1. **Create a new sidebar template in a text editor such as Notepad.**

   See Chapter 9 for information on template tags and themes.

2. **Save the file as** sidebar2.php.

   In Notepad, choose File⇨Save on the menu. When you're asked to name the file, type sidebar2.php and then click Save.

3. **Upload** sidebar2.php **to your** themes **folder on your Web server.**

   See Chapter 6 for FTP information and review Chapter 9 for information on how to locate the themes folder.

Now that you have your new Sidebar Template added to your themes folder, you should see that template listed in your theme files when you log in to your WordPress Administration panel, click the Presentation tab, and click the Theme Editor subtab.

To include the `sidebar2.php` template in one of your page templates, find this code:

```
<?php get_sidebar(); />
```

And replace it with this `include` code:

```
<?php include('sidebar2.php'); ?>
```

Using that `include` statement, you can include virtually any file in any of your WordPress templates. You can use this method to also create Footer Templates for pages on your site. To do this, first create a new template with the filename of `footer2.php` and then find this code in the template you wish to accomplish this for:

```
<?php get_footer(); ?>
```

And replace that with this code.

```
<?php include('footer2.php'); ?>
```

You can do multiple things with WordPress to extend it beyond the blog. This chapter gives you a few practical examples, using the default Kubrick theme. The point here is to show you how to use WordPress to create a fully functional Web site using a CMS platform that's well known for its applications in the blogging world. You can use WordPress to create a fully functional Web site that can handle anything from the smallest personal Web site to a large business Web site.

Chapter 10 shares some other exiting ways to extend your Web site by adding multimedia tools such as podcasting, videos, and photo galleries.

Optimizing Your WordPress Blog

Search engine optimization (SEO) is the practice of preparing your site to make it as easy as possible for the major search engines to crawl your site and cache your data in their systems so that your site appears as high as possible in the search returns.

For example, if you visit Google's search engine page at http://google.com and do a search using the keywords *WordPress designer,* my own site at E.Webscapes is the first site in the search results for those keywords (at least, it is as I'm writing this). Those results can change from day to day, so by the time you read this book, someone else may very well have taken over that coveted number-one position. That is the reality of chasing those high-ranking search engine positions. It's here today, gone tomorrow.

This is the goal for search engine optimization: to make sure that *your* site ranks as high as possible for the keywords that you think people will use to find the content that your site contains. After you've attained those high-ranking positions, the next goal is to keep them. (Check out *Search Engine Optimization For Dummies,* by Peter Kent [Wiley Publishing] for some valuable information on keeping those high ranks through ongoing optimization of your site.)

Right out of the box, WordPress comes equipped and ready to create an environment that is friendly to search engines by allowing them easy navigation through your archives, categories, and pages. This is accomplished through a clean code base, content that is easily updated through the WordPress interface, and a good, solid navigation structure.

To extend search engine optimization even further, you can tweak five elements within your WordPress posts, pages, and templates. They are:

- ✔ **Custom permalinks:** Check out Chapter 8 for information on WordPress permalinks. Using custom permalinks, rather than the default Word-Press permalinks, fills your post and page URLs with valuable keywords.

- ✔ **Posts and page titles:** Creating descriptive titles for your blog posts and pages will provide rich keywords in your site.

- ✔ **Text:** The text (content) of your blog posts and pages is filled with keywords that search engines will find and index. Keeping your site updated with descriptive text and phrases helps the search engines find keywords to associate with your site.

- ✔ **Category names:** Using descriptive and identifying names for the categories you create in WordPress places great keywords right in the URL for those category pages, if you use the custom permalinks.

- ✔ **Images and** `ALT` **tags:** You can place `ALT` tags in your images to further define and describe the images on your site. You can accomplish this easily by using the description field in the WordPress image uploader, as I describe in Chapter 8.

Planting keywords in your Web site

If your site is hosted by a provider that has the Apache `mod_rewrite` module enabled, you can use the custom permalink structure for your WordPress-powered site — and if you're interested in a higher ranking for your site, I strongly recommend using custom permalinks. By using custom permalinks, you're automatically inserting keywords in the URLs of your posts and pages, allowing search engines to include those posts and pages in their databases of information on the Web on those topics. (I explain setting up and using custom permalinks in full detail in Chapter 8 of this book.)

Keywords are the first step on your journey toward great search engine results. Search engines are dependent on keywords. People use keywords to search for the content they're looking for.

The default permalink structure in WordPress is pretty ugly, if I'm being honest here. They certainly won't win any beauty contests. When you're looking at the default permalink for any post, you should see a URL that looks something like this:

```
http://yourdomain.com/p?=105
```

You can see that the URL has no keywords of worth. By changing to a custom permalink structure, your post URLs automatically include the titles of your posts, providing keywords, which search engines absolutely love. For example, a custom permalink might appear in this format:

```
http://yourdomain.com/2007/02/01/your-post-title
```

Optimizing your post titles for search engine success

Search engine optimization isn't completely dependent on how you set your site up. It's also dependent on you, the site owner, and how you present your content.

One way to present your content in a way that will allow search engines to catalog your site is to give your blog posts and pages titles that make sense and coordinate with the actual content being presented. If you're doing a blog post on a certain topic, make sure that the title of your blog post contains at least one or two keywords about that particular topic. This gives the search engines even more ammunition to list your site in the returns on searches relevant to the topic you discuss in your post.

The more people who find your site, the more popular your site can become as you gain new readers who find you through search engine results.

A blog post with the title A Book I'm Reading isn't going to tell anyone about what book it is, making it difficult for people searching for information on that particular book to find by searching for it in one of the major search engines.

However, if you gave the post the title WordPress For Dummies: My Review, this not only provides keywords in the title, it also automatically inserts those keywords into the URL (if you're using custom permalinks), giving the search engines a triple keyword play:

✔ Keywords exist in your blog post title.

✔ Keywords exist in your blog post URL.

✔ Keywords exist in the content of your post.

Making sure you keep your keywords in mind when giving your blog posts and pages titles will go further in helping people who are searching for those topics find your site.

Writing content with readers in mind

When you write your posts and pages and are interested in making sure your content appears in the first page of search results so that your readers, or potential readers, find your site, you need to keep those people in mind when you're composing the content for your blog posts and pages.

When search engines visit your site to spider or crawl through your content, they aren't seeing how nicely designed your site is. What they're looking for are words — and they're grabbing those words from your site to include in their databases. You, the site owner, want to make sure that you're using the words and phrases in your blog posts and page content that you want included in search engines.

If your blog post is about a recipe for fried green tomatoes, for instance, in order for people to find your recipe in the search engines, you need to be sure to add some keyword phrasing that you think people will use when they search for the topic. For example, if you think people might use the phrase *recipe for fried green tomatoes* as a search term, you may want to include that phrase in the content and title of your post.

You can see, by now, that a title such as A Recipe I Like isn't as effective as a title such as A Recipe for Fried Green Tomatoes, right? Including it inside your post or page content gives the search engines a double keyword whammy.

Let me give you an example. I once wrote a post about a rash that I developed on my finger, under my ring. I wrote that post well over a year ago, not really meaning to attract a bunch of people to that particular post. However, it seems that many women around the world suffer from the same rash because that post still gets at least one comment a week, a year after the fact. When people do a Google search using the keywords *rash under my wedding ring*, out of a possible 1,460,000 results returned, my blog post appears in the number-one slot, as shown in Figure 16-11.

This is how great blogs are! I was actually able to completely solve my problem with the rash under my finger because one woman from Australia found my blog through Google, visited my blog post, and left a comment with a solution that worked. Who says blogs aren't useful?

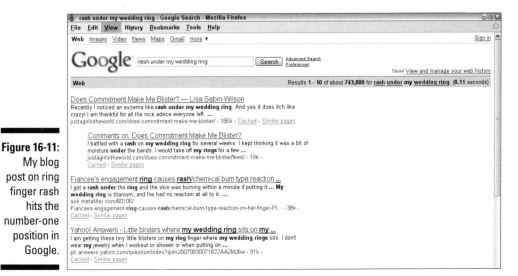

Figure 16-11:
My blog
post on ring
finger rash
hits the
number-one
position in
Google.

Creating categories that attract search engines

One little-known SEO tip for WordPress users: The names you give to the categories you've created on your blog provide rich keywords that attract search engines like bees to honey. A few services on the Web — Technorati.com being one of the biggest — treat categories in WordPress like tags. Services such as Technorati use those categories to classify blog posts that have been recently made on any given topic. The names you give to your categories in WordPress can serve as topic tags used by Technorati and other similar services.

Search engines also see your categories as keywords that are relevant to the content on your site. In this regard, it's important to pay attention to what you're naming your categories and making sure that you're giving them names that are relevant to the content you're providing on your site.

For instance, if you sometimes blog about your favorite recipes, you can make it easier for search engines and services such as Technorati to find your recipes if you create categories that are specific to the recipes you're blogging about. Instead of having one Favorite Recipes category, you can create multiple category names that correspond to the types of recipes you blog about — for example, Casserole Recipes, Dessert Recipes, Beef Recipes, and Chicken Recipes. This narrows the field quite a bit for your readers — and for search engines.

You can also consider having one category called Favorite Recipes and creating subcategories (also known as *child categories*) that give a few more details on the types of recipes you've written about. (See Chapter 8 for information on creating categories and child categories.)

Categories use the custom permalink structure, as well. So, links to your WordPress categories also become keyword tools within your site to help the search engine — and ultimately, search engine users — to find the content. Using custom permalinks gives you category page URLs that look something like this:

```
http://yourdomain.com/category/Category_Name
```

It's the `Category_Name` portion of that URL that puts the keywords you want right into the hands of search engines, where you want them.

Using the ALT tag for images

When you use the WordPress image uploader to include an image on your post or page, you're given a Description text box to enter a description or phrase about the image. (I cover using the WordPress image uploader in detail in Chapter 8.) This automatically becomes what is referred to as the `ALT` tag.

Its real purpose is to provide a description of the image for people who, for some reason or another, can't actually see the image. For instance, with text-based browsers that don't display images, the visitor sees the description, or `ALT`, text that describes what image would be there if only he could see it. Also, it assists people with impaired vision, who rely on screen-reading technology, because the screen reader will read the `ALT` text from the image to describe the image to the visitor. You can read more about Web site accessibility for the disabled and vision impaired at the W3C Web site here: `www.w3.org/WAI/References/Browsing`.

An extra benefit to `ALT` tags is that search engines gather data from images through the `ALT` tags used to further classify the content of your site. The following is the code for inserting an image, and I've bolded the `ALT` tag of the code to demonstrate what I'm talking about:

```
<img src="http://yourdomain.com/image.jpg" alt="This is an
         ALT tag within an image" />
```

Search engines harvest those `ALT` tags as keywords. The WordPress image uploader gives you an easy way to include those `ALT` tags without having to worry about inserting them into the image code yourself. Just fill out the Description text box before you upload and add the image to your post. (Figure 16-12 shows the Description text box that accompanies the WordPress image uploader.)

Figure 16-12:
Fill out the
Description
box to auto-
matically
add ALT
tags to your
images.

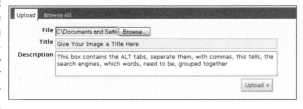

Places to Bookmark

Several resources in the WordPress codex can help you understand some of
the advanced techniques used for the development of unique WordPress
sites (see Table 16-2).

Table 16-2	Resources from the WordPress Codex to Help You Get Started with Some Advanced WordPress Hackery	
Location	*Resource Title*	*Resource Description*
http://codex. wordpress.org/ Creating_a_ Static_Front_ Page	Creating a Static Front Page	You don't want your blog to be on the front page of your site? It's possible with a static front page.
http://codex. wordpress.org/ Category_ Templates	Create Category Templates	WordPress lets you create a unique page for each category within the blog.
http://codex. wordpress.org/ Using_Custom_ Fields	Using Custom Fields	WordPress lets post authors assign custom fields to a post.

Part VI
The Part of Tens

The 5th Wave · By Rich Tennant

DENISE AND JERRY LEVIN — AUTHORS OF "LOST IN THE MALL PARKING LOT," "THE MISPLACED GALLERY INVITATION," AND, "THE BAD HAIRCUT — WHY ME?"

Truthfully? If it weren't for WordPress, many of our adventures would have remained untold.

In this part . . .

Welcome to the Part of Tens! In this section, I tell you about ten fabulous WordPress themes and let you know where you can get them. I also give you a list of great plugins that you can use to enhance your WordPress blogging.

Chapter 17

Ten Great — and Free — WordPress Themes

In This Chapter

▶ Finding good WordPress themes

▶ Using popular WordPress themes to style your blog

As a WordPress theme developer and designer, this chapter was probably the most difficult for me to put together. I know, I know, I was thinking the same thing as you — "Ten Great WordPress themes — no big deal!" And yet, it's a very big deal because the themes available for WordPress number in the thousands, if not hundreds of thousands. Many of these themes are excellent, and it was really tough to pick a mere ten. The list I present here isn't exhaustive by any means. Chapter 9 gives you a few more resources for use in finding a theme that suits your needs.

The criteria I kept in mind when choosing the following themes are the following:

- ✔ **User friendly:** The best themes incorporate as much detail as possible to allow the theme user to just load the theme and start blogging without a whole lot of fuss and muss. You can use these themes directly out of the box, and usually, they have a whole lot more to offer if you want to tinker. The key here is this: You don't *have* to tinker.

- ✔ **Compatibility with widgets:** Themes that are set up to use WordPress Sidebar Widgets are the most user friendly. Widgets are wonderful, and they make your blogging life incredibly easy by giving you drag-and-drop functionality and control over the content that appears in your sidebar. (If you don't know what widgets are, flip back to Chapter 10.)

- ✔ **Administrative options:** Most of the themes on my list provide you with an options menu in the theme editor, located in the administration panel. These options give you even more control over your blog theme settings and make it extremely easy for you to make changes without having to tinker with the code.

✔ **Valid code:** A set of standards for Web design and code called the W3C standards, developed by the World Wide Web Consortium (`http://w3c.org`), serves as a sort of proofreading for the code on all Web site designs. Although you may not notice it, valid XHTML code goes a very long way toward ensuring that the theme you're using meets that set of standards, and you can be relatively confident that your blog site isn't causing errors in different browsers. Designers who pay attention to valid code are the designers to look for when choosing a theme for your site because they understand validation and your need to make sure your site is reaching all of your visitors, no matter what browser they're using to view your content. You can tell whether a designer has used valid code on his or her site by using the site validation tools located on the W3C Web site here: `http://validator.w3.org` for HTML code validation and `http://jigsaw.w3.org/css-validator` for CSS code validation.

With these things in mind, I present to you the top-ten free WordPress themes available for you to download and try on your site. These themes aren't listed in any particular order; each one is just as good as the next.

Cutline

Theme designer: Chris Pearson

`http://cutline.tubetorial.com`

The highlights of this theme are the following:

✔ It has a very clean, uncluttered, two-column layout.

✔ Small details in this theme make the big picture shine: detailed treatment of lists, block quotes, pull quotes, and comment links, to name just a few.

✔ It supports the WordPress Widgets plugin (which you can find at `http://automattic.com/code/widgets`).

✔ It supports the FlickrRSS Plugin (you can find FlickrRSS at `http://eightface.com/wordpress/flickrrss`).

✔ It supports the Random Header Images plugin, allowing you to switch header images easily without even knowing how to manipulate the code to do it. (Random Header Images at `http://www.tubetorial.com/downloads/random_header.zip`.)

Cutline is included in the themes available for WordPress.com bloggers. Cutline makes it to the top of my list because I think it's one of the most functional, versatile, and friendly free themes available.

Tarski

Theme designers: Ben Eastaugh and Chris Sternal-Johnson

`http://tarskitheme.com`

The highlights of this theme are the following:

- ✔ The admin options menu gives you several options to customize your theme and includes several nicely designed header graphics.
- ✔ Its print style sheet maximizes paper output of your site, for people who are interested in printing your blog posts.
- ✔ It has a two-column layout.
- ✔ Its sidebar is widget ready.

The Tarski theme designers make it very easy for you to personalize your blog without being required to know a lick of HTML, CSS, or coding that is usually required to accomplish the changes necessary to personalize your blog theme. The Tarski theme comes with a choice of header artwork for you to choose from, and to change the header artwork, you just select the artwork in the theme options page. The options page for the Tarski theme, found in your WordPress Administration panel under the Presentation tab, also provide you with several options you can select to further personalize the theme to suit your needs.

The theme's Web site has comprehensive information on using the theme and its features.

SandPress

Theme designer: Arpit Jacob

`http://www.clazh.com/sandpress-free-wordpress-theme`

The SandPress theme was the first-place winner of a recent WordPress theme design competition held in June/July 2007 at `http://sndbox.org`. SandPress provides you with a very clean, three-column layout. The theme designer paid some very special attention to the small details of the theme, such as fantastic icons that call colorful attention to various sections of your site (such as comments, page navigation, RSS feeds, and so on).

xMark

Theme designer: Lisa Sabin-Wilson

http://blogdesignsolutions.com

The highlights of this theme are the following:

- ✔ It's a fully fluid three-column theme. *(Fluid* means that it expands and contracts to fill your browser page, no matter what size your browser is.)

- ✔ It displays blog content on the left and two widget-ready sidebars on the right.

- ✔ Its admin options menu allows you to choose various settings for your theme.

- ✔ The theme supports several popular WordPress plugins. The integration is *seamless,* meaning that if you have the plugins installed on your WordPress installation, they'll automatically work; if you don't have them installed, you won't even notice the functionality is there. (This is an especially good function if you want to use this theme with WordPress MU.)

After you activate the xMark theme, you see the xMark tab in the top navigation menu. Click that tab and you'll find a few options that you can set for your blog. These options allow you to make significant choices for how certain features are displayed on your blog, without having to tinker with the actual code inside the template. xMark doesn't require plugins; it works perfectly for you straight out of the box. However, the theme does support several popular WordPress plugins, with full documentation on the theme Web site explaining how to take full advantage this feature. xMark also provides support for Google AdSense.

Another important feature is that the theme is SEO optimized, which gives you an edge when it comes to the popular search engines finding and listing your site in their search results.

Blog.txt

Theme designer: Scott Wallick

www.plaintxt.org/themes/blogtxt

This theme has a theme options menu that allows complete user control over text size and layouts. It offers nine different layout possibilities and has a robust style sheet with a separate print style sheet. Its sidebars are widget ready. It also has an elastic, two-column layout that is minimal: fewer than 300 lines of CSS. It's perfect for customizing, with a theme options menu that includes a feature for easily using it like a Content Management System.

Rounded V2 Blue

Theme designer: Ghyslain

http://itcouldbethisone.com

This theme has a two-column layout with playful rounded boxes that make up the sidebar; the sidebar on this theme is fully widget ready. The detailed treatment of the comments area of this theme makes it a fun alternative to other themes available. Its fluid design makes full use of your entire browser window, no matter what size monitor or screen resolution you use. A variation of the Rounded theme was adopted at WordPress.com and is available to you if you're running a WordPress.com blog.

Almost Spring

Theme designer: Becca Wei

http://beccary.com/goodies/wordpress-themes

This theme has a two-column layout and its sidebar is widget ready. Its Admin Options menu gives you several options to change some elements of the theme — such as the font size for the blog title, post author options, and the date format — without having to worry about manipulating the template code. Becca's Almost Spring theme was adopted by WordPress.com as one of its selected themes, so if you're running a blog at WordPress.com, you may want to check this one out.

Redoable

Theme designer: Dean J. Robinson

www.deanjrobinson.com/wordpress/redoable

Redoable is the only dark theme that made my list of top tens. The light-text-on-a-dark-background type of theme has gained popularity among designers and theme fans across the blogosphere. However, it can make your blog difficult for some visitors to read. I include this theme in my list because of the popularity of this type of look. Aside from readability issues, Redoable is a beautiful theme with a lot of detailed treatment. This theme was built on the very popular K2 theme, which I tell you about later in this chapter.

This theme has a two-column layout, and its sidebar is widget ready. It supports multiple popular WordPress plugins. (See the theme's Web page for details.) This theme also gives detailed treatment to many design classes, letting you create a unique blog site.

Anaconda

Theme designer: Angsuman Chakraborty

`http://anaconda.taragana.net`

This theme has a three-column layout with content in the middle and sidebars on each side. It posseses a fluid layout that expands and contracts with your browser window, taking up the full width of your screen. Both sidebars are widget ready, and the Admin Options menu lets you control features such as search, comments, asides, archives, and more. The theme also has gives detailed treatment of different elements on the design with snappy-looking icons.

K2

Theme designers: Chris J. Davis and Michael Heilemann

`http://binarybonsai.com/wordpress/k2`

Named after one of the deadliest mountains in the world, the K2 WordPress theme is by far the most popular among WordPress theme fans, as well as theme designers. A good majority of the best WordPress themes available today are based on the K2 code base, including many of the themes listed in this chapter (Cutline, Tarski, and Anaconda, to name a few). Many designers and developers have taken their inspiration from K2, which is why no top-ten WordPress themes list would be complete without mentioning it. The K2 Web site contains comprehensive information on the theme and how to use it, including a helpful community forum.

Chapter 18

Ten Great WordPress Plugins

In This Chapter

▶ Finding popular WordPress plugins

▶ Using plugins to enhance your blog

*I*n this chapter, I give you a list of ten of the most popular plugins available for use on your WordPress blog. This list of plugins isn't exhaustive, by any means. Hundreds of excellent WordPress plugins can, and do, provide you with multiple ways to extend the functionality of your blog. And if these ten plugins aren't enough for you, you can find many more WordPress plugins at the official WordPress Web site here: `http://wordpress.org/extend/plugins`.

The greatest plugin of all is Akismet, which I describe in Chapter 10 when discussing comment spam and the management of comments and trackbacks on your blog. I don't include Akismet in this list of great WordPress plugins because Akismet stands alone as an absolute must on any WordPress blog; in addition, Akismet comes packaged with the WordPress software and requires only activation and an API key. (See Chapter 10 for more details on activating Akismet.) Akismet is the answer to combating comment and trackback spam. It kills spam — dead.

Chapter 10 contains information on how to locate, download, unpack, install, activate and manage plugins within your WordPress blog.

Related Entries

Developer: WASABI

`http://wasabi.pbwiki.com/Related-Entries`

This plugin outputs a list of related posts on your blog based on keyword matching. For example, if I'm visiting your blog and reading your latest post about your favorite espresso, the Related Entries plugin gives me (the reader) a list of related posts on your blog, just in case I want to read more of your blog posts about espresso. And, trust me, I *love* reading about espresso almost as much as I love consuming it.

This plugin works only if you had or have a permalink schema with the post titles in it — for example, `/archives/2006/01/02/post-title` or similar (See Chapter 8 for more information on using permalinks.) The plugin strips out everything but the post title and uses it to find entries that are related to the topic they are currently reading about.

To install this plugin on your WordPress blog, download and unpack the plugin files, upload the plugin file to your Web server into the `/wp-content/plugins` folder, and activate the Related Entries plugin.

After activation, click the Plugins tab in the Administration panel and you'll notice a new Related Posts Options subtab in the Plugins submenu. Click Related Posts Options and scroll to the bottom. In the SQL Index Table Setup paragraph, click the This Script link to run the script necessary to prepare your database to store related entries information. You need to do this only once, when you install the plugin.

The Related Posts Options page also gives you some options for how you'd like WordPress to display your related posts. Here are some tips on configuring the display options:

- **How Many Related Posts Would You Like To Show?:** Pick a number and enter it in this text box. Anywhere from 5–15 posts is usually sufficient.

- **Before/After (Post Title):** Tell WordPress what, if any, HTML tags you want inserted before and after each post title in the list of related posts.

  For example, if you want the list of related posts to appear as an unordered (or bulleted) list, you enter **<li>** in the first box and **</li>** in the second box. Doing so surrounds each title in the list with the HTML tag, as in `<li> . . . </li>`. (For more about HTML, see *HTML 4 For Dummies*, 5th Edition, by Ed Tittel and Mary Burmeister [Wiley Publishing].)

- **Show Excerpt?:** Select True or False in the drop down menu. True tells WordPress to display a short snippet, or excerpt, of each post in the related posts list. False tells the script only to display the title of the post, without the post excerpt.

- **Excerpt Length (No. of Words)?:** Type in the number of words you want shown in the excerpt. Do this only if you have selected True in the Show Excerpt drop-down menu. (If you selected False in the Show Excerpt drop down menu, just leave this box blank.)

- **Before/After (Excerpt):** Type the HTML tags that you want to be inserted before and after the excerpt. For example, `<p>` in the first box and `</p>` in the second inserts the paragraph tags before and after the excerpt. Of course, if you chose False for the Show Excerpt? option, leave this blank.

- **Show Password Protected Posts?:** If you have posts on your blog that are protected by a password, do you want them to show up in the related posts list? Select True or False in the drop-down menu here.

Remember to click the Save! button to save your options.

Now it's time to add the plugin code to your template so that the list of related posts will show up on your site. You *must* place the code within The Loop. (Flip back to Chapter 9 for a review of The Loop.) You can insert the code into any WordPress template, as long as it is inserted within The Loop.

Insert the following Related Entries plugin code within The Loop of the template file:

```
<? related_posts(); ?>
```

Be sure to save your template after you've made these changes. And that's it — you're done. Now you can sit back and watch the plugin do its work. If you have a new blog with just a handful of posts on it, the plugin may not pick up a list for each post yet. In that case, you'll see the message No Related Posts.

If your WordPress theme has a 404 template (404.php), you can insert the following code in your 404 template (within The Loop) to display a list of related posts on your 404 page:

```
<?php related_posts_404(); ?>
```

Why this plugin is called *Related Entries* and yet every single reference to the plugin, after you have it installed, is *Recent Posts,* I don't know. But that's the way it is, so there you have it.

Subscribe to Comments

Developer: Mark Jaquith

http://txfx.net/code/wordpress/subscribe-to-comments

The Subscribe to Comment plugin adds a very nice feature to your blog by allowing your visitors to subscribe to individual posts you've made to your blog. When they do this, they receive notification, via e-mail, whenever some-one leaves a new comment on the post. This goes a long way toward keeping your readers informed and making the discussions lively and active! The plugin includes a full-featured subscription manager that your commenters can use to unsubscribe to certain posts, block all notifications, or even change their notification e-mail address.

To install this plugin on your WordPress blog, download and unpack the plugin files, upload the subscribe-to-comments.php file to your Web server into the /wp-content/plugins folder, and activate the Subscribe to Comments plugin on the Plugins page in your WordPress Administration panel.

The plugin comes with a few additional options:

- ✔ If you want to manually determine where in your comments form the subscribe check box appears, insert the following code in the Comments template (`comments.php`) where you want it to display: `<?php show_subscription_checkbox(); ?>`.

- ✔ If you want to enable users to subscribe to comments without having to first leave a comment, place the code somewhere in your Comments template (`comments.php`), but make sure it's *outside* the comments form. A good place would be right after the ending `</form>` tag for the comments form, as in the following: `<?php show_manual_subscription_form(); ?>`.

Subscribe to Comments gives you a very nice administration options menu. You can find this by clicking the Options tab in the top menu of the WordPress Administration panel and then clicking the Subscribe to Comments subtab in the navigational menu. This displays the Subscribe to Comments Options page, where you set up the different options for the plugin, including the name and e-mail reply address that you want to use for the notifications that are sent.

Share This

Developer: Alex King

`http://alexking.org/projects/wordpress`

Share This is a relatively new plugin to emerge onto the scene, but its developer isn't so new. Alex King was one of the original WordPress platform developers before he left the project to pursue his own, very successful consulting business, Crowd Favorite. Alex designed the Share This plugin as a combined "e-mail this" plugin and social bookmarking service, allowing visitors to share content through e-mail and popular social bookmarking services such as Technorati, del.icio.us, and Digg.

If you're using a version of WordPress prior to version 2.1, you need to upload the included `prototype.js` to your `wp-includes/js/` directory. By default, the Share This link is added at the very end of your blog post, and the Share This form is added to the footer of your site. If you'd like to control exactly where these go in your template, you can do so by disabling the auto-output and using the Share This template tags to place the link exactly where you want them to appear.

To disable the auto-output, you need to edit the `share-this.php` file in the `/wp-content/plugins/share-this/` folder. At the time of this writing, Alex hasn't developed an easier method, such as an options menu in the

WordPress Administration panel. This would be a very nice feature for the future development of this plugin so that users aren't required to edit PHP files. Not everyone is comfortable opening a PHP file and trying to find her way.

WordPress does try to make it a bit easier for you to edit plugin files. (See Chapter 10 for more information on managing and editing plugins.) To begin editing this file, click the Plugins tab in the WordPress Administration panel, find the Share This plugin link, and click the Edit link to the far right.

To disable the auto-output of the Share This link, find the following two lines of code in the Share This plugin file:

```
@define('AKST_ADDTOCONTENT', true);
@define('AKST_ADDTOFOOTER', true);
```

Find them? Now change them to this:

```
@define('AKST_ADDTOCONTENT', false);
@define('AKST_ADDTOFOOTER', false);
```

When you have the auto-output disabled, use the following template tags to your Main Index Template (index.php) and/or the Single Page template (single.php) and add them in the place you want the link to appear.

For the Share This link; add this tag:

```
<?php akst_share_link(); ?>
```

For the Share This form, add this tag:

```
<?php akst_share_form(); ?>
```

This plugin requires the wp-footer() call in the Footer template (footer.php) of your template. If your theme doesn't include a wp_footer() call, you can add it easily by opening the footer.php template and adding this bit of code:

```
<?php wp_footer(); ?>
```

Every social bookmarking service out there has its own icon. Before Share This, people put these icons on their blogs as a way to let their visitors know that they could share their content with each social bookmarking service. This was a really good concept when only a handful of services existed; however, these services started popping up everywhere! Pretty soon, people were putting a dozen or two bookmarking icons on their site to encourage their visitors to submit their content to the all those different services.

Sharing is good. It's great, as a matter of fact. However, all those icons can begin to look pretty cluttered and messy on one blog template. The Share This Icon Project (`http://shareicons.com`) seeks to provide a solution to this messy clutter by gathering all those services and icons and wrapping them all up into one neat and clean package.

WP ShortStat

Developer: Jeff Minard

`http://blog.happyarts.de/wp-shortstat`

WP ShortStat isn't a complicated plugin at all, but it's very robust and powerful and provides you with some detailed information about the traffic and visitors to your blog. Such information is extremely helpful if you're interested in tracking who is visiting your blog, where they are coming from, and how many visitors you have daily and even monthly. All the statistics data is stored in your WordPress database, and that process is all set up during the installation of the plugin.

To install this plugin, download and unpack the plugin files, upload the `wp-shortstat.php` file to your Web server into the `/wp-content/plugins` folder (Optional: If your blog isn't published in the English language, copy the correct language file [`*.mo`] into the same folder), and activate the WP-ShortStat plugin.

After you install the plugin, you can view your statistics by clicking the Dashboard tab in the WordPress Administration panel and then clicking the Short Stat subtab. It will take a while for stats to display because, after all, it takes visitors to your site in order for the ShortStat plugin to return the details of those visits. However, after a day or so, you can see details on unique visits and hits to your site and RSS feed, the keywords that people use to find your site, the most popular resources on your site, and much more.

WordPress Mobile Edition

Developer: Alex King

`http://alexking.org/projects/wordpress`

Another great plugin from the talented Alex King is called WordPress Mobile Edition, which provides a custom display of your blog for a mobile device. Mobile browsers are automatically detected; no configuration is needed.

Have you ever browsed the Web with a mobile device such as a BlackBerry or mobile phone with Internet capabilities? Even if you haven't, you can bet there are hundreds of thousands of people who have, and do. As mobile Web browsing becomes more and more popular, you want to make sure that your site renders decently in your readers' mobile browser. This plugin will do it for you. It's fast. It's easy. And it does its job.

To install this plugin, download and unpack the plugin files, upload the `wp-mobile.php` to your Web server into the `/wp-content/plugins` folder, upload the `wp-mobile` folder to your Web server into the `/wp-content/themes` folder, and activate the WordPress Mobile Edition plugin.

SRG Clean Archives

Developer: Shawn Grimes

`www.sporadicnonsense.com/2005/04/28/clean-archives-plug-in`

SRG Clean Archives is a simple plug-in designed to display your archive lists in a clean and uniform fashion. It lists the Month/Year (links to that months archives), the day of the month the article was published, the title of the article (permalink to article), and the number of comments that have been made on each article. It also keeps password-protected articles from showing up in your archives list.

To install this plugin, download and unpack the plugin files, upload the `srg_clean_archives.php` to your Web server into the `/wp-content/plugins` folder, and activate the SRG Clean Archives plugin. After you install the plugin, insert the following string of code where you want the archives to be displayed, such as in your sidebar or on a separate archive page template:

```
<?php srg_clean_archives(); ?>
```

WP Ajax Edit Comments

Developer: Ronald Huereca

`www.raproject.com/wordpress/wp-ajax-edit-comments/`

Using the WP Ajax Edit Comments plugin is a way for you to do a huge favor to the readers of your site. This plugin allows readers to edit their own comments that they have left on your blog. I don't know about you, but I have days when I could be considered the queen of typos and spelling errors, and when I've made such an error in a comment on someone's blog, I've wished that I could log in to his WordPress Administration panel to edit my comment. For those of you who have this plugin installed on your blog, please accept my gratitude!

This plugin does not require your readers to log in to your WordPress Administration panel to edit their comments — they can do it right on the Comments page of your blog. To install this plugin, download the plugin file from the plugin home page and unpack the files on your computer. Upload the `wp-ajax-edit-comments` folder to the plugins directory on your Web server (`/wp-content/plugins`) and then activate the plugin. After activation, you find the WP Ajax Edit Comments page by clicking Options in the WordPress Administration panel and then clicking the AJAX Edit Comments subtab. On this page, you can set the amount of time you allow your readers to edit their comments (for example, within 30 minutes of leaving the comment). The developer provides full instructions, including video guides, on the plugin's home page.

Translate

Developer: Trevor Creech

`http://trevorcreech.com/blog/2006/04/27/translate-widget`

¿Hablas español? ¡Ningún problema!

Translate does just what the title of the plugin states: It translates! The Translate plugin currently supports the following languages: English, French, German, Spanish, Italian, Portuguese, Japanese, Chinese, Arabic, and Russian.

Translate is a widget plugin only, so if your theme doesn't support Sidebar Widgets, you can't use this plugin on your site. You can, however, find a similar plugin that provides translation services: `http://blog.taragana.com/index.php/archive/angsumans-translator-plugin-pro-for-word press-blogs-released/`.

To install the Translate plugin, download and unpack the plugin files, upload the `translate.php` file and the Flags folder into the plugins folder (`/wp-content/plugins/`) of your WordPress installation, and then activate the Translate plugin. After activation, you can use it in your sidebar by clicking the Presentation tab and then clicking the Widgets subtab. Add the Translate widget to your sidebar by dragging it from Available Widgets to your sidebar.

Random Quotes

Developer: Zombie Robot

`http://www.blogmotron.com/wp-quotes`

This is a fun plugin that lets you show a new quote on your blog each time your blog is loaded. Do you have any favorite quotes you'd like to share with your visitors? This plugin will do it for you. This plugin uses the database to store quotes, not a text file. It has a spiffy administrative interface (screenshot). You can call up a random quote, or a specific quote in your pages. You can make a page with all your quotes, and you can turn certain quotes off without actually deleting them. The quote layouts are done with CSS, so you can stick them anywhere in your theme template(s) and style them yourself.

WordPress.com Stats

Developer: Andy Skelton

`http://wordpress.org/extend/plugins/stats`

With the rise in popularity of the hosted WordPress.com service came a huge demand for the statistics that WordPress.com provided to its users within each of its Dashboard pages. Users of the self-hosted WordPress.org software would drool when they saw the stats available to WordPress.com users, and the cry for a similar stats plugin for WordPress.org could be heard across the WordPress blogosphere. Andy Skelton answered that call with the release of the WordPress.com Stats plugin for WordPress.org users. This plugin, once installed on your WordPress.org blog, starts collecting all the important statistics that any blogger would want to know about the activity on her blog, including the number of hits to your site per hour, day, month; your most popular posts; the sources of the traffic on your blog; and the links people click to leave your site.

The stats are provided for you on one easy-to-view page. This plugin also does not count your own visits to your blog, so you can be assured that the counts are accurate, not inflated because your own visits.

To install the plugin, download it from the plugin's home page and unpack it onto your own computer. Upload the `stats.php` file to the plugins directory on your Web server (`/wp-content/plugins/`). Activate the plugin in your WordPress Administration panel.

As with the Akismet Spam plugin, you need a WordPress.com API key for the stats plugin to work. See Chapter 10 for information on the Akismet plugin, as well as information on how and where to obtain a WordPress.com API key. This key gets entered in the WordPress.com Stats page in your WordPress Administration panel: Just click the Plugins tab in the Administration panel, click the WordPress.com Stats subtab, and enter the API key there.

After you've activated the plugin and inserted your WordPress.com API key, click the Dashboard tab in the Administration panel to see the Blog Stats subtab. Click this subtab to view your stats.

Appendix

Configuration Options

● ●

*I*n Part IV of this book, I cover the installation, configuration, and use of the WordPress MU software. Chapter 13 of that part addresses the initial setup of your options after you have the WordPress MU software installed on your own Web server. This appendix provides you with information on the settings options available for editing a user blog within your WordPress MU network.

To get to this section within your WordPressMU Administration panel, click the Site Admin tab in the Administration panel and then click Blogs. Doing so takes you to the Blogs page, which displays all the blogs within your network. Clicking the Edit link to the right of any of the blogs listed there opens the Edit Blog page, where you find the various settings you can configure for the blog. Table A-1 presents each of these settings, along with a description of the setting and an example.

Values in Table A-1 marked as Serialized Data mean that the data is fixed and can't be changed. Typically, this is data that's fixed and set in the WordPress MU database, program files, or both.

Table A-1	Configuration Options for Individual Blog Settings	
Edit Option	*Description*	*Example of Settings*
URL	The URL of the blog.	`user.yourdomain.com`
Path	The server path to the blog.	Most often set to /
Registered	Date and time the user registered this blog.	2007-04-22 22:20:21
Last Updated	Date and time the user last updated this blog.	2007-04-22 22:20:21
Public	Determines whether the public can view the blog.	Yes or No
Archived	Indicates whether the blog is archived.	Yes or No
Mature	Indicates whether the blog contains adult content.	Yes or No

(continued)

Table A-1 *(continued)*

Edit Option	Description	Example of Settings
Spam	Indicates whether the blog is considered spam.	Yes or No
Deleted	Indicates whether the blog is deleted.	Yes or No
Siteurl	The Internet address of the blog.	`http://user.yourdomain.com`
Blogname	The name of the blog.	My Blog Name
Blogdescription	The tagline of the blog.	My tagline
Users Can Register	Determines whether registration to the blog is open to the public.	0 = No (`False`) 1 = Yes (`True`)
Admin Email	E-mail address of the user who registered the blog.	`user@theirdomain.com`
Start of Week	The day of the week the WP Calendar begins.	1 = Monday 2 = Tuesday 3 = Wednesday 4 = Thursday 5 = Friday 6 = Saturday 7 = Sunday
Use BalanceTags	Determines whether WordPress automatically corrects invalidly nested XHTML.	0 = No (`False`) 1 = Yes (`True`)
Use Smilies	Determines whether WordPress converts emoticons — such as :-) and :-P — to graphics.	0 = No (`False`) 1 = Yes (`True`)
Require Name Email	Determines whether a commenter is required to submit a name and e-mail address.	0 = No (`False`) 1 = Yes (`True`)
Comments Notify	Determines whether WordPress sends the blog owner a notification when a visitor leaves a comment.	0 = No (`False`) 1 = Yes (`True`)

Edit Option	*Description*	*Example of Settings*
Posts per RSS	Sets the number of posts to display in the RSS feed.	Enter numeric value. 10
Mailserver URL	Internet address of the mail server, which is used for blogging by e-mail.[1]	`user@theirdomain.com`
Mailserver Login	The login name for the user's mailserver, which is used for blogging by e-mail.[1]	`username@their domain.com`
Mailserver Pass	The password for the user's mailserver, which is used for blogging by e-mail.[1]	theirpassword
Mailserver Port	The port for their mailserver; used for blogging by e-mail.[1]	110
Default Category	The category that uncategorized posts are assigned to by (Category ID).	1
Default Comment Status	Sets the default for comment status.	Options: Open Closed
Default Ping Status	Sets the default for ping/trackback status.	Options: Open Closed
Default Ping Flag	Determines if WordPress will attempt to notify any blogs linked to posts.	0 = No (`False`) 1 = Yes (`True`)
Default Edit Post Rows	Determines the height of the text edit window where bloggers write their blog posts.	Default value is 10. The larger the number, the bigger the height of that text box.
Posts Per Page	Sets the number of posts displayed on the front page of the blog.	Default value is 10
What to Show	Determines what type of content is displayed on the front page.	Posts: Show blog posts Page: Show static page
Date format	The format of the date that appears on the posts and comments.	Default: F j, Y

(continued)

Table A-1 *(continued)*

Edit Option	*Description*	*Example of Settings*
Time format	The format of the time that appears in the posts and comments.	Default: g:i a
Links Updated Date Format	The format of the time that appears on updated links.	Default: F j, Y g:i a
Links Recently Updated Prepend	Determines what should appear before a recently updated link.	You can place anything (or nothing) here. A popular mark is the asterisk (*) to mark a recently updated link.
Links Recently Updated Append	Determines what should appear after a recently updated link.	You can place anything (or nothing) here. A popular mark is the asterisk (*) to mark a recently updated link.
Links Recently Updated Time	Sets how often the server checks for updated links (in seconds).	Default is 120 seconds.
Comment Moderation	Determines whether all comments are placed in the moderation queue to be approved.	0 = No (False) 1 = Yes (True)
Moderation Notify	Determines whether the blog admin should be notified when there are comments awaiting moderation.	0 = No (False) 1 = Yes (True)
Permalink Structure	Determines the permalink structure the blog uses.	/%year%/%monthnum%/ %day%/%postname%/
Gzipcompression	Determines whether Gzip (a UNIX utility for reducing the size of data files) is on.	0 = Off (False) 1 = On (True)
Hack File	Determines whether the blog uses a my-hacks. php file.	0 = No (False) 1 = Yes (True)
Blog Charset	The charset setting for the user's blog.	No reason to change this. UTF-8 is the recommended charset.

Edit Option	Description	Example of Settings
Moderation Keys	The keywords that the user has placed in her comment moderation settings.	If the user has any moderation words set in the Options menu on the Discussion Options page under the Comment Moderation header, they will be listed in this box.
Active Plugins	Lists the plugins that are activated for this blog.	If the user has activated any plugins, the plugin name is listed here.
Home	The Internet address for the blog.	`http://user.your domain.com`
Category Base	Sets special permalink rules for category display.	`/category/` If no special permalink rule is set for categories, this field is blank.
Ping Sites	Determines which ping, or update, services are notified when the user makes a new post.	`http://rpc. pingomatic.com/`
Advanced Edit	Determines whether the uses the visual editor (WYSIWYG) when writing.	0 = No (`False`) 1 = Yes (`True`)
Comment Max Links	The number of links that the user has set in the Discussion Options for his blog for comment moderation.	2
Gmt Offset	The user's GMT offset.	0 for those in London
Default Email Category	The category any posts made via e-mail will be assigned to.[1]	1
Use Linksupdate	Determines whether WordPress should indicate when the links in the user's blogroll were last updated.	0 = No (`False`) 1 = Yes (`True`)
Template	The name of the template used on the blog.	default

(continued)

Table A-1 *(continued)*

Edit Option	Description	Example of Settings
Stylesheet	The name of the template that contains the style sheet (CSS) used on the blog.	default
Comment Whitelist	The setting that the user has selected for her blog under Discussion Options concerning whether a comment author must have a previously approved comment.	0 = No (False) 1 = Yes (True)
Page Uris	The URLs for static pages within the users blog.	SERIALIZED DATA
Blacklist Keys	The list of key words, e-mail addresses, or IP addresses the user has set in the Comment Blacklist section in her Discussion Options (by clicking the Options tab and then the Discussion tab in the Administration panel).	spam@spammer.com If the user has made no blacklist entries, this field is blank.
Comment Registration	Determines whether users need to be registered and logged in to comment.	0 = No (False) 1 = Yes (True)
HTML Type	Captures the recommended practice for the HTML for basic Web standards.	text/html This is recommended and shouldn't be changed.
Use Trackback	Determines whether the user is using the trackback features available in WordPress blogs.	0 = No (False) 1 = Yes (True)
Default Role	Determines the default user role assigned to new registrants.	Default: subscriber Options: Subscriber Contributor Editor Author Administrator

Edit Option	Description	Example of Settings
Uploads Use Yearmonth Folders	Determines whether WordPress MU sorts image uploads in folders by year and month on the Web server.	0 = No (`False`) 1 = Yes (`True`)
Upload Path	Sets the server path for uploaded files.	`wp-content/uploads` This is the default, and recommended.
Secret	This is encrypted data that contains the user's database password, username, name, host, and absolute path.	This value is set when the blog is created. There's never a reason to change this value.
Blog Public	Determines if the blog is visible to the public.	0 = No (`False`) 1 = Yes (`True`)
Default Link Category	The default category for links that users add to their blogroll.	Assign a category ID here 1
Show On Front	This setting shows whether the user is displaying the latest blog posts or a static page on the front page of his blog.	Options: Posts Page
Fileupload Url	The Internet address of the location of all files the user uploads using the image uploader.	`http://user.your` `domain.com/files/`
Post Count	Displays the number of posts to the blog.	2 No reason to change or adjust this setting.
Rewrite Rules	The `mod_rewrite` rules in the `.htaccess` file of the user's blog account, as determined by the permalinks option the user has set under Options and then Permalinks.	SERIALIZED DATA
Allowedthemes	Lists the themes the blogger is allowed to use for his blog.	default

(continued)

Table A-1 *(continued)*

Edit Option	Description	Example of Settings
New Admin Email	This is the administrative e-mail address for the user.	`user@theiremail.com`
WPLANG	The language setting for the user's blog account.[2]	Option is blank; WordPress MU assumes the default language of English
Cron	This is the Cron setting for the user's blog, if any.	SERIALIZED DATA

[1]*A word about blogging by e-mail with WordPress MU: Users can't, at this time, configure their own settings for blogging by e-mail. They have to rely on the WordPress MU site administrator to set it up for them, using the configuration settings on the Edit Blog page. In order for blogging by e-mail to work, you (the site administrator) insert the mail information in the mail server URL, mail server login, mail server password, and mail server port text boxes. Next, you need to access the* `http://user.yourdomain.com/wp-mail.php` *file each time a user publishes a post via e-mail — but it's unrealistic for you to manually access that file on a regular basis in order to retrieve the e-mail for the post, so you need to set up a CRON job on your Web server to handle this. If you're unaware of how to set up CRON jobs on your Web server, contact your Web hosting provider for assistance.*

[2]*WordPress MU doesn't currently support languages other than English. Some community users, however, have translated it for different languages. You can learn more by visiting the WordPress MU Forums here:* `http://mu.wordpress.org/forums/tags.php?tag=language.`

Index

BUSINESS, CAREERS & PERSONAL FINANCE

0-7645-9847-3

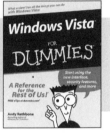

0-7645-2431-3

Also available:

- Business Plans Kit For Dummies
  0-7645-9794-9
- Economics For Dummies
  0-7645-5726-2
- Grant Writing For Dummies
  0-7645-8416-2
- Home Buying For Dummies
  0-7645-5331-3
- Managing For Dummies
  0-7645-1771-6
- Marketing For Dummies
  0-7645-5600-2

- Personal Finance For Dummies
  0-7645-2590-5*
- Resumes For Dummies
  0-7645-5471-9
- Selling For Dummies
  0-7645-5363-1
- Six Sigma For Dummies
  0-7645-6798-5
- Small Business Kit For Dummies
  0-7645-5984-2
- Starting an eBay Business For Dummies
  0-7645-6924-4
- Your Dream Career For Dummies
  0-7645-9795-7

HOME & BUSINESS COMPUTER BASICS

0-470-05432-8

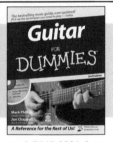

0-471-75421-8

Also available:

- Cleaning Windows Vista For Dummies
  0-471-78293-9
- Excel 2007 For Dummies
  0-470-03737-7
- Mac OS X Tiger For Dummies
  0-7645-7675-5
- MacBook For Dummies
  0-470-04859-X
- Macs For Dummies
  0-470-04849-2
- Office 2007 For Dummies
  0-470-00923-3

- Outlook 2007 For Dummies
  0-470-03830-6
- PCs For Dummies
  0-7645-8958-X
- Salesforce.com For Dummies
  0-470-04893-X
- Upgrading & Fixing Laptops For Dummies
  0-7645-8959-8
- Word 2007 For Dummies
  0-470-03658-3
- Quicken 2007 For Dummies
  0-470-04600-7

FOOD, HOME, GARDEN, HOBBIES, MUSIC & PETS

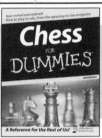

0-7645-8404-9

0-7645-9904-6

Also available:

- Candy Making For Dummies
  0-7645-9734-5
- Card Games For Dummies
  0-7645-9910-0
- Crocheting For Dummies
  0-7645-4151-X
- Dog Training For Dummies
  0-7645-8418-9
- Healthy Carb Cookbook For Dummies
  0-7645-8476-6
- Home Maintenance For Dummies
  0-7645-5215-5

- Horses For Dummies
  0-7645-9797-3
- Jewelry Making & Beading For Dummies
  0-7645-2571-9
- Orchids For Dummies
  0-7645-6759-4
- Puppies For Dummies
  0-7645-5255-4
- Rock Guitar For Dummies
  0-7645-5356-9
- Sewing For Dummies
  0-7645-6847-7
- Singing For Dummies
  0-7645-2475-5

INTERNET & DIGITAL MEDIA

0-470-04529-9

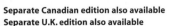

0-470-04894-8

Also available:

- Blogging For Dummies
  0-471-77084-1
- Digital Photography For Dummies
  0-7645-9802-3
- Digital Photography All-in-One Desk Reference For Dummies
  0-470-03743-1
- Digital SLR Cameras and Photography For Dummies
  0-7645-9803-1
- eBay Business All-in-One Desk Reference For Dummies
  0-7645-8438-3
- HDTV For Dummies
  0-470-09673-X

- Home Entertainment PCs For Dummies
  0-470-05523-5
- MySpace For Dummies
  0-470-09529-6
- Search Engine Optimization For Dummies
  0-471-97998-8
- Skype For Dummies
  0-470-04891-3
- The Internet For Dummies
  0-7645-8996-2
- Wiring Your Digital Home For Dummies
  0-471-91830-X

Separate Canadian edition also available
Separate U.K. edition also available

Available wherever books are sold. For more information or to order direct: U.S. customers visit www.dummies.com or call 1-877-762-2974. U.K. customers visit www.wileyeurope.com or call 0800 243407. Canadian customers visit www.wiley.ca or call 1-800-567-4797.

SPORTS, FITNESS, PARENTING, RELIGION & SPIRITUALITY

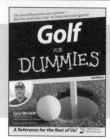

0-471-76871-5

0-7645-7841-3

Also available:
- Catholicism For Dummies
  0-7645-5391-7
- Exercise Balls For Dummies
  0-7645-5623-1
- Fitness For Dummies
  0-7645-7851-0
- Football For Dummies
  0-7645-3936-1
- Judaism For Dummies
  0-7645-5299-6
- Potty Training For Dummies
  0-7645-5417-4
- Buddhism For Dummies
  0-7645-5359-3

- Pregnancy For Dummies
  0-7645-4483-7 †
- Ten Minute Tone-Ups For Dummies
  0-7645-7207-5
- NASCAR For Dummies
  0-7645-7681-X
- Religion For Dummies
  0-7645-5264-3
- Soccer For Dummies
  0-7645-5229-5
- Women in the Bible For Dummies
  0-7645-8475-8

TRAVEL

0-7645-7749-2

0-7645-6945-7

Also available:
- Alaska For Dummies
  0-7645-7746-8
- Cruise Vacations For Dummies
  0-7645-6941-4
- England For Dummies
  0-7645-4276-1
- Europe For Dummies
  0-7645-7529-5
- Germany For Dummies
  0-7645-7823-5
- Hawaii For Dummies
  0-7645-7402-7

- Italy For Dummies
  0-7645-7386-1
- Las Vegas For Dummies
  0-7645-7382-9
- London For Dummies
  0-7645-4277-X
- Paris For Dummies
  0-7645-7630-5
- RV Vacations For Dummies
  0-7645-4442-X
- Walt Disney World & Orlando
  For Dummies
  0-7645-9660-8

GRAPHICS, DESIGN & WEB DEVELOPMENT

0-7645-8815-X

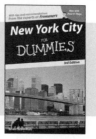

0-7645-9571-7

Also available:
- 3D Game Animation For Dummies
  0-7645-8789-7
- AutoCAD 2006 For Dummies
  0-7645-8925-3
- Building a Web Site For Dummies
  0-7645-7144-3
- Creating Web Pages For Dummies
  0-470-08030-2
- Creating Web Pages All-in-One Desk
  Reference For Dummies
  0-7645-4345-8
- Dreamweaver 8 For Dummies
  0-7645-9649-7

- InDesign CS2 For Dummies
  0-7645-9572-5
- Macromedia Flash 8 For Dummies
  0-7645-9691-8
- Photoshop CS2 and Digital
  Photography For Dummies
  0-7645-9580-6
- Photoshop Elements 4 For Dummies
  0-471-77483-9
- Syndicating Web Sites with RSS Feeds
  For Dummies
  0-7645-8848-6
- Yahoo! SiteBuilder For Dummies
  0-7645-9800-7

NETWORKING, SECURITY, PROGRAMMING & DATABASES

0-7645-7728-X

0-471-74940-0

Also available:
- Access 2007 For Dummies
  0-470-04612-0
- ASP.NET 2 For Dummies
  0-7645-7907-X
- C# 2005 For Dummies
  0-7645-9704-3
- Hacking For Dummies
  0-470-05235-X
- Hacking Wireless Networks
  For Dummies
  0-7645-9730-2
- Java For Dummies
  0-470-08716-1

- Microsoft SQL Server 2005 For Dummies
  0-7645-7755-7
- Networking All-in-One Desk Reference
  For Dummies
  0-7645-9939-9
- Preventing Identity Theft For Dummies
  0-7645-7336-5
- Telecom For Dummies
  0-471-77085-X
- Visual Studio 2005 All-in-One Desk
  Reference For Dummies
  0-7645-9775-2
- XML For Dummies
  0-7645-8845-1

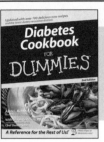